SEEING FORESTS FOR TREES
Environment and Environmentalism in Thailand

edited by

Philip Hirsch

A joint project of the
National Thai Studies Centre
Australian National University
and the
Asia Research Centre on Social,
Political and Economic Change
Murdoch University

SILKWORM BOOKS
CHIANG MAI

To my mother,
who knows that forests and trees both matter

First published in 1997, reprinted in 1998 by
Silkworm Books
54/1 Sridonchai Road, Chiang Mai 50100, Thailand
silkworm@pobox.com

ISBN 974-390-007-1

Cover photograph: Ban Mae Hang, Mae Sarieng, Mae Hong Son
© 1996 by Chatchawan Thongdeelert
Design by T. Jittidejarak
Set in 10 pt. Palatino by Silk Type

Printed in Thailand by O.S. Printing House, Bangkok

CONTENTS

III

PREFACE AND ACKNOWLEDGEMENTS

Hardly a day goes by without a significant environment-related issue making news in Thailand's media. The issues concerned tend to have little to do with global warming or holes in the ozone layer. In Thailand today, environmental concern has to do with problems closer to home, more directly and immediately connected with livelihoods and quality of life. That is not to say that they are parochial; on the contrary, environmentalism in Thailand reflects many of the key wider issues affecting and concerning Thais in rural and urban areas alike – namely the impact of rapid economic and cultural change, the inequalities associated with rapid economic growth, and nagging questions as to whether Thailand's change is bringing irrevocable losses along with the gains of development.

A significant feature of environmentalism in Thailand - and indeed elsewhere – is its variegated character, sometimes to the point where everything and anything becomes an environmental issue. The Thai term for environment, singwaedlom, is hugely encompassing, literally translatable as "surrounding things". At one level, this can make analysis of environmentalism a study of such a disparate set of issues as to become apparently meaningless. At another, though, the very discourse of environment helps to bind seemingly fragmented phenomena, hence the "forest for the trees" in the title of this book. Within the discourse of environment, a quite differentiated set of interests and sub-discourses is revealed, reflecting patterns of differentiation of Thailand's increasingly complex socio-political makeup, and it is this differentiation of Thai environmentalism that defines the book.

The chapters in this book emerged from a conference and follow-up workshop at the Asia Research Centre on Social, Political and Economic Change at Murdoch University. The Centre provided financial support for several of the participants, and it also provided a congenial environment in which to commence the editing process. The National Thai Studies Centre also contributed generously to the workshop, while the Department of Anthropology at the School of Oriental and African Studies, University of London, provided the environment in which much of the editorial work was completed. Other than the diverse set of authors themselves and the numerous participants in Thai environmental issues who have given generously of their time and ideas to assist the editor in forming the key ideas that shape this collection, particular thanks is due also to Craig Reynolds and Peter Jackson at the National Thai Studies Centre for first proposing the workshop, and to Trasvin Jittidejarak for her support as publisher. As on many previous occasions, my family has been exceptionally accommodating to my perpetually peripatetic existence.

Philip Hirsch

Sydney
November 1996

CONTRIBUTORS

Anan Ganjanapan is a Lecturer in Anthropology at the Faculty of Social Sciences, Chiengmai University

Apichai Puntasen is Associate Professor in the Faculty of Economics, Thammasat University

Roger Attwater has recently completed a PhD at the Centre for Resource and Environmental Studies, Australian National University

Philippa England is a Lecturer in Law at Griffith University

Timothy Forsyth is a Lecturer in Geography at the London School of Economics, University of London

Charles Greenberg is a Lecturer in Geography at Capilano College, Vancouver

Philip Hirsch is a Senior Lecturer in Geography at the University of Sydney

Nitasmai Tantemsapya is a researcher at the Thailand Environment Institute, Bangkok

Pratuang Narintarangkul Na Ayudhya is researcher based at the Social Research Institute, Chiengmai University

Rapin Quinn is completing a PhD at the Department of Human Geography, Research School of Pacific and Asian Studies, Australian National University

Helen Ross is a Research Fellow at the Centre for Resource and Environmental Studies, Australian National University

Santita Ganjanapan is a Lecturer in Geography at the Faculty of Social Sciences, Chiengmai University

Jim Taylor is a Lecturer in Anthropology at the School of Social Sciences, Curtin University

SEEING FORESTS FOR TREES
Environment and Environmentalism in Thailand

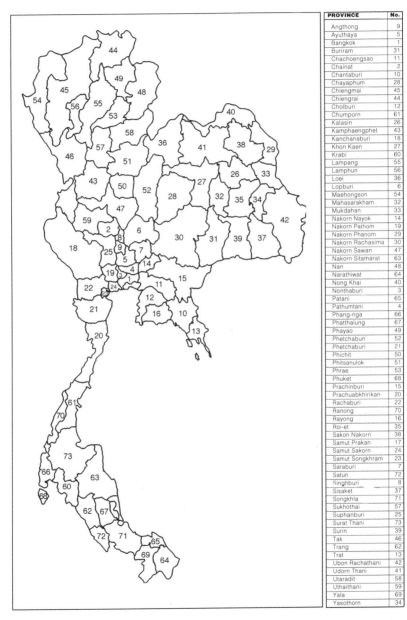

PROVINCE	No.
Angthong	9
Ayuthaya	5
Bangkok	1
Buriram	31
Chachoengsao	11
Chainat	2
Chantaburi	10
Chayaphum	28
Chiengmai	45
Chiengrai	44
Cholburi	12
Chumporn	61
Kalasin	26
Kamphaengphet	43
Kanchanaburi	18
Khon Kaen	27
Krabi	60
Lampang	55
Lamphun	56
Loei	36
Lopburi	6
Maehongson	54
Mahasarakham	32
Mukdahan	33
Nakorn Nayok	14
Nakorn Pathom	19
Nakorn Phanom	29
Nakorn Rachasima	30
Nakorn Sawan	47
Nakorn Sitamarat	63
Nan	48
Narathiwat	64
Nong Khai	40
Nonthaburi	3
Patani	65
Pathumtani	4
Phang-nga	66
Phatthalung	67
Phayao	49
Phetchabun	52
Phetchaburi	21
Phichit	50
Phitsanulok	51
Phrae	53
Phuket	68
Prachinburi	15
Prachuabkhirikan	20
Rachaburi	22
Ranong	70
Rayong	16
Roi-et	35
Sakon Nakorn	38
Samut Prakan	17
Samut Sakorn	24
Samut Songkhram	23
Saraburi	7
Satun	72
Singhburi	8
Sisaket	37
Songkhla	71
Sukhothai	57
Suphanburi	25
Surat Thani	73
Surin	39
Tak	46
Trang	62
Trat	13
Ubon Rachathani	42
Udorn Thani	41
Utaradit	58
Uthaithani	59
Yala	69
Yasothorn	34

THAILAND'S PROVINCES AS REFERRED TO IN THE TEXT

INTRODUCTION:
SEEING FORESTS FOR TREES

Philip Hirsch

This book is not about trees. Nor, specifically, is it about Thailand's forests, or rivers, or clean air, or even nature in general. Rather, this is a book that looks at the wider significance of a phenomenon *whose constituent parts tend to hide the bigger picture*. The book examines various modes of response to environmental degradation in Thailand, in order to show how comprehensively environmentalism has become woven into the country's social, political and economic fabric. It finds environmental awareness, action and activism to be as differentiated as Thai society itself. Moreover, like the socio-political milieu that contains it, environmentalism in Thailand is becoming yet more diverse as nuances of environment enter ever further into the country's political and developmental discourse.

ENVIRONMENT AND ENVIRONMENTALISM

When we speak of environmentalism in Thailand or elsewhere, we usually refer to a collective social response to environmental degradation. The physical changes manifest in the natural and living environment are themselves a response to the actions of individuals who have used resources in particular ways, but also to social, economic and political systems that have fostered a particular path of development. Not surprisingly, given the wide range of social interests and value systems involved, environmentalism is a complex and multifarious phenonmenon.

1

Environmentalisms

The roots of environmentalism spread in many directions. Western environmentalism has antecedents in Henry Thoreau's back-to-nature endeavours and liberal utopian responses to the industrial revolution in North America and Europe. Engels' abhorrence of "dark satanic mills" of northern England and acknowledgement of adverse impact of humans on their surroundings contain an implicitly environmental critique of early industrial capitalism (cf Redclift 1984: 8-9). Kropotkin's anarchist position and proposals for smaller scales of social, economic and political organisation resonate in more recent work such as that of Schumacher (1973). One strand of western conservation derives from North American notions of wilderness (cf Fraser-Darling 1971). From a non-western perspective, Buddhism is essentially environmentalist in its philosophy of limited wants and harmony between humans and their natural surroundings (Sulak 1992). This has entered western environmental thought as epitomised in Shumacher's notion of "Buddhist economics" (Schumacher 1973). In a similar vein, some environmental movements seek inspiration from principles that reflect shared characteristics with non-western, subsistence oriented pre-industrial society, particularly those with animist belief systems: diversity, smallness of scale, adaptation *to* rather than *of* physical surroundings. In contrast, a technocratic-rationalist approach to the environment has it origins in the emergence of the managerial state and the ascendence of scientism. Environmentalism in Thailand has anterior roots in several of these traditions, based in part on the joint influence of western education of the elite and Buddhist values, and in part on countervailing elite and subaltern influences.

If environmentalism has emerged out of many traditions, then not surprisingly it also takes on many forms. O'Riordan (1976) identifies two types of environmentalism, ecocentric and technocentric. Ecocentric environmentalism starts from the position that humans and the societies they create are part of nature. In order to maintain the environment, humans must adapt to and live in harmony with their surroundings, rather than trying to dominate them. The ecocentric critique targets the domineering and arrogant aspects of modernism that place humanity outside and above nature. It is based on two key moral principles, concerned with the natural world and human society respectively. *Bioethics* asserts the inherent worth and rights of plants and animals on the same level as those of humans. Meanwhile, *self-reliance* asserts the superiority of small-scale social and economic organisation, in direct opposition to the centralism and gigantism of modern society.

Technocentric environmentalism, on the other hand, starts from the perspective of controlling and managing an environment that is fundamentally separate from humans and their social, economic, technological and political systems. The environmentalist task is to foster an equilibrium by controlling and managing both the environment itself and our impact on it. The technocratic critique is usually of "irrational", unscientific use of the environment that fails to maximise utility and economic benefit. This approach is thus inimical to traditional, small-scale, low-technology use of the environment.

O'Riordan's dichotomy has been further refined with the emergence of distinctive movements, strands or "paradigms" of environmentalism and environmental management. Thus the deep ecology movement (Naess 1988) on the one hand, and "frontier economics" on the other, sit in contradiction along a spectrum. Between these extremes lie approaches to environmental stewardship that Colby (1988) represents as environmental protection (an essentially reactive managerial response to depredations made on the environment), resource management (more pro-active, but often working within a zero-sum framework) to the more optimistic and positive-sum eco-development paradigm. As a classificatory exercise, this schema tends toward reductionism, in that it views eco-development as an emerging consensus paving the way forward for all concerned. Such an approach fits well with the environmental initiatives of the World Bank, which seek to play down contradictions between mainstream development trends and environmental integrity. In Thailand there is also discernible an environmental rationalism that allows business, technocratic think tanks and government departments to adopt the environmentalist mantle and to dismiss overtly politicised environmentalism as irrational or "emotional" (see also Chapter 2 of this book).

First versus third world environmentalism?

Environmentalism was long considered primarily as a response to industrial capitalist society, and thus essentially as a "first world" phenomenon (eg Thurow 1980: 104-5). There are several underlying reasons for this. First, the target of the environmentalist critique is primarily the transformation of the natural world inherent in industrialism. Second, environmentalism has been thought of as a kind of "luxury", an aesthetic that can only make itself felt when societies have attained a level of wealth that allows them to look beyond immediate survival issues. This rationale also supports the notion that *within* particular socio-economic orders, it is the wealthier middle classes who dominate environmentalism. Third, environmentalism as a movement is sometimes considered to be contingent on liberal democracy, representing the emergence of a civil society that is limited outside the advanced capitalist world. This book fundamentally challenges these notions, whose obsolesence is clear as it has become blatantly apparent that the "developed" world has no monopoly on environmentalism and, less obviously, that within the developing world environmentalism often has its base in the livelihood struggles of the rural poor rather than the aesthetics of emerging middle classes (cf Gadgil and Guha 1994: 130).

In a world prone to simplification through dichotomies, and following the emergence of environment and environmentalism onto the global agenda, we hear increasingly of a schism between first and third world environmentalism. As Indian and Latin American environmentalists emerge onto the world stage, their critique is marked by linkage with basic development concerns of poverty and subsistence (Agarwal et al., 1987), subordination of women (Mies and Shiva 1993) and other issues that are part of a wider concern with the impact of capitalist development on third world societies and economies as well as environments. Nevertheless, the notion of a third world environmentalism is problematic on at least two main counts. First is the declining relevance of the notion of "third world" itself (Arnold 1993), as the differences between countries in East and Southeast Asia, on the one hand, and those of sub-Saharan Africa, on the other, belie the notion of a bipolar global division of wealth among countries. Thailand is one country whose development over the past couple of decades has helped make this distinction problematic. The second difficulty with the contraposition of western environmentalism and a third world equivalent is that *within* individual countries there is a great diversity of environmentalist thought and action, as the studies in this book testify.

The ambivalent position of the "third world" or "South" was highlighted at the United Nations Conference on Environment and Development (UNCED), where Malaysia's Prime Minister Mahatir galvanised the "group of 77" to oppose a binding treaty on forests, presenting this as the South's position. Philippa England's chapter 4 in this volume shows the contradictions of Thailand's stance here. The case of Thailand also illustrates the wider paradox, that radical "third world" environmentalism stands in opposition to the development agenda of nation states represented in Mahatir's position just as vehemently as it differentiates itself from "first world" environmentalism, for example that of the World Resources Insititute (Agarwal and Nain 1991). In this book, we delve into the complexities of environmentalism in one country in order to illustrate this point in much greater detail. The multiple modes, ideologies, socio-economic bases and socio-political agendas of environmentalism within a single country demonstrate the need for caution in setting up simple dichotomies.

Environmentalism and power

The political content of environmentalism is similarly complex. As a social movement, environmentalism has emerged as a powerful challenge to dominant industrial capitalism (cf Touraine 1985; Ekins 1992). In Thailand, social movements have included the student uprising and activism of the 1970s, together with peasant-based social justice movements during this liberal period. The ruthless crackdown in 1976 polarised opposition into alliance with the Communist Party of Thailand (CPT), temporarily removing the political space for opposition from within the system. With the eclipse of the socialist world, and the crisis in neo-Marxist critique more generally, environmentalism has galvanised a major strand of opposition to dominant forces of state and capital in a wide range of geographical, social and political circumstances (Eckersley 1994). In Thailand, similarly, the decline of the CPT in the early 1980s was matched by a new role for non-governmental organisations (NGOs), initially in poverty and livelihood issues but increasingly in the environmental arena. In this sense, environmentalism represents countervailing power, a challenge to the dominant forces of state and capital. While this challenge has yet to pose a serious threat to the *modus operandi* of global industrial capitalism and the state structures that support it, significant victories, such as the June 1995 action by Greenpeace to stop Shell's sinking of the Brent Spar oil platform, demonstrate the potential of galvanised environmental resistance. In Thailand, cancellation of the Nam Choan Dam represents a similar seminal victory (Hirsch and Lohmann 1989). Less direct, but perhaps more significant, is the role of environmental activism in shifting the political centre of gravity within the mainstream in regard to environmental controls and standards that affect decision making. In Thailand, the creation of a new Ministry of Science, Technology and Environment and progressive provisions within the 1992 National Environmental Quality Protection and Enhancement Act were in part a response to environmental activism. Least noisy of all, but in cumulative effect and by virtue of mass participation perhaps most significant as a social movement, are the myriad environment-focused actions throughout the world – and particularly widespread in Thailand – by marginalised groups whose livelihoods are threatened by further expropriation of their resource base, whether it be by eucalyptus plantations, large dams, industrial pollution or even national parks. This last example represents a reverse side to environmentalism that can be regressive in its implications for poorer countries or social groups within them.

Environmentalism has been as prone to co-optation, both as an ideology and as a movement, as have other critiques and modes of activism (Chatterjee and Finger 1994). The national parks and protected areas example is a case in point. At an international level, the concept of national parks as wilderness, by definition thereby regarding any human occupation as pernicious, is an outcome of North American conservation ideology being imposed in very different cultural and socio-economic contexts. In many countries including Thailand, this has often led to alienation of marginal people's resource base (see Pratuang's Chapter 7 in this volume). It represents the use of an environmental rationale to justify extension of state control over resources at the expense of local communities (Wells and Brandon 1993). The same has been true of reforestation programs with fast-growing species for industrial pulp and paper operations (Lohmann 1991). Technocratic approaches to environmental management also demonstrate the adaptability of those in power to usurp and incorporate, but also substantively transform, countervailing ideologies. This has been institutionalised within bureaucracies, think tanks and international organisations. Business has also painted itself green, reflected in the Business Council for Sustainable Development (BCSD) set up in advance of the UNCED conference, responding in part to the new commercial opportunities presented by application of environmental technology. Thailand now has its own BCSD.

Environmentalism is thus defined and refined by geographical, historical, social and political context. The purpose of this book is to take a contextual approach, to examine environmentalism in a country whose pace of social, economic, political and environmental change in recent years has been dramatic. Among trends that have served to promote environmentalism in its various guises are the rise of the middle class, increased involvement of peripheral rural populations in mainstream discourses, and Buddhist and social movements that have grown in response to the rapid changes associated with a restructuring of the country's economic base. Meanwhile, environment and environmentalism have become institutionalised in various forms, both within and outside government.

ABOUT THIS BOOK

While it is important to consider environmental politics in their international context, it is also useful to distinguish global environmental politics *per se* (Porter and Brown 1991) from the international comparative context in which more local environmental politics are shaped and played out. This book is primarily concerned with the latter, although Thailand's politics of environment have taken on an increasingly significant international dimension in recent years.

The book is organised thematically, differentiating contexts of environmentalism in two main ways. The first is to examine national and local contexts in which environmental politics are played out. The discourse of national versus local interest is a recurrent theme that reflects the tensions inherent in different scales of environmentalism. The second part of the book's organising framework is based on the rural versus urban contexts in which environmental problems arise and responses emerge. In some respects, this is out of step with the increasingly fuzzy demarcation between urban and rural economy and society in Thailand. Yet the case studies reveal quite different bases and characteristics of urban and rural environmentalism. In part, this represents a continuing managerial approach to the former and activist basis for the latter. Participation in environmental struggles is more broadly based in rural than in urban areas, although this is likely to change rapidly in coming years.

Environment has become closely entwined in the discourse of community, culture, society and nation in Thailand. Environmental discourse both reflects and influences social, economic and political process. Phil Hirsch's Chapter 2 provides an overview of these interrelationships, and it investigates the differentiated social basis for environmentalism with reference to material and ideological underpinnings. In Chapter 3, Jim Taylor focuses on a central pillar of the Thai nation, Buddhism, to show how environmental struggles have been boosted by the legitimating influence of religious association, notably through the role of individual monks. The case of Phra Prajak also shows the limits to such in the face of wider state and capital interests. Taylor also reveals how environment and poverty alleviation have been used by the state (in this case the military) as a pretext to try to evict large numbers of farmers from their unregistered lands. The discourse of nation is treated at quite a different level by Philippa England in Chapter 4, with an analysis of the interacting influences between national and international environmental agendas in the case of Thailand. The complexities of accommodating national positions to global agreements lie in part in the multiple interests within each country, posing significant questions concerning the "national" stance of countries in international environmental negotiations.

While the public face of environmentalism is often most apparent at the national level, much of the country's everyday environmental activism is played out in much more local arenas. Some of these receive attention through the press, such as the case of Phra Prajak reported by Taylor in Chapter 2; the vast majority remain local (eg Hirsch 1995). In the section on local politics of environment, three types of local initiative are examined: state-initiated, non-governmental organisations (NGOs) and self-organisation of farmers. In Chapter 5, Apichai Puntasen discusses the role of *tambon* councils to show the potential and limitations of local organs created by state machinery in the specific context of community forest management. A significant finding is the importance of local socio-economic context, notably power structures and relative differentiation of communities, in determining the effectiveness of bodies that are simultaneously state organs and people's organisations. Rapin Quinn presents in Chapter 6 a local case study that shows how NGOs have moved from rural development to environmental concerns. In so doing she reveals the micro-differentiation of environmental approaches, both by demonstrating the significance of local history and ecological context, and also by illustrating the different ideologies and approaches brought by four organisations from *within* the NGO movement. The range of NGO impacts and responses exemplifies the diversity of NGO environmentalism in Thailand, in terms of NGO analysis of problems and solutions, scales of action and analysis, and structural relationship with villagers, the state and commercial interests. Pratuang reports in Chapter 7 on recent networking initiatives in northern Thailand. The case study shows how local action in one watershed, initially based on the specific and localised issue of community forestry, has developed into a wider movement on grassroots watershed management and resistance to state encroachment in the guise of national parks.

Environmentalism in Thailand is largely a response to the depredations made on resources, livelihoods and quality of life by the country's rapid economic development in recent decades, and this is particularly striking in the rapid pace of urban development and environmental degradation. Often the tensions in Thailand's rapid growth path are represented in terms of the urban-rural divide, the assumption being that cities and their inhabitants have benefited at the expense of the countryside and peasantry. The environmental nightmare of Bangkok belies this simplification, and it is further challenged by the quite different environmental impact of urban development on various social groups and places within the city. In line with the thrust of this book in examining environmentalism in Thailand as a socially differentiated response to environmental problems, Helen Ross in Chapter 8 takes a "stakeholder" approach to show the range of players in the capital city's environmental politics and management. She reveals how Thailand's rapidly developing political situation has opened spaces for participation of new stakeholders. Charles Greenberg takes a similar approach for the Extended Bangkok Metropolitan Region in Chapter 9, presenting a social analysis of environmental costs and their social and geographical distribution in the context of peri-urban development. He frames responses in terms of "eclectic environmentalism". The diverse nature of environmental voices has both strengths and weaknesses – strengths in being encompassing and flexible, weaknesses in being fragmented and containing internal contradictions. The socially regressive side of elite environmentalism is illustrated in the case of proposals for an urban park at Bang Kachao. Both Ross and Greenberg conclude on optimistic notes, seeing the potential for increasingly participatory environmentalism and thus a broadening of the social base of urban environmental decision making. In Chapter 10, Tim Forsyth looks critically at the rhetoric and reality of government policy on industrial pollution. He shows how the country's industrialisation has brought with it quite new environmental challenges, with which technocratic management signally fails to deal because of the political dominance of pro-industry branches of government. The chapter is an interesting illustration of the differential environmental agendas within the bureaucracy, and it is a strong case for promoting the role of professionals and citizen groups in tempering the worst abuses. An interesting aspect of this study is that it moves beyond a simple state/civil society division, showing the potential and need for alliances between pressure groups and sympathetic individuals or agencies within the bureaucracy.

If urban and industrial growth represent the leading edge of development and concentration of environmental degradation, rural development and its environmental implications nevertheless remain the fundament of environmental activism in Thailand. In reality, many rural environmental problems can be linked to urban and industrial expansion, whether as a result of direct impact, as related in the case of peri-urban development in Chapter 9 and provincial industrial estates in Chapter 10, or in less direct demands on the rural resource base in the form of logging, energy development and other extractive economic activities. In Chapter 11, Anan Ganjanapan shows the links between politics of environment and politics of ethnicity in the context of highland development programs. Struggles for control over resources raise human and community rights issues most sharply in the case of upland minorities, many of whom still do not hold Thai citizenship. Ethnicity can sometimes divert attention from more fundamental material conflicts over resources between various social actors. Anan's discussion reinforces the point that environment lends legitimacy both to government agencies, for example in resettlement programs, and to communities in their struggle for resources. It also brings home the point made in other chapters about divisions internal to the bureaucracy. Roger Attwater's Chapter 12 shares with Anan's study a focus on watersheds, which have become a common unit for analysis, management and activism – as also indicated in Chapter 7 by Pratuang. Attwater's study of catchment management deals with a small watershed in Phetchabun, on the North-Northeast border. The stakeholder approach resonates with Ross's Chapter 8 on Bangkok, in this case demonstrating the differentiated set of actors concerned with resource and environmental management in a watershed setting. The chapter shows how a stakeholder analysis can be used positively to facilitate dialogue between diverse interests in pursuit of improved watershed management. In Chapter 13, Santita Ganjanapan investigates the contrast between scientific and indigenous classification systems. While this follows in Conklin's (1957) ethnological tradition, it is also central to the discussion at hand in showing the different meanings of environment and environmental degradation to different social actors. The contrast between indigenous and scientific classification offers a case of competing, and sometimes conflicting, interpretations of environment and legitimacy of claims to manage it. Chapter 14, by Nitasmai Tantemsapya, also shows the value of indigenous modes of resource use, but in this case with reference to the sustainable agriculture movement in Thailand. She discusses how sustainable agriculture has emerged as a direct response, if not yet a real challenge, to destructive mainstream practices. She also indicates the wide range of social actors involved in the movement, including some within the bureaucracy.

The wider picture thus shows a diverse environmental movement with multiple agendas, which are manifest from local to international scales. Like other social movements, Thai environmentalism reflects the social, economic and political milieu in which it is located. Concomitantly, it is instrumental in setting directions and limits to the country's development path. As part of the emerging political economy, environment increasingly serves as a legitimising discourse for a range of socio-political actors. Environmentalism in its various manifestations is thus a response to, but also an influence on, the country's ecological fortunes and emerging social forces at different levels.

Yet the very incorporation of environmentalism into a range of mainstream as well as peripheral discourses also indicates some of its limits within the bigger picture of Thailand's development juggernaut. The very diversity of actors and material interests articulating environmental concern itself produces contradictions that limit the unity of environmentalism as a movement. As a legitimising discourse, moreover, environmentalism has a limited "shelf life" that may be approaching its use-by date in certain circumstances, for example as more powerful voices utilise environmental discourses to their own ends. Most powerfully, the dominant material forces behind Thailand's ecologically unsustainable development path are so strong that environmentalism ultimately may do little other than to allow a tinkering at the edges. And finally, the internationalisation of Thailand's economy within its regional context and through globalisation limits the role of a nationally bound social movement. To this end, internationalisation of environmentalism in a form that preserves the role of local voices is perhaps the movement's greatest challenge.

REFERENCES

Agarwal, Anil; D'Monte, Darryl; and Samarth, Ujwala, eds., 1987, *The fight for survival: people's action for environment*, New Delhi, Centre for Science and Environment.

Agarwal, Anil and Narain, Sunita, 1991, *Global Warming in an Unequal World: a case of environmental colonialism*, New Delhi, Centre for Science and Environment.

Arnold, Guy, 1993, *The End of the Third World*, Basingstoke, Macmillan.

Chatterjee, Pratap and Finger, Matthias, 1994, *The Earth brokers: power, politics and world development*, London, Routledge.

Colby, Michael, 1988, *Environmental Management in Development*, World Bank Discussion Paper No. 80, Washington, D.C., World Bank.

Conklin, Harold, 1957, *Hanunoo agriculture: a report on an integral system of shifting cultivation in the Philippines*, Rome, Food and Agricultural Organisation of the United Nations.

Eckersley, Robyn, 1994, *Environmentalism and political theory: toward an ecocentric approach*, London, University College Press.

Ekins, Paul, 1992, *A new world order: grassroots movements for global change*, London, Routledge.

Fraser-Darling, Frank, 1970, *Wilderness and Plenty*, London, British Broadcasting Corporation.

Gadgil, M. and Guha, R., 1994, "Ecological Conflicts and the Environmental Movement in India", in D Ghai, ed, *Development and Environment: Sustaining people and nature*, Oxford, UNRISD and Blackwell

Hirsch, Philip, 1995, "A state of uncertainty: political economy of community resource management at Tab Salao, Thailand", *Sojourn*, 10(2), pp 172-97.

Hirsch, Philip and Lohmann, Larry 1989, "The Contemporary Politics of Environment in Thailand". *Asian Survey* 29(4) pp 439-51.

Lohmann, Larry, 1991, "Peasants, plantations and pulp: the politics of eucalyptus in Thailand", *Bulletin of Concerned Asian Scholars*, 23(4), pp 3-17.

Mies, Maria and Shiva, Vandana, 1993, *Ecofeminism*, London, Zed Books.

Naess, Arne, 1988, "Deep ecology and ultimate premises", *The Ecologist*, 18(4/5), pp 128-31.

O'Riordan, Timothy, 1976, *Environmentalism*, London, Pion.

Porter, Gareth and Brown, Janet 1991, *Global Environmental Politics*, Boulder, Westview.

Redclift, Michael, 1984, *Development and the environmental crisis: red or green alternatives?*, London, Methuen.

Schumacher, Ernst, 1973, *Small is beautiful: a study of economics as if people really mattered*, New York, Harper and Row.

Sulak Sivaraksa, 1992, *Seeds of peace: a Buddhist vision for renewing society*, Berkeley, Parallax Press.

Thurow, Lester, 1980, *The Zero Sum Society: Distribution and the Possibilities for Economic Change*, New York, Basic Books.

Touraine, Alain, 1985, "Social Movements and Social Change", in Orlando Fals Borda, ed., *The Challenge of Social Change*, London, Sage, pp 77-92

Wells, Michael and Brandon, Katrina, 1993, *People and Parks: Linking Protected Area Management with Local Communities*, Washington, D.C., World Bank.

ENVIRONMENT AND ENVIRONMENTALISM IN THAILAND: MATERIAL AND IDEOLOGICAL BASES

Philip Hirsch

INTRODUCTION

The environment in Thailand has become an issue of major local, national and international interest and concern. Rapid growth in the country's economy has placed enormous stresses on the natural environment, both through natural resource depletion and through pollution associated with industrial development. A number of social, economic and political forces have combined to bring the environment into mainstream public debate within Thailand. Commonly, environmentalism is seen to be based both on response to material aspects of environmental change and on responses emanating from ideological position. In a society that is undergoing such rapid economic and ecological change, what is subsumed under the term "environment", and what are the material and ideological bases for environmentalism?

This chapter considers the role of environment and environmentalism within Thailand's rapidly changing circumstances. It starts with an overview of environment and development, suggesting that various manifestations of development help to explain not only degradation of the country's natural environment, but also changing socio-political structures that have shaped environmentalist responses. A framework for examining the material and ideological bases for Thai environmentalism is set out, recognising the need for a socially differentiated approach to the "environmental movement". A conclusion suggests that environmentalism in Thailand needs to be seen as a multi-faceted discourse that deals with key social, economic and political issues, including questions of control over resources by empowered and disempowered groups.

DEVELOPMENT, ENVIRONMENTAL DEGRADATION AND ENVIRONMENTALISM

Economic growth and the environment

The relationship between development and the environment is often considered in terms of impacts that technology and economic growth have on natural resources and amenities such as clean water and air. The question of development *versus* the environment has received attention in the lead-up to, during and in the aftermath of the United Nations Conference on Environment and Development, and the notion of sustainable development immediately raises issues of the compatibility or otherwise of particular approaches to development with environmental integrity (eg WCED 1987; Redclift 1987; World Bank 1992; Redclift and Sage 1994). In Thailand, the impact of economic growth has been such that there do appear to be unequivocal trade-offs, at least as seen in retrospect. Broadly, the environmental impact of rapid economic development in Thailand can be seen in two main aspects: natural resources depletion and pollution.

Resource depletion

Thailand's development path has led both directly and indirectly to depletion of the country's natural resources. Depletion of forests has been commented on most widely (eg Uhlig 1984; TDRI 1987; Feder et al., 1988; Hirsch 1990a; PER 1992; Rigg and Stott forthcoming). One of the main issues of contention in explaining deforestation in Thailand is whether logging should be seen as the principal cause. In other words, is it resource extraction *per se* that has led to depletion, are other development-related processes more relevant, or should we look elsewhere? In the case of deforestation, encroachment by agriculturalists engaged in cash cropping often appears more significant, yet here too we find competing explanations; on the one hand *under*development in the form of population growth among small scale farmers, on the other development in the form of commercial agriculture facilitated – indeed promoted – as part of agricultural modernisation and diversification. While the intention is not to go into details of the arguments here (see Hirsch 1987), the point to emphasise is that competing discourses of blame emanate from different perspectives on development and underdevelopment. Those perspectives are based both on ideological position and material interest.

Thailand's rapid growth from the 1960s until the present day has been built in part on an unsustainable pattern of resource depletion. Other than timber, and the export income from crops grown on land where the forests once stood, a host of other resources have been harnessed to support the country's agricultural expansion and export oriented industrialisation. Energy has been a key issue, and the construction of large dams has been the major demand on Thailand's natural resources in this sector. Mining has also made localised demands. Perhaps most vital of all, however, and likely to become even more critical in coming years, is the issue of water. Both agricultural and industrial growth have relied on harnessing the country's once seemingly abundant water resources. In recent years, the absolutely limited nature of this resource has become apparent, and water is now a constraint to further development in areas ranging from intensive agriculture, through tourism, to the continued growth of Bangkok and other urban centres. Doubtless, the shortage has been exacerbated by periods of unusually low rainfall, but rates of growth in consumption that are directly related to development driven patterns of demand are such that a crisis has pending for some time. The latest trend is for the country to fuel further natural resource based growth by turning to neighbouring countries' timber, energy, mineral and water resources, an important facet of Thailand's increasingly internationalised approach to development (cf Hirsch 1993, Chapter 11).

Pollution

Pollution is another direct consequence of Thailand's rapid economic growth path. Pollution takes many forms, including fouling of the country's waterways with industrial and domestic effluent, airborne emissions from industry and automobiles, despoliation of coastal areas by tourism and poorly regulated construction, and effects of increasingly chemical-intensive agriculture. Congestion is a another facet of unregulated growth, most notably on Bangkok's streets, but increasingly also in regional centres such as Chiang Mai. The costs of pollution are spread unevenly, both geographically and socially, and this has contributed to the politicisation of pollution issues.

There are different schools of thought on whether pollution is an inevitable consequence of growth-oriented development. Certain types of pollution are commonly associated with low-technology industries that may become cleaner with economic development, for example sulphur emissions from coal burning (cf Mingsan 1994 : 13). Up to a certain point, such pollution increases with growth in energy consumption, but a certain level of affluence brings cleaner technologies in the so-called "inverted U-curve" (Dhira and Olsen 1994 : 7). On the other hand, much depends on the regulatory and policy environments in which industrialisation and urban growth takes place, and in Thailand there has been little effective legislation – the 1992 National Environmental Quality Protection and Enhancement Act nowithstanding (see Forsyth's Chapter 10 in this book).

Pollution may also be seen as appropriation or depletion of resources, in this case the public goods of clean air and water or uncongested roads. Conceptually, resource depletion and pollution may be seen as part and parcel of the same phenomenon, that is use of uncosted or undercosted public goods, usually to private ends. Access to such goods is governed by political and social processes, as is the question of who benefits or suffers most from the effects of their (ab)use. In this way, physical deterioration of the environment is inherently a socio-political issue and one which has a direct bearing on relative equity or inequity in development, depending on how costs and benefits are distributed socially and geographically.

This is not to suggest that environmental protection is a zero-sum game; rather, it is to point toward socio-political explanatory factors as realities that serve as an effective drag on more positive outcomes.

Socio-political development and environment

The physical impact of development on the environment is the most obvious background to environmentalism in a country whose economy is growing as rapidly as that of Thailand. However, the purpose of this chapter is not to dwell on well-covered ground or further elaborate on the often shocking details of depredations made in the name of development (see Rigg 1995). Rather, the major focus is on a sometimes overlooked facet of development, particularly in reference to environment and environmentalism, and that is the way in which social and political forces have emerged as part and parcel of the country's development path (see Hewison 1993). Changing class structure and composition, altered power relationships between business and bureaucracy, city and countryside, military and civilians, government and NGOs, labour and capital, together with new political spaces for disempowered groups and emerging politics of alliance (see Gagnon et al. 1993), all have a bearing on environmentalism.

Despite increased awareness of the socio-political nature of environmental questions, an ambivalence is implicit in the way in which environmentalism is represented and popularly understood in Thailand. On the one hand, environmentalism is often seen to be the product of Thailand's rapidly growing middle class. It is commonly assumed, not only in the Thai case, that a combination of education, increased concern over quality of life issues and the leisure to reflect beyond immediate survival questions all give the middle class a key role in environmentalism. The implication is that environmental concern is a luxury, vested mainly in the middle class, that comes at a particular level of development (Dhira and Olsen 1994 : 7). This is an approach that often seems compelling in the Thai case, given the rapid and coincident emergence of environmentalism as a socio-political force and the numerical and political growth of Thailand's middle class within a rapidly growing economy.

On the other hand, many of the very problems that environmentalism in Thailand has set out to address arise directly or indirectly from the patterns of growth that have helped to create this middle class. Moreover, basic livelihood issues affecting the country's still mainly rural population lie behind the more politicised environmental campaigns of recent years. Increasingly, Thailand's rural, peripheral, marginalised groups have been drawn into the environmental arena and are actively participating in – and sometimes providing the driving force behind – environmental politics. In such instances, issues that are played out as environmental politics often reveal a more fundamental social basis, with control over resources situated at the heart of many disputes.

What, then, is the socio-political basis of Thai environmentalism? Should we be looking primarily to the middle class, primarily to marginalised social groups, or to other social and political dynamics produced by Thailand's recent pattern of development?

The middle class and globalisation

One of the major changes concomitant with Thailand's recent socio-economic development is the emergence of a strong middle class. While there are debates over what the middle class actually consists of or represents, it is beyond question that a relatively affluent and educated professional and business stratum has increased in size and relative political influence since the 1970s. Technocratic elements within the bureaucracy are in some respects part of the growth of this middle class, which is often portrayed as a progressive force for change – particularly in the aftermath of the May 1992 upheaval.

On the surface, there is much to support the notion that environmentalism in Thailand is a middle class phenomenon. Many of the more strident campaigns are articulated through the Bangkok based media, which identify closely with the rather loosely defined middle class as a progressive, democratising force in Thai society (notably *The Nation* and *Krung Thep Thurakij* [Bangkok Business]), with the editorial influence of key figures such as Suthichai Yoon. Middle class interests in environmentalism are evident in a number of business-based environmental initiatives in recent years. Within the bureaucracy, and in policy-oriented think-tanks, recent environmental initiatives are associated with technocratically inspired moves toward a more ecologically informed approach to development. The buzzword of globalisation in the Thai context is used to help explain the increasingly cosmopolitan character of Thai middle classes and their adoption of current progressive thinking, in areas including environmental concern.

However, the notion of a middle class basis for environmentalism is complicated by several contradictions. Until the 1980s, business and environmentalists were more often assumed structurally and strategically to be on opposite sides of the major environmental debates rather than in alliance. This was true globally, and it was reflected in Thailand in some of the early environmental struggles such as the TEMCO issue (Hirsch and Lohmann 1989). More recently, business has been keen to be seen, at least, as concerned about the environment. Global initiatives such as the Business Council on Sustainable Development, which played an important role at the 1992 United Nations Conference on Environmental and Development, have been mirrored in Thailand (see *Thailand Environment Institute Quarterly* 2[1]).

Several prominent business groups and individuals have taken up environmentalist stands of one sort or another in recent years. Among the best known are: Sophon Suphaphong, President of Bangchak Petroleum, an important sponsor of the Thailand Environment Institute (see below); Khunying Chodchoy Sophonpanich, daughter of Bangkok Bank founder Chin Sophonpanich, who has become known for her "Magic Eyes" [*Taa Wiseet*] anti-litter campaign, and more recently for her role in the skytrain controversy, even venturing into an unlikely alliance with Kraisak Choonhavan (*The Manager*, March 1994 : 26-9); Pornthep Pornprapha, founder of the environmental organisation Think Earth, who is President of Siam Motors – a major player in an industry that is itself heavily implicated in the country's pollution problems. Other business-based environmental initiatives are more directly related to the business activity itself. The Regent Hotel, for example, has sought the assistance of the Faculty of Environmental and Resource Studies at Mahidol University, together with the Local Development

Institute, to develop an environmentally sound "master-plan" for its Cha-am site.

Business-based environmentalism in Thailand can be interpreted in a number of ways, ranging from ingenuous assumptions of altruism on the part of business, to conspiracy-inspired assumptions of cynical concern for image alone. Doubtless there is a spectrum of underlying reasons for individual business involvement in environmental initiatives, which vary from one individual, one business and one initiative to another (Hirsch 1994). It is also likely that there are multiple motivations behind each. Among the range of motivations that may be identified are: idealism based on genuine concern for the environment; a trendy or socialite "feel good" activity for those with time and money to spare from business activities; image, where environmental concern is seen to improve the selling power of business; business interest in environmentally sound practice, either through resource and energy savings or through the business of environmental technology; and vested interest where, for example, superficial environmental arguments may be used to oppose a development that threatens business interest.

The complexity of issues raised by business-based environmentalism illustrates the wider difficulty of sorting out ideological and material interest in environment. The political economy approach rests more with the latter, but needs also to be informed by the former. That is to say, social class, questions of access to resources and pecuniary benefits may shape particular environmental stands, but these should not be seen entirely in isolation from the influence of environmental concern that is to some degree independent of narrow self-interest.

Business is often counterpoised with bureaucracy, with the latter seen as conservative and antithetical to the emergence of civil society, and as such going against the grain of growth in the role of middle class influence. Nevertheless, within the bureaucracy, it is necessary to distinguish between old-style, entrenched modes based on patronage and bureaucratic power *per se*, and those informed by technocratic concerns. Recent legislation in key areas has been informed by more or less genuine attempts to respond to some of the concerns raised by critics of Thailand's rapid – and sometimes rapacious – development path.

An important bureaucratic reform has been the changed role of the National Environment Board (NEB). The NEB was established in 1975 under the first National Environmental Quality Act. As a separate body reporting directly to the Prime Minister's Office, the NEB had little enforcement power and a limited bureaucratic role. In 1992, the Ministry of Science, Technology and Environment was created, with three new Departments specifically concerned with environment added to the old Ministry of Science and Technology. These new Departments took on many of the functions of the old NEB, and the NEB was reconstituted as a prime-ministerial advisory board. The powers of the new MOSTE were enhanced by the potentially far-reaching National Environmental Quality Protection and Enhancement Act of 1992. It has even been suggested that an entire ministry be devoted to environment, and that this Ministry take on functions, such as flora and fauna protection, that sit uncomfortably with the primary function of other ministries in which they are currently based (see interview with MOSTE Permanent Secretary Kasem Snidvongs in *TEI Environmental Quarterly Journal* 2(1): 67).

One of the more significant institutional interfaces between public and private middle class influence, particularly in the area of environmental policy and legislation, is to be found in independent policy oriented think tanks. Two of the most significant of these, the Thailand Development Research Institute and the Thailand Environment Institute, have environment high or at the centre of their policy and research agendas. The professional orientation of these institutes can be characterised as technocratic / rationalist. In the environmental arena, this means development of centrally located information systems and policy instruments that make for more sound environmental management. A recent trend has been to push for a move away from the old "command and control" approach to environmental legislation and standards, which has been ineffectively applied and subject to abuse, toward more market oriented principles such as polluter-pays approaches that rely on business self-interest. Of course, for such approaches to work, an effective monitoring system is still necessary, and to date little has been achieved in this area.

Democracy, participation and NGOs

While think tanks and new bureaucratic approaches place emphasis on more rational and flexible environmental management, they do not take on board the wider concern of citizen participation. To the extent that citizens do have a role, there is a heavy bias toward educated groups. Essentially the task of environmental management is seen as a technocratic task of getting the market signals right, internalising externalities and finding the right level of compromise where there are unavoidable conflicts between environmental and developmental objectives.

Yet development in Thailand has brought with it new political spaces. Democracy and participation have become buzzwords, opening up new avenues for expression of power and dissent. Nevertheless, there are still limits to opposition, together with both more and less legitimate discourses for its expression. In this light, environmentalism can be seen as a legitimising discourse that has offered marginalised groups, and those acting on their behalf in an only partially liberalised political atmosphere, opportunities to reclaim control over resources usurped or encroached on by external forces.

In an organisational sense, environmentalism in Thailand is associated primarily with non-governmental organisations (NGOs). NGOs include many types of organisation and environmental ideology and activity. NGOs sit somewhere on the divide between elitist, middle class and grass-roots, peasant- or working-class based social and political action. On the one hand, most NGO workers are from urban, educated backgrounds. On the other, NGOs commonly work to an anti-bureaucratic, egalitarian ideology born of opposition to the mainstream development path that has marginalised less priveleged sections of society and done so much to damage the country's natural environment.

There is an increasing number of NGOs specifically concerned with environmental issues in Thailand. Others have become involved in environmentalism either incidentally or through re-orientation of activities, ideologies and practical concerns as resource and environmental issues have become part of the development agenda (cf Rapin's Chapter 6 in this book). A recent study provides an excellent reference for the range of NGOs involved in environmental issues in Thailand (Pfirrman and Kron 1992).

NGOs are ideologically diverse, with some firmly committed to advocacy and thus political action, while others have a more project-based alternative development agenda. Among the former, organisations range from those that work closely with government agencies (for example, Wildlife Fund Thailand) to those that tend to challenge government policy, programmes and projects (for example, Project for Ecological Recovery). Personnel also vary between those based in Bangkok and staffed mainly by university graduates, and more locally based NGOs run by monks, schoolteachers or other prominent local figures. NGOs also vary according to the issues with which they deal, the level at which they operate, their interaction with other NGOs and so on.

Of late, a key issue that has drawn NGOs into the environmental arena is the close association of livelihood issues with environmental degradation. Because most NGOs working in the area of rural development are concerned with people's welfare and with approaches to development that depend on low-technology, high-natural-resource content production alternatives, together with issues of resource management and tenure rights, environmental degradation has found its way onto the NGO agenda as a logical outcome of Thailand's declining environmental fortunes and increasing conflict over natural resources.

Incorporation of peripheries

While many of the prominent actors in environmental policy and politics in Thailand – including NGO staff – are indeed middle class, defined in the broadest sense, a study of the key environmental issues suggests a more complex picture. Briefly stated, a grassroots environmentalism has emerged as a combination of two related trends. The first is the impact of Thailand's development path on rural livelihoods, in particular as it has affected peripheral and marginalised people and areas. This has been most apparent in forest reserve areas, where resource competition between state, capital and local people's interests has intensified greatly (Hirsch 1993 : Ch. 6). The second trend is the incorporation of people living in more marginal areas into mainstream political and economic arenas, and the role of environment as a legitimising discourse for their claims over resources.

The past three decades of economic growth in Thailand have affected rural and urban dwellers' livelihoods in multifarious ways. The overall thrust of Thailand's development path has been incorporative, as the mainstream polity and economy has drawn in peripheral people and resources (Hirsch 1990b). A consequence is steady encroachment on the country's land, forest and water resources. In a country where, despite rapid industrial growth and urbanisation, a majority of the population is still rural and depends at least in part on local environmental resources for day to day livelihood needs, it is thus difficult to separate the issues of development, environmental degradation and impacts on welfare.

Examples of resource encroachment, degradation and competition that have led to environmental disputes include large dams, logging, eucalyptus planting, mining, industrial and tourist developments and a host of other resource exploitation activities. The grassroots responses to these have been exercised at a number of levels. It is important to recognise that those that find their way into the national press, frequently as they do, are still only the tip of the iceberg. More typically, resource disputes remain local and are resolved or left to fester at the local level. It is usually when related disputes involve wider environmental politics that they become publicised, sometimes as *causes celebres*. This is an important point in interpreting the nature of environmental politics as perceived through the Bangkok media, for it tends to imply that there are non-local (or non grassroots) players acting as catalysts, coordinators, instigators, or even *agents provocateurs* – depending on point of view – in most disputes.

Disputes are not the only arena in which local initiatives in resource and environmental management come into play. Much more long term and generalised, but receiving less written attention outside specialised academic circles, is the wide range of traditional resource management practices that are the historical basis for environmental stewardship in Thailand. Local irrigation systems in northern Thailand (*meuang faai*) and sacred forests in the Northeast (*paa puu taa*) are among the various means by which local people have managed resources and environment over a long period of time (Siam Society 1989).

In recent years, local resource management has been politicised as contradictions have emerged between local interests, on the one hand, and centralised state management and control over resources, on the other. Decentralisation is an issue that has recently taken on wider political significance, and there are important implications for local environmental and resource management (Apichai 1994). Community resource management has become an important focus for development work of NGOs, and some promising moves in a similar direction are also the subject of new government initiatives. A notable example is the Sam Mun Highland Development Project, a watershed management scheme that emphasises participatory approaches to conflict resolution among the communities involved. Elsewhere, support for community forests makes use of traditional and innovative approaches that often involve aspects of empowerment, since the question of community control over forest resources is as much socio-political as organisational. Networks ("horizontal" linkages) are an important aspect of recent grassroots approaches in such areas, and NGOs have had an important facilitating role here (see Pratuang's Chapter 7 in this volume). The issue of community versus state management of forest and other resources was central to a symposium held at the Parliament building in February 1993 (Wiwat 1993).

While much of the grassroots activism in the environmental arena has been in peripheral rural areas and has arisen as people and resources have been affected by resource competition arising from mainstream development trends, marginalised groups in urban areas have also been drawn onto the stage of environmental politics. A recent example is the community of Ban Krua, a longstanding Muslim settlement in the heart of Bangkok that would be dislocated by the construction of an expressway extension. Opposition by those to be affected led to the setting up of an inquiry, which found the expressway to be unwarranted on a number of grounds. An important claim of opponents was that the expressway was built to serve private rather than public interest, as it would have linked the main expressway network with the new World Trade Centre. Here, too, an environmental dispute turns out to be based on livelihood concerns and questions of economic interest of poorer vesus wealthier sections of society.

Centralisation and decentralisation

A final socio-political angle on development and the environment in Thailand is the question of centralised versus decentralised power and decision making over resources. Recent developments point in somewhat contradictory directions. On the one hand, centralisation is inherent in historical processes of national integration as part of incorporative development, and in current mainstream processes of globalisation, economic integration, industrialisation and rationalisation of resource management within increasingly rational-legalistic frameworks.

On the other hand, decentralisation is promoted through attention to participatory approaches to resource management and is an increasingly significant item on the wider political agenda in Thailand, notably in debates over election of provincial governors and granting of legal status to *tambon* councils. NGOs and grassroots environmentalism are also firmly based within an agenda of decentralised resource management.

DISCUSSION : BASES OF THAI ENVIRONMENTALISM

An organisational or institutional approach to Thai environmentalism reveals many recent developments that reflect on trends in Thailand's society, economy, polity and ecology. The environment has been institutionalised in several forms – a new Ministry of Science, Technology and Environment, together with a wide-ranging National Environmental Quality Act; independent think-tanks with a major focus on the environment; and a host of NGOs with primary or secondary concerns in the environment. However, such an approach tends to restrict our focus to outward form or expression of environmentalism and, while it helps to point toward the considerable diversity within the so-called environmental movement, it leads toward an instrumentalist rather than structural understanding of the movement. In the remainder of this chapter, the social background to Thai environmentalism is considered in terms of material and ideological rather than institutional bases. While these are only touched on briefly here, the chapters that follow serve to enhance our understanding of environment and environmentalism in Thailand in a way that contributes to this perspective.

Material bases

Materially, there are two main angles from which environmentalism can be examined. The first is to look at actual bio-physical impacts of human activity in order to understand who is affected, where and how, and with what response. The second is to consider the livelihood and resource bases of different societal groups as a background to their involvement in environmentalism in its various manifestations. Most discussions pay greater attention to the former than the latter, seeing environmentalism as a logical outcome of depredations made on nature by the development process. Less attention has been given to the material basis for a socially differentiated Thai environmentalism.

Bio-physical impacts

Some of the bio-physical impacts of Thailand's development path have been described above. In rural areas, deforestation, increasingly chemical intensive agriculture, decline in water availability, encroachment of large resource projects such as dams, reforestation with exotic species, soil erosion and salinisation are prominent among the list of problems that can be related directly to patterns of development experienced over the past few decades. In urban areas, air and water pollution and congestion rank among the principal features of environmental degradation. There is significant geographical concentration of each of these problems within rural and urban areas. In rural areas, degraded forest reserve land has become the focus of much attention. In urban areas, slums and transport corridors are targeted.

If we see environmentalism principally as an attempt to deal with such issues when and as they occur, it is not difficult to identify the main loci of Thai environmentalism in the past few years. Thung Yai, Huai Kha Khaeng, Nam Choan, Pak Mul, Dong Yai, Doi Suthep, Khlong Toey, Ban Krua – all conjure up reminders to those familiar with Thai environmental politics of the active responses made by local and wider actors to environmental degradation or threats of such. As we catalogue these isolated struggles, it should be possible to discern a more structured social basis for an emerging environmentalism, in which material interest is significant.

Livelihood, class and control over resources

For most Thais, concrete livelihood issues at a very local level are the most significant consequence of environmental degradation. Since environmental impacts of development affect diverse social groups and people living and working in different places unequally, impacts themselves, and means to deal with them, are determined in large part by control over resources by those groups. Impacts that affect more affluent, politically vocal or influential groups naturally tend to attract high profile coverage, notably problems of traffic congestion and air pollution in Bangkok (Ross 1993). This in part explains the common expectation that it is mainly the middle classes at a certain stage of development who initiate and dominate environmentalism. However, such an expectation flies in the face of the reality that the majority of Thais whose livelihoods are most threatened by environmental and resource degradation are poorer people living in rural areas.

The way in which bio-physical impacts are manifested depends on socio-economic perspective. Deforestation is a "problem" for different social groups and for urban and rural dwellers in quite different ways (cf Blaikie 1985 : Ch 2.). For wealthy Bangkokians, the loss of the country's forests means primarily loss of a recreational and aesthetic amenity. For upland minorities, deforestation may mean total loss of livelihood. For lowland rice farmers, destruction of headwater forests may mean less certain irrigation supplies and reduced opportunities for gathering subsistence foods and medicinal plants.

Responses depend on a combination of the nature of bio-physical impact, the group most affected and the way in which impacts are felt. Typically, those with the financial resources to do so have tended to buy themselves out of the problem at an individual level rather than engage in social or political action for change. Houses are built on raised land or dykes are built to surround new housing estates to "solve" the problem of flooding; more expensive and luxurious cars are bought to ameliorate the discomfort of traffic jams; air conditioning provides at least superficial protection against air pollution; and exclusive resorts are built as islands of nature for the wealthy to enjoy. Middle class mobilisation over environmental issues tends to be precisely in those areas where private, individual responses are least effective, notably in areas such as traffic congestion.

Collective responses by poorer, more marginal sections of the community are based both on the power in numbers and the difficulty of solving the problems at hand through individual responses. Thus protest over logging in headwater forests, resistance to eucalyptus plantations and opposition to large dams take collective form. Moreover, alliance with NGOs and other middle class actors is increasingly common. The politics of alliance are an important aspect of recent Thai environmentalism that belies simple class- or interest-based approaches (Gagnon et al., 1993).

Class is a problematic category in explaining the differentiated material basis for environmentalism. On the one hand, class is classically defined in terms of control over means of production, lending itself readily to an analysis that focuses on differential control over environmental resources. On the other, the complexities of class in a rapidly industrialising society whose population nevertheless remains predominantly rural, and whose elite structure also shows cleavages and overlap between business and bureaucracy, defy definitive class analysis (cf Turton 1989). Moreover, in the context of place-specific environment and resource issues, territorial interest also comes into play and transcends local class structure (Gagnon et al., 1993). In this respect, control over natural resources is a more relevant differentiating category to structure investigation into the material basis for environmentalism.

Ideological bases

Environmentalism is sometimes thought of *as* an ideology. However, Thai environmentalism is ideologically differentiated. Rigg and Stott (forthcoming) identify western and indigenous antecedents for modern environmentalism in Thailand (see also Siam Society 1989). The plural nature of Thai environmentalism is most evident in the range of environmental organisations that has emerged. Diversity in underlying ideology is also explained by the differentiated material basis for environmentalism, in particular as relates to the politics of legitimacy in control over resources.

Western environmentalism

Western environmental thought underlies many aspects of environmentalism in Thailand today. Rigg and Stott (*op.cit.*) suggest that an important channel of environmentalist thought has been the range of ideas imported by western trained elites since the beginning of the twentieth century. More recently, what O'Riordan (1976) refers to as techno-centric environmentalism has become integrated to an increasing degree into the policy and *modus operandi* of key government departments and think tanks as outlined above. Certain NGOs, although they emphasise the importance of indigenous discourses on environment as a substantive part of their campaign work, nevertheless have taken on a socio-political role with parallels to western environmental groups, and several such groups are well integrated through various networks with the international environmental movement. Nevertheless, the adcendancy of environ-mentalism elsewhere in Southeast Asia, and also in India and Latin America, is such that internationalisation does not simply mean westernisation.

Buddhism and traditional environmentalism

In counterpoint to western, educated, middle class, urban-based, techno-centric ideologies of environment, specifically Thai approaches are also identifiable. Some of these are based on Buddhist ideas of nature and the role of monks in an increasing number of well publicised environmental disputes, such as at Mae Soi (Phra Pongsak) and Dong Yai (Phra Prajak – see Taylor in the next chapter), as well as in a host of less well publicised cases (Taylor 1991). Other indigenous ideological bases for environmentalism are identifiable in local, traditional approaches to resource management such as *muang-faai* irrigation systems of northern Thailand.

Legitimacy and resource tenure : a new moral economy?

There is clearly some value in trying to disentangle endogenous from exogenous ideological bases for Thai environmentalism. For NGOs, it also makes political sense to promote an environmentalism grounded in Thai society and culture rather than imported from overseas. However, such an approach misses a significant dimension of the differentiated ideological basis for environmentalism, which is the different view of resources and their legitimate use by different social actors within Thailand.

Many of the environmental disputes of recent years are, in fact, claims over resources between more and less powerful actors. Actors at all levels have invoked environment to justify such claims. The legitimising role of environmentalism evident in marginalised groups' claim to forest reserve land and associated resources has already been alluded to, but it is not only disempowered groups who seek to legitimise claims via environmental discourse. The *Isan Khiew* (Greening of the Northeast) program, and its successor *Khor jor kor*, both of which sought to increase control of powerful players (the Army and Royal Forest Department respectively – the latter in cohorts with private business investors), have used environment as a public rationale. Moreover, in each case, there is a genuine belief in the right to the resource in question on behalf of the claimant – whether it be the dispossessed farmer who has been paying land tax on forest reserve land that was purchased from earlier settlers and "improved" through backbreaking labour; or the government official who believes in the "right of state" (cf Anderson 1987 : 1) to the same resource.

In light of the above, we should be looking at ideology of environment in its wider contemporary socio-political role, and not simply in ways limited to conventional and essentialist notions of what is indigenous Thai or what constitutes an environmental issue. In this sense, a latter-day moral economy of control over resources may be seen to underlie much of the "peripheral environmentalism" which, though more hidden and perhaps counter-intuitive than middle-class environmentalism, forms the backbone of the environmental movement in Thailand today

.

CONCLUSION

In summary, the environment in Thailand, as indeed elsewhere, is not a singular or unambiguous concept. Practitioners concerned with environment in Thailand are working in diverse institutional settings and have different – sometimes competing – objectives. There are multiple ideologies of environment, whose material and cultural bases require structured investigation. Environment serves as a legitimising discourse, among empowered as well as disempowered groups. Control over resources, and the right to use and manage them, is at the heart of Thai environmentalism today.

REFERENCES

Anderson, Benedict, 1987, "Introduction", *in Southeast Asian Tribal Groups and Ethnic Minorities, Cultural Survival Report 22*, Cambridge, MA., Cultural Survival.

Apichai Puntasen, 1994, "Decentralisation and local government initiatives towards environmental management", *TEI Quarterly Environment Journal*, 2(2).

Blaikie, Piers, 1985, *The Political Economy of Soil Erosion in Developing Countries*, London, Longman.

Dhira Phantumvanit and Erik Olsen, 1994, "The relationship between business and environment", *TEI Quarterly Environment Journal*, 2(1) pp 5-11.

Feder, Gershon, Tongroj Onchan, and Yongyuth Chalamwong, 1988, "Land policies and farm performance in Thailand's forest reserve areas". *Economic Development and Cultural Change*, 36, 483-501.

Gagnon, Christiane; Philip Hirsch; and Richard Howitt, 1993, *"Can SIA Empower Communities?,"* *Environmental Impact Assessment Review*, 13, 229-53.

Hewison, Kevin, 1993, "Of regimes, state and pluralities : Thai politics enters the 1990s", in Kevin Hewison, Richard Robison and Gary Rodan, eds., *Southeast Asia in the 1990s*, Sydney, Allen and Unwin.

Hirsch, Philip, (1987), "Deforestation and Development in Thailand". *Singapore Journal of Tropical Geography*, 8(2) 129-138.

Hirsch, Philip, 1990a, "Forests, Forest Reserve, and Forest Land in Thailand", *Geographical Journal*, 156, 2, pp 166-74.

Hirsch, Philip, 1990b, *Development Dilemmas in Rural Thailand*, Singapore, Oxford University Press.

Hirsch, Philip, 1993, *Political Economy of Environment in Thailand*, Manila, Journal of Contemporary Asia Publishers.

Hirsch, Philip, 1994, "Where are the roots of Thai environmentalism?", *TEI Quarterly Environmental Journal*, 2(2) 5-15.

Hirsch, Philip and Larry Lohmann, 1989, "The Contemporary Politics of Environment in Thailand", *Asian Survey* , 29(4) 439-51.

O'Riordan, Timothy, 1981, *Environmentalism*, London, Pion.

PER [Project for Ecological Recovery], 1992, *People and the Future of Thailand's Forests*, Bangkok, PER.

Pfirrman, Claudia and Dirk Kron, 1992, *Environment and NGOs in Thailand*, Bangkok, Thai NGO Support Project and Friedrich-Naumann-Stiftung.

Redclift, Michael, 1987, *Sustainable Development: Exploring the Contradictions*, London, Methuen.

Redclift, Michael and Colin Sage, eds., 1994, *Strategies for Sustainable Development: Local Agendas for the Southern Hemisphere*, Chichester, Wiley.

Rigg, Jonathan, ed., 1995, *Counting the Costs: Economic Growth and Environmental Change in Thailand*, Singapore, Institute of Southeast Asian Studies.

Rigg, Jonathan and Philip Stott, forthcoming, "Forest Tales: Politics, Environmental Policies and their Implementation in Thailand", in Udai Desai, ed., *Environmental Policy and Politics*.

Ross, Helen, 1993, "Environmental and Social Impacts of Urbanisation in Bangkok", paper presented at *Fifth International Conference on Thai Studies*, London.

Siam Society, 1989, *Culture and Environment in Thailand*, Bangkok, Siam Society

Sutharin Koonphol, 1994, *TEI Quarterly Environmental Journal*, 2(2).

Taylor, Jim 1991, "Living on the Rim : Ecology and forest monks in Northeast Thailand", *Sojourn*, 6(1), 106-25.

TDRI [Thailand Development Research Institute], 1987, *Thailand Natural Resources Profile : Is the resource base for Thailand's development sustainable?*, Bangkok, TDRI.

Turton, Andrew, 1989, "Local Powers and Rural Differentiation". In Gillian Hart, Andrew Turton and Benjamin White, eds., *Agrarian Transformations : Accumulation, social conflict, and the state in Southeast Asia*. Berkeley, University of California Press.

Uhlig, Harald, ed. 1984, *Spontaneous and Planned Settlement in Southeast Asia*. Hamburg, Institute of Asian Affairs.

Wiwat Khatithammanit, ed., 1993, *Sitthi Chumchon: Kaan krajaay amnaat jadkaan sapyakorn [Community Rights and Decentralisation of Natural Resource Management]*, Bangkok, Local Development Institute.

WCED [World Commission on Environment and Develoment], 1987, *Our Common Future*, Oxford, Oxford University Press.

World Bank, 1992, *World Development Report*, Washington, D.C., World Bank.

"THAMMA-CHAAT": ACTIVIST MONKS AND COMPETING DISCOURSES OF NATURE AND NATION IN NORTHEASTERN THAILAND

Jim Taylor

INTRODUCTION

Following the Thai government's review of its 1985 forest policy, the recently liberalised national print-media focused considerable attention on equity and quality-of-life issues, relating in particular to social justice and the environment. At the interactive centre were the newly politicised urban middle-class "greens" or environmentalists mediating between traditional elitist interests and the indigenous worldview of frontier peasants. The environmentalists, in turn, supported the work and local leadership of a number of activist monks engaged in forest conservation and village development, particularly in the impoverished northeast region. In this chapter I argue that the issues of social justice, equity, and conservation in Thailand have been frequently articulated in the matrix of a religio-political discourse, which has provided an alternative arena in the exercise of power. This autonomous and potentially integrative (in the Gramscian sense) alternative social field has been seen by dominant forces as a threat to the state and market forces.

RELIGION, CULTURE AND SOCIAL ACTION

In looking at Thai religion, many observers have misread the possibilities for alternative discourses and have often presented religious ideas and practices as monolithic and hegemonic, little worthy of serious attention. This position has failed to understand the nature of historical reforms, instances of resistance, and the impact of local ideas informed by an active cosmology. Here, the dynamic Buddhist concept of *Kamma* (volitional or intentional action and its multiple consequences) is related to a "fatalistic" hierarchical cosmic order; an ideological conception justifying social inequalities. As an "otherworldly" religion,[1] it is elitist, politically remiss and disinterested in conventional realities. In other words, it is a soteriology of "resignation and escape". This normative cosmology constitutes a total meaning system or theodicy in a Weberian sense, with organic-like social ethics for the actors which legitimates and simultaneously moderates privilege and power.

However, this "otherworldly" perspective on living religion is unable to make sense of internal (emic) perspectives of local discourses, or understand the underlying meanings and dialectics of social, cultural and political life. It has also failed to link small scale Buddhist worlds to wider systems and to the discursive processes of change and resistance. In fact the Theravadin religion is an elaborate ideological system which includes multiple possibilities informed by everyday experience, intellectual ideas, consciousness (of the human actors), as well as institutionalised thought-systems and social discourses (cf Therborn 1980: 2).

In this paper I view the Theravadin religion from an emic perspective as a totality, as a discursive system, internally and instrumentally differentiated by sub-systems (which would include non-normative religious expressions) within the same greater tradition. I argue that the Theravadin religion in Thailand has provided alternative ideological structures, through a reinterpretation of Buddhalogical meanings and symbols, to those of the

---

[1]   Worsley (1957: 223). Also, Troeltsch (1957: 152) remarked that "Buddhism ... presents the opposition to the spirit of politics in its most acute form ...". For many contemporary Marxist writers on Thailand, the problem of dealing with a peasant oppositional consciousness and religious experience is acute. For example, Shigeharu Tanabe talks about living Buddhism etically as though it constituted two distinct non-related religious systems: "hegemonic" and "heterodox" Buddhism. A hegemonic Buddhism is a manipulative system which has been able to regulate "popular consent to the karmic order of the world through a highly organized system at all social levels, and it has succeeded in fostering the popular belief that salvation comes in the other world in accordance with the individual accumulation of merit (bun) in this world..." (Tanabe 1984: 86).

state and its elites. I present my argument by showing how the politico-religious functions of three well-known rural activitist monks have been couched in a notion of *Dhamma*-truths (the teachings of the Buddha concerned with conditioned existence). In a Gramscian sense, this has in turn provided a conscious direction for social action, in each case supported by an "eco-*dhammic*" discourse. Such an interpretation is a radical departure from conventional understandings of Thai religion.

ACTIVIST MONKS, DISCOURSES OF POWER, AND THE ENVIRONMENT

Phra Prajak

Perhaps the most contentious case involving an activist monk in recent years has been that of a hitherto unknown forest monk named Phra Prajak Khuttajitto, at Pakham District in the northeastern province of Buriram. It is to this particular case that I first turn.

Prajak first gained national attention in 1991 by taking a stand against the civil and military bureaucracy and related capitalist interests in the now failed *Khor jor kor* (a relocation scheme for the poor in degraded forest lands). This scheme, ostensibly to protect reserved degraded state forests from intensified encroachment, actively promoted the establishment of monoculture commercial tree-farming. It was inspired by the government's economic policies and the world-wide demand for wood chips and paper pulp (Lohmann 1990: 9-17). As a consequence, Prajak and other monks and peasants, who resisted the military-led eviction, were accused of engaging in anti-statist activities and of hindering national prosperity and development.

In fact, as I have shown elsewhere (Taylor 1993: 3-17; Taylor 1994), the Prajak case has been as much a localised dispute involving subordinate groups and government officials with issues such as traditional rights to land and resources, conservation and commercial forestry, as one that contrasts centralised capitalist development interests and state policies with local human needs and autonomous social space. In the context of a diminishing frontier and, as a consequence, increasingly insecure peasant ways of life, these collective needs have been articulated through an invigorated national "green" consciousness more recently informed by an alternative Buddhist discourse.

In Thailand, this active religious orientation has presented itself as an oppositional consciousness within the context of a democratising and increasingly pluralistic political milieu. This new "green" theology has entailed the reinterpretation of communalistic Buddhist social ethics espoused by a late leading Buddhist monastic thinker named Phra Phutthathaat [Buddhadasa Bhikkhu] (Jackson 1988). Phutthathaat has been an immense influence on many clerical and secular Buddhist activists in the past three decades, including Prajak, especially in his notion of a grass roots Buddhist "socialism" (*sangkhom-niyom*). In this conception, as Swearer (in Bhikkhu Buddhadasa 1986: 33-38) has suggested, there are three main principles: the principle of the good of the whole and the interdependence of society, culture and nature; the principle of restraint (from personal greed), social equity and generosity; and the principle of respect for the community and loving-kindness. The first informs all political, economic and social structures; the second governs individual behaviour; and, the third prescribes the correct attitude towards all forms of life. Essential to this pragmatic action philosophy is the need for living a simple and satisfying life in harmony with nature as a counter-force to the inequities and injustices of modernisation; in Saneh's (1993: 100) terms, a kind of "spiritual way out". This alternative eco-*dhammic* discourse differs radically from Western conceptions of planned social change and modernisation embedded in capitalist development glibly pursued by the Thai state. However, it may be argued that the state has little option but full economic participation in a globalisation process dominated by "First-World" states and their international banks. The post-colonial modernisation discourse can be seen as an integral component in the exercise of power and domination. It implies a disciplined, individualistic, economic rationality in an unrestrictive global application.

At the periphery of globalisation are the disaggregated peasants and a reformulated politico-religious counter-ideology, articulated by activist monks such as Prajak. Discursively, the social and political ramifications of Prajak's case had important judicial implications and involved many actors, not least the personal interests of the civil and military elites. But recent politicised "green" issues in Thailand have also generated considerable concern from the pro-democratic middle-classes (Malee 1991). These issues have converged in a cauldron of competing discourses in relation to conserved forests, traditional access rights to these forests, commercial forests and national development. The social, economic and environmental implications of these interventions and competing interests have been largely ignored.

Prajak saw his presence at the 34,000 hectare Dongyai forest reserve (which the Royal Forestry Department wants to incise into the neighbouring Thablaan National Park) as necessary in order, as he said, to "protect the destruction of nature by 'selfish' people". We also gain further insights into the activist monk's discourse on action in the following remark: "even though the body is broken into dust (an allusion to resistance), we must be here to take care of nature for the future of the masses . . ." (Prajak 1991: 60).

Prajak's religio-political (and politico-moral) discourse of social action informed by reformulated Buddhist-truths (*Dhamma*; Thai: *tham*), and the strategy of conservation, concerns the long term interests of an impoverished frontier people. This implies the need for decentralization, localised and more equitable resource control and management, participation, sustainable cultural practices and self-reliance. However, this is somewhat idealistic as the problem was confounded by the fact that many of the settlers did not share Prajak's long term view. The exigencies of survival in a harsh social, political and economic milieu have meant that many of the local people were easily bought by capitalist interests, illegal loggers, commercial foresters, timber merchants and the like. As well, survival tended to favour convenient though environmentally debilitating cash crops such as cassava.

This divisive situation, which saw the community ideologically split along eco-political grounds, made it easy for the state to manipulate the situation to its own advantage. It is another reason why activist monks teach at multiple levels, from the elites and political power bases, to the grass roots and the local villagers. Prajak was well aware of internal divisions within the local community on ecological matters where self-interest predominated. Among many of the impoverished villagers, environmentally-friendly alternatives had to be seen in the context of an immediate, practical and culturally appropriate manner.

Prajak, encamped in the Dongyai forest, saw the way the local settlers and the forest ecosystem were exploited by the state and capitalist interests and decided to stay and help the people. In the first instance, Prajak had to convince the villagers of the importance of maintaining the ecosystem and protecting the forest for the future well-being of the local community. As mentioned above, this has not been without localised tensions due to conflicting community interests relating to both the historical conditions of settlement and contemporary livelihood realities. The relocated and spontaneous settlers around Dongyai consist largely of dispirited and disempowered non-kin groupings from many northeastern provinces. This has weakened the natural formation of collective action groups and a sense of integral autonomy.

Prajak, intent on consciousness-raising for collective action, was never afraid to speak out on moral and politico-environmental issues. He simultaneously taught religion to villagers as it related to the practical mundane problems of the local community. Prajak, as with a number of other development monks, incorporated his *Dhammic* knowledge with a distinctive grass-roots orientation to practice. This reformulated praxis did not endear him to the state or the military.

As a projected scenario of the problem in the countryside, the 1985 National Forestry Policy Committee proposed the establishment of monoculture eucalyptus plantations over 61,600 square kilometres of reserve forest lands by the year 2020, of which at least two-thirds (though this was later revised in the policy review to one-third) were to be planted by commercial firms (Lohmann 1991: 6n12). Interestingly, in 1993 and early 1994 farmers in the central provinces of Northeast Thailand started to win long battles against the provincial state apparatus to remove eucalyptus from community forest lands (traditionally used for public grazing and the collection of firewood) and replant with native species. Prajak felt that the continued promotion of eucalyptus in the countryside can only lead to social unrest. He went on to say that there are many powerful persons "buying land everywhere in the country, frequently contested by the local inhabitants, to plant eucalyptus and establish paper pulp factories . . . ". And, in an ominous prediction shortly before he disrobed, Prajak (1991: 102) said that in the future the land will be "full of blood".

Prajak has been at the centre of nation-wide publicity on conservation and community managed forests in the northeast region. As a consequence he has lived in constant fear from company ruffians, the army and police. The use of fear by state apparatus and the disappearance of certain informal leaders fits the extreme logic of what Ben Anderson called "extra-political" killings by state interests. This peaked in the mid-1970s but has remained a persistent – if muted – feature of modern Thai political life (Anderson 1990; Handley 1992: 20). For reasons not hard to see, the impoverished northeast region has long had a higher incidence of peasant resistance and corresponding state-initiated political killings than any other region (Turton 1976: 284).

As a means of discrediting Prajak, the military accused him of being a "Russian monk" and "communist monk", asocial epithets which indicate negative and potentially threatening categories. This is an extreme form of ideological restriction by the state (Turton 1984: 50) in which the accused is delegitimated to a condition described by Therborn (1980: 83) of "ideological non-existence" and "excluded from further meaningful discourse as being insane, depraved, traitorous, alien, and so on". As expected, the local religious authorities declined to support Prajak.

In early 1994, some months before he disrobed and disappeared, Prajak was awaiting the outcome of a court case and attempting to entrench himself more deeply into the forest (Aranya 1994: 13-15). A warrant for his arrest had been issued by the state for his alleged felling of trees in the reserve to make a new monastery dwelling. He claimed that these were dead trees. There is no doubt that this had caused Prajak considerable concern. The International Network of Engaged Buddhists noted in a widely circulated facsimile in July 1994 that there seemed to be a concerted effort by the state, some influential local people with interests in logging and the military-controlled television and radio media to discredit the monk once and for all.

As early as March 1992, Prajak had said that the problem of forest conservation at Dongyai was becoming too great, the forest rapidly disappearing, the settlers increasingly factionalised, and that he alone was not able to maintain resistance against the state, capitalist interests, and the disaggregated settlers (Sanitsuda 1992b). Prajak also admitted that he underestimated the complexity and disagreement between the state's policy-makers and their implementers, especially the influential local-based middle-ranking government officials. This was one reason why the promises made to him by the Chuan government in late 1993 were unable to be kept, in particular that resulting from a meeting with Deputy Interior Minister Suthat on ensuring protection of the Dongyai forest.

Despite the democratising but still highly centralised bureaucratic political system, on the frontier little is likely to change in the foreseeable future. However, the ramifications of the May 1992 revolt have forced the military to back down (if not out) on its ambitious nation-wide proposals for the coerced relocation of frontier peasants from degraded, and sometimes not-so-degraded, forest land. But simply to blame the military is to obscure the multiple political and economic interests in a new democratic guise involved in the intensified exploitation of natural resources.

The events following the democratising revolt of May 1992 failed to provide Prajak with the support he needed. Nor did the position of the "subaltern" or disaggregated peasants, or that of local conservation movements, improve greatly after this event. For Prajak, events became so complex and problematic that he decided to disrobe shortly before the rains retreat period in July 1994 and, at the time of writing, his whereabouts are unknown.[2]

---

[2] It appears that Prajak and an activist monk called Phaisaan (mentioned below) visited Japan to talk about conservation and the consequences of monoculture plantation forestry in Thailand (spearheaded by Thai-Japanese interests). On his

As shown in the recent attempts at constitutional reform, established social hierarchies and institutional power structures continue to seek order and legitimation in a given rationality, a hegemonic system which allows at best only a tinkering at the edges. Prajak's aim at the empowerment of conservation-minded local people through *Dhamma*-truths, and an attempt at shifting the institutionalised architecture of power, was clearly opposed to the regulated, development-oriented, state.

Prajak's presence at Dongyai since 1989 has challenged the moral basis of the new semi-democratic polity. In so doing he has also tested the capacity of the state to incorporate competing discourses. In Prajak's case, these alternative discourses invert statist notions of modernisation and ordered human progress and show the interrelationship between ideology, practice, and nature.

The forests have long been seen by wandering forest monks as special places, not only in normative religious terms for spiritual practice, but as total ecological systems, important for all life forms. In this mutuality, no single life form should dominate another. Prajak saw the forest as important for all interdependent living beings in its regulation of the four basic elements of life (earth, air, water and fire). Prajak went on to say that,

"nowadays we don't understand ourselves, where we are (spiritually) in relation to nature; but if we practice meditation we will understand ourselves and the relationship between forests and our body . . . even the Buddha and his disciples knew the importance of the harmony and interdependence between man and nature" (1991: 98-99).

Although the case of Prajak is somewhat extreme, there is nevertheless a continuing struggle on the frontier between the interests of

return in July 1994, Prajak was obstructed from returning to the Dongyai forest, and he subsequently disrobed. The *Matichon* newspaper (Saturday 19 August 1994) suggested that Prajak had been in debt and had even been considering suicide, and in a report the following day that he had disrobed. The *Bangkok Post* (Friday 19 August, 1994) mentioned that Prajak had withdrawn some money from a bank and left Buriram province, confirming that there were ongoing problems confronting the monk at the Dongyai forest.

subordinate groups, together with locally managed conservation strategies supported by activist monks, and the state and capitalist interests. The latter interests are presented in the guise of an interventionist developmental discourse, one which espouses the virtues of continuing national economic growth regardless of social and environmental cost.

Luang Phor Naan and Luang Phor Khamkian

The following accounts are of the rather less controversial – but no less effective – activist northeastern monks named Luang Phor Naan (65 years of age with 45 years as a monk), from Surin Province (Noraset and Sak n.d.: 83-7; Seri 1988: 54-65), and Luang Phor Khamkian (58 years of age with 27 years as a monk), from Chaiyaphuum Province. First I turn to Naan, one of the pioneers of monastic-led small-scale development work in northeastern villages. Naan is also one of the founding figures of the active grass-roots voluntary organisation called Sekhiyatham, established in 1990 (see Taylor 1994: 43-45).

In an interview given to the author in 1993, Naan remarked that he undertook a step by step approach in attempting to alter some of the more socially and environmentally destructive cultural practices among the villagers. At the same time, he would identify local knowledge which can be incorporated into rural change programs. He said that monks can be good local leaders, and are needed as much today as in the past when the outside world had minimal impact on the village.

In fact, Naan noted that some problems are greater than before, and others, such as localised corruption, are at least as great. In recent times, there has been considerable ill-feeling over multi-level corruption in the planting of eucalyptus. In general, Naan said that corruption in any form tends to inhibit the growth of democracy at the grass roots. In regard to commercial tree farming using eucalyptus, he noted that there are many vested interests pushing for the promotion of this tree crop throughout Northeast Thailand. Echoing the concerns more radically expressed by Prajak, Naan said that these state and capitalist interests do not have local people's customary rights, local ecology or that of conservation at heart, only personal greed. In turn this negative feature flowed into the village and affected local attitudes and traditional community values.

To Naan, spiritual and material development must go side by side. As he says, "we need the spiritual dimension in all development activities" and without first having a clear vision of ourselves, and the root causes of poverty, "how can we then develop the community?" (Seri 1988: 57). For the future, he remarked that he intended to continue working for the people towards the goal of community-based self-reliance, to enable them to be independent of unreasonable demands from the state and the consequences of market capitalism. In turn he hopes that his ideas and practices will diffuse widely in the northeastern countryside.

As in the case of Naan, Luang Phor Khamkian similarly became involved in community development based on first hand experience of deprivation among frontier-dwellers. He has two main branch monasteries in Chaiyaphuum Province, one headed by the charismatic former student radical turned development monk, Phra Phaisaan Wesaalo, who has written on the role of monks and rural democracy (Phaisaan 1992: 37-50). Both of these branch monasteries contain some valuable natural forest and have been continually under threat from encroachment and illegal logging over the years. Alongside one monastery, for instance, there is the ever present threatening eucalyptus plantation established some fifteen years ago by the Royal Forestry Department. This severely eroded, hot and lifeless plantation contrasts with the neighbouring rich, biologically diverse and moist forest monastery in a way which social critic and writer Sanitsuda Ekachai (1992a: 3-4) colourfully describes as a juxtaposition of hell and heaven.

Khamkian, like Naan, is very active and travels widely throughout the country at the invitation of NGOs, academic insti tutions and village conservation and development groups. He is vice-president of the Seklyatham movement (Taylor 1994: 44). In contrast to Prajak, who Khamkian admires but feels is too critical and intolerant of government officials, Khamkian tries to work alongside state agencies as much as possible, especially the Royal Forestry Department. However, Khamkian also dislikes the promotion of eucalyptus plantations and says that there are many fast growing indigenous alternatives (such as the trees known in the local idiom as *Sadao* [known elsewhere as the neem tree, *Melia indica*], *Kathin Yak* [a member of the *leguminaceae* family, genus *Leucaena*], *Kha-thong*, *Khao-mong*, and *Phayung* [*Dalbergia cochinchinensis*]).

Regarding some of the obstacles to alternative rural development, Khamkian considers the political machinations of the state and modernisation are the cause of most problems confronting the villagers (Noraset and Sak n.d.: 16). One of the most important approaches to alternative development stressed by Khamkian and other activist monks is to show by example. His teaching mode is to relate the Buddha's teaching as praxis to the everyday life experiences of the villagers.

In a similar position to Naan, Khamkian believes that monks cannot ignore their social responsibilities to the laity. "And we are also to blame if the villagers are trapped in indebtedness. It is our duty to show the way" (Sanitsuda 1990: 67; 1992a: 3-4; Seri 1988: 111-21). Khamkian feels that the villagers have had a constant struggle with poverty and hunger because they have followed the main-stream, greed-motivated capitalist economy. The villagers cleared much of the surrounding forest encouraged by the state to get land to plant cassava, because it was quick money. In the end this left them in a condition of increasing hunger and indebtedness.

Khamkian, as with Prajak, Naan, and other alternative development monks seen as generating a counter-ideology and discourse of resistance, was labelled a communist at various times by the state. He says, this is

> "understandable, because what I am preaching is different from traditional folk understanding about Buddhism . . . (M)y answer is to stay here, keep on working, and let people see, understand and judge for themselves" (Sanitsuda 1990: 69).

Khamkian's two branch forest monasteries consist of the only greenery visible amid vast areas of cassava growing. Khamkian's close affinity with nature and the forest is obvious, as he says, "(N)ature is our greatest teacher . . . (N)ature teaches us the value of simplicity as well as the essence of life". Khamkian has expressed great concern about the disappearing biodiverse forests. He says this is another reason for staying in the area. Meditation practice, as well as the natural forest environment, can "free our minds, if we can see through to (the practical implications of) nature" (ibid.). This, according to all three of these monks, is the essence of Dhamma.

CONCLUSION

Ingold (1993) describes an externalising "global" attitude of mind in which the world is to be conquered, controlled and manipulated. It is not a world within which we dwell but a place where interventions may be launched from outside and above, as though humankind were somehow able to live on or off the environment rather than within it. Indeed, this action towards the environment as planned intervention underlies the western notion of production. History itself becomes a process wherein "human producers, through their transforming reaction on nature, have literally constructed an environment of their own making" (Ibid.:39). Modern western ideas and technologies have placed humankind and its interests outside of the material world and provided the means for the former to control the latter (Ibid.:41). In contrast, traditional Buddhist cosmology (and other indigenous cosmologies of engagement) see humankind as a part of an ordered universe of meaningful relations.

The Theravadin order of monks has long been an extremely important local institution and focus of collective identity through rituals, and one where the secular and religious dimensions of life are seen as a totality. Indeed, to a Buddhist villager, religion cannot be readily separated from wider social, economic and political concerns. As a parallel to the civil administrative hierarchy, and regulated closely by the state, the national order of monks has been used from time to time to disseminate officially sanctioned policies. However, as in the case of monks like Prajak, "deviant" counter-ideological individuals who have given "too much attention to the protection of their flock . . . are subject to discipline and punishment" (Girling 1984: 393). Therefore, while the religious totality provides a coherence and meaning to human experiences, hierarchy and conceptions of order, it has also been a matrix for the emergence of alternative or competing discourses. In a sense, it has explained both stability and, in normative Buddhist terms, impermanence or inherent instability among all conditioned phenomena (*anicca*; Thai: *anit*).

The importance of the spiritual dimension in popular development and conservation has not been lost in alternative development in much of the so-called Third World. This has led, in Rahnema's (1992: 129-130) words, to a "revival of the sacred in . . . everyday relationships with the world" and to a regeneration of "people's space". Wherever the spiritual dimension has been present in Buddhist Southeast Asia, it has led to a creative means of mass mobilisation. Prajak, Khamkian and Naan, for instance, use meditation as a base for building community consciousness and an awareness of individuality before encouraging involvement in collective action. Another activist-monk talked about the necessity of individuals to "green the mind" first before "greening" the countryside. This alternative consciousness entails, in Sulak Sivaraksa's (1988:96) terms, a return to the "sacred" (or at least a reinvigoration and reformulation of the sacred), and will enable ordinary people to resist the disruptive effects of economisation.

In recent years activist-monks, such as Prajak, Naan and Khamkian, have become totalising symbols of an eco-*dhammic* resistance movement that has questioned the moral basis of the state and market capitalism.

REFERENCES

Anderson, B., 1990, "Murder and Progress in Modern Siam", *New Left Review*, No. 181, May/June.

Aranya Siriphon, [1994] 2537, "Phra Prajak Khuttajitto, Huai-nam phut, Amphoe Pakham, Jangwat Buriram", *Sayaamrat Sapdaawijaan*, Year 40, Vol. 46, Week 17-23 April.

The *Bangkok Post*, 1994, Friday 19 August.

Bhikkhu Buddhadasa, [2529] 1986, *Dhammic Socialism*, trans. and ed. Donald K. Swearer, Bangkok: Thai Inter-religious Commission for Development.

Girling, J., 1984, "Thailand in a Gramscian Perspective", *Pacific Affairs*, 57 (3).

Handley, P., 1992, "Have gun, will kill", *Far Eastern Economic Review*, 27 February.

Ingold, T., 1993, "Globes and spheres: The topology of environmentalism", in *Environmentalism: The view from anthropology*, Milton, K., (ed.), London: Routledge.

Jackson, P.A., 1988, *Buddhadasa: A Buddhist thinker for the modern world*, Bangkok: Siam Society.

Lohmann, L., 1990, "Commercial tree plantations in Thailand: Deforestation by any other name", *The Ecologist*, 20 (1), Jan/Feb.

Lohmann, L., 1991, "Peasants, Plantations, and Pulp: The Politics of Eucalyptus in Thailand", *Bulletin of Concerned Asian Scholars*, 24(4), Oct-Dec.

Malee Traisawasdichai, 1991, "The Young Greens", in *The Nation*, Bangkok, 14-15 October.

The *Matichon* newspaper, 1994, Saturday 19 August.

Noraset Phisitphanphorn, and Sak Prasaandii, n.d., *Thamniab Phrasong nakphathanaa Phaak-Isaan* (A list of development monks in Northeast Thailand), Bangkok: Mahaachulalongkorn University.

Phaisaan Wesaalo, Phra Ajaan, [1992] 2535, "Santiwithi nai khwaamrunraeng" (Peaceful method in violence), *Waansaan Phor Sor Lor* (World Buddhist Fellowship Journal), Year 25, Vol. 177.

Prajak Khuttajitto, Phra Ajaan, [1991] 2534, *Satja Jaak Dongyai* (The truth from Dongyai), Bangkok: Eco Press.

Rahnema, M., in Sachs W., 1992, *The development dictionary: A guide to knowledge as power*, London: Zed Books.

Saneh Chamarik, 1993, *Democracy and Development: A cultural perspective*, Bangkok: Local Development Institute.

Sanitsuda Ekachai, 1990, *Behind the Smile: Voices of Thailand*, Bangkok: The Post Publishing Co. Ltd.

Sanitsuda Ekachai, 1992a, "Man and the Forest", *Bangkok Post*, Friday, 24 January.

Sanitsuda Ekachai, 1992b, "Conservationist monk afraid for his life", *Bangkok Post*, 12 March.

Seri Phongphit, 1988, *Religion in a Changing Society*, Hong Kong: Arena Press.

Sulak Sivaraksa, 1988, *A socially engaged Buddhism*, Bangkok: Thai Inter-Religious Commission for Development.

Tanabe, S., 1984, "Ideological practice in peasant rebellions: Siam at the turn of the twentieth century", in *History and Peasant Consciousness in South East Asia*, Turton A., and Tanabe S., eds., Senri Ethnological Studies, No.13, Osaka.

Taylor J. L., 1993, "Social activism and resistance on the Thai frontier: The case of Phra Prajak Khuttajitto", *Bulletin of Concerned Asian Scholars*, 25 (2), pp 3-17.

Taylor J. L., 1994, "A social, political and ethnoecological study of community forests and rural leadership in Northeast Thailand", Indian Ocean Centre for Peace Studies, Occasional Paper, No. 36.

Therborn, G., 1980, *The Ideology of Power and the Power of Ideology*, London: Verso Editions.

Troeltsch, E., 1957, *Christian Thought: Its History and Application*, New York: Living Age Books.

Turton A., 1976, "Northern Thai Peasant Society: Twentieth-century transformations in political and jural structures", *The Journal of Peasant Studies*, 3 (3), April.

Turton A., 1984, "Limits of Ideological Domination", in *History and Peasant Consciousness in South East Asia*, Turton A., and Tanabe S., eds., Senri Ethnological Studies, No. 13, Osaka.

Worsley, P., 1957, *The Trumpet Shall Sound*, London: Paladin.

UNCED AND THE IMPLEMENTATION OF FOREST POLICY IN THAILAND[1]

Philippa England

INTRODUCTION

This chapter explores trends in forest policy in the international fora of the United Nations Conference on Environment and Development (UNCED) and at the national level in Thailand. Where relevant, it draws links between developments at these two levels, highlighting the common issues which make forest conservation so illusory. It demonstrates that despite the upsurge of environmental awareness at all levels of governance, forest policy presents unresolved dilemmas for which no easy solutions exist. Inconsistent policies, failed forestry initiatives and continuing deforestation are the main results of the failure to address inherent conflicts in the forest sector. The impressive recent commitment of many states, including Thailand, to environmental protection has not led to meaningful solutions for forest conservation. On the contrary, as environmental concerns have become more mainstream, as governments and businesses have taken on board the environmental agenda, issues which challenge the economic imperatives of mainstream society have been pushed to the side lines. In Thailand, the logging ban and the revival of interest in community forestry projects are laudable initiatives, but they offer only a belated and inadequate response to deforestation, especially when viewed in the light of other, more dominant trends in forest policy. The overall conclusion is that,

[1] The author would like to thank her research assistants, Ms Deborah Lamb and Ms Nikolina Babic, for help in researching this paper and Mr. Keiran Tranter for his help with editing the final text.

while environmental awareness is on the increase in Thailand as elsewhere, fundamental issues of resource exploitation are yet to be addressed in any meaningful way. The deadlock in international negotiations on a forest treaty at UNCED is simply indicative of dilemmas which confound initiatives at both international and national levels.

FOREST ISSUES AT UNCED

Preparations for UNCED began in 1989 with the passing of General Assembly Resolution 44/228, calling for a Conference on Environment and Development in 1992 at Rio de Janeiro. The purpose assigned to the Conference was the formulation of strategies to integrate environment and development in every aspect of economic life (Johnson 1993:19).

The result of three years of intensive preparations, the Rio Conference was the largest gathering of heads of state in history. The achievements of the Conference include the preparation and signing of two new international treaties and the production of important declarations and documents, including the *Rio Declaration on Environment and Development* and Agenda 21. Developed countries left the Conference, however, without realising their ambitions for a separate treaty on forest conservation. In part this was because developing countries, led by the Malaysian Prime Minister, Dr Mahathir, refused to abandon the terms of the *Kuala Lumpur Declaration*, issued by the Group of 77 shortly before the Conference began.

The Kuala Lumpur Declaration

In April 1992, developing countries met to finalise their collective policy stance for the UNCED. Their deliberations showed that developing countries had serious reservations about the UNCED, especially on forest related matters. These reservations, which eventually came to great prominence at Rio, are comprehensively stated in the *Kuala Lumpur Declaration* issued by the Group of 77 in

April. The Declaration makes it clear that, in the eyes of developing countries, environmental and development issues are inseparable. It contains serious qualifications on the support of developing countries generally for environmental protection. For example, the Declaration affirms the commitment of the developing countries to addressing environment and development issues in an integrated, comprehensive and balanced manner. This enthusiasm is heavily qualified, however, by frequent reference to the need to protect the national sovereignty of developing countries and the need for developed countries to shoulder the main burden of environmental protection:

"We call for a new global partnership based on respect for sovereignty and the principles of equity and equality among states for the achievement of sustainable development, taking into account the main responsibility of developed countries for the deterioration of the environment and the need for sustained economic growth and development of developing countries." (Para 3)

On the question of conservation of forests, the *Kuala Lumpur Declaration* made three points – that forest resources are part of the national patrimony subject to sovereign rights of control; that the conclusion at Rio of a *Non Legally Binding Authoritative Statement of Principles on the Management, Conservation and Development of All Types of Forests* would render unnecessary the negotiation of a binding international treaty and that, while developed countries should increase their national forest cover they should avoid unilateral measures such as bans and restrictions on international trade in tropical forest products (Cl.15-17). On the question of NGO participation in forest conservation and environmental policy-making generally, the *Kuala Lumpur Declaration* was notably silent.

It is significant that this meeting was convened by and took place in Malaysia at a time so close to the final Conference. By April 1992, the Malaysian Prime Minister, Dr. Mahathir bin Mohamad, had made clear his concerns about the pending Conference at Rio. Having earlier considered boycotting UNCED altogether, the Prime Minister demonstrated at the Kuala Lumpur meeting that he had now decided to take an active role in the deliberations and to push for an outcome not prejudicial to Malaysia's continuing involvement in the international timber trade.

In summary, the *Kuala Lumpur Declaration* made it clear that the Rio Conference was not going to avoid the bitter North-South political confrontation that has so frequently characterised United Nations activities. As an active member of ASEAN and the Group of 77, Thailand was locked by the *Kuala Lumpur Declaration* into this collective, confrontational stance.

Outcomes of UNCED on Forest Policy

Throughout the Rio Conference, the Malaysian Prime Minister, on behalf of the Group of 77, stood in opposition to international involvement in tropical forest conservation, including the adoption of a legally binding treaty. Dr Mahathir resolutely championed the terms of the *Kuala Lumpur Declaration*, showing no leeway in his negotiating stance. Although only India was as vocal in its opposition to an international treaty, the developed countries failed to divide the Group of 77 and to win over the support of those governments, including Thailand, which stood to gain from the United States' last minute offer to double international forest conservation assistance. The general environment of hostility created by the developed world's reluctance to put up significant new finance and the United States' procrastinations on climate change and technology transfer also help to explain the failure of the proposal for a forest treaty (Panjabi 1992: 88, 89-103, 134-136; Kindall 1993: 73-76). The fact that the United States, which was so clearly unwilling to accept any restraints on its own economic freedom, was firmly in favour of a forest treaty only served to highlight the apparent hypocrisy of the developed countries and to entrench the Group of 77 in their opposition to a forest treaty. The developed countries were far from agreement among themselves on many issues (Johnson 1993: 103). Their performance, and that of the United States in particular, provided no justification for developing countries with views less confrontational than Malaysia to break away from the fold (Panjabi 1992: 99-101).

The principal outcome of this political deadlock on forest issues was the adoption of the *Non-Legally Binding Authoritative Statement of Principles for a Global Consensus on the Management, Conservation and Sustainable Development of All Types of Forests*. This Non Legally Binding Statement simply declares that it represents a first global consensus on forests (Preamble Cl(d)). A closer inspection of its terms, however, shows what little real consensus there was. For example, the Statement opens with an affirmation of national sovereignty over natural resources, but this is immediately followed by a call for increased international co-operation for forest conservation and sustainable development (Principle 1). The need for a cross sectoral, integrated environment and development approach is acknowledged at several points and there is also an ambitious call for the "greening of the world" (Principle 8(a)), but these environmentally commendable principles sit side by side with Principles Thirteen and Fourteen which deal with the international timber trade and unilateral measures to prevent free trade in forest products. Principle Thirteen states that open and free international trade in forest products should be facilitated and the local processing of forest products should be encouraged. Principle Fourteen states:

"Unilateral measures, incompatible with international obligations or agreements, to restrict and/or ban international trade in timber or other forest products should be removed or avoided, in order to attain long term sustainable forest management."

The inclusion of Principles Thirteen and Fourteen led many NGOs immediately to condemn the Statement as a "Chainsaw Charter" (Johnson 1993:5-6). Perhaps the most that can be said for this Statement is that it represents a very weak compromise, in which the need to protect and conserve forests is heavily tempered by the short term economic interests of some timber exporting countries in maintaining a free market for tropical timber products. This basic dichotomy, between the need to protect and the desire to exploit tropical forests, accounts for the inclusion of such potentially contradictory principles as the encouragement of "open and free international trade in forest products", alongside the denunciation of "fiscal, trade, industrial, transportation and other policies and practices that may lead to forest degradation" (Principle Thirteen).

The emphasis on national sovereignty and the rejection of an international treaty are further evidence of the lack of any real international political consensus on forest issues.

The *Convention on Biological Diversity* and the *Framework Convention on Climate Change* touch marginally on forest issues. The first of these Conventions requires each contracting party to establish a system of protected areas (Article 8) and to develop national strategies, plans or programs for the "conservation and sustainable use of biological diversity" (Article 6). The *Framework Convention on Climate Change* allocates the leading responsibility for combating climate change to developed countries (Article 1; Principle 3). It does, however, commit all contracting parties to promoting the conservation and sustainable management of "sinks and reservoirs" for greenhouse gases including forests (Article 4(1)(d)). The Convention calls for special consideration of the needs and circumstances of countries which shoulder an abnormal burden under the Convention (Article 3(2)).

In summary, UNCED adopted some progressive principles on forest conservation but at a high price. The Conference polarised views along a North-South divide, generated insufficient finance and gave credence to the view that sustainable timber exploitation is both feasible and desirable (Shiva 1993: 78). Critics who regard the Conference as a retrogressive step (Panjabi 1992: 276; Pallemaerts 1993: 1-19; Porras 1993: 20-34), at least on the forest issue, have good grounds for their pessimism.

Thailand, UNCED and International Forest Policy

It is clear that UNCED helped to create a new level of environmental awareness in Thailand. The country's National Report to UNCED describes the extensive national and regional consultations which preceded the Conference (National Report 1992: 7). It gives Thailand's support to the *Convention on Biological Diversity* and the *Convention on Global Climate Change*. It describes Thailand's commitment to reforestation and forest conservation as measures which will help to implement the goals of these treaties. The Seventh National Economic and Social Development Plan and the Master

Plan for the Forestry Sector are presented as further evidence of Thailand's commitment to environmental goals, including forest conservation (Thailand National Report 1992: 19).

In addition to the submission of a National Report to the UNCED, Thailand participated actively in regional negotiations arranged prior to and in preparation for the Rio Conference. In the two years leading up to UNCED, Thailand hosted the Regional Forum on Business and Environment, the Ministerial Conference on Environment and Development in Asia and the Pacific, the Technical Workshop to Explore Options for Global Forestry Management and the International Conference on Global Warming and Sustainable Development. Thailand's ambitions to play a regional leadership role were also furthered by the establishment of the Environmental Research and Training Centre (ERTC) in Bangkok in March 1992 (Thailand National Report 1992: 10).

Thailand's preparatory activities at national and regional levels illustrate its enthusiasm for the goals of UNCED generally. Nevertheless, when the Rio Conference finally took place, Thailand's stand on forest issues, as with many developing countries, can only be described as ambivalent. For example, the Thai delegation to the Conference was led by Professor Dr Her Royal Highness Princess Chulaborn Mahidol. Her statement to the Conference included general observations on the need for sectoral integration and area specific development programs taking into account local factors (1992: 236). The diplomatic overtones of the Thai delegation are in marked contrast to the Malaysian Government's contribution, especially on forest matters. Nevertheless, Thailand, like other developing countries, was not lured away from the Group of 77's hard line on forest issues by the offer of additional financial assistance for forest conservation (Shiva 1993: 81). This position appears incongruous in the light of Thailand's National Report to UNCED. This documents Thailand's commitment to a massive reforestation programme and calls for increased international assistance for reforestation and conservation projects (National Report 1992: 70). The imperatives of regional politics are only partially to blame for Thailand's ambivalence on forest issues at

UNCED. Factors at the national level, as discussed below, also contributed significantly to this result.

FOREST POLICY IN THAILAND

Are the conflicts and contradictions apparent in international forest policy reflected in the national sphere? In the remainder of this chapter, factors which frustrate the realisation of forest conservation in Thailand and their relation to the international dilemmas which emerged at UNCED are explored. Three areas of Thai forest policy are afforded special attention: the logging ban; the "new partnership" between government and NGOs; and the reforestation programme.

Deforestation and the Logging Ban

Thailand is no newcomer to problems of forest conservation. On the contrary, it can boast one of the worst records of deforestation in Southeast Asia to date. Forest cover has decreased from 72% (36.9 million ha) in 1938 to 29% (14.8 million ha), in 1985. Some estimates put the remaining area of natural forest as low as 22% (Hurst 1990:81). The rate of deforestation in Thailand is shown in Table 1.

Table 1:

Comparison of Existing Forest and Changes Between 1961-1985.

YEAR	AREA OF FORESTED LAND (ha)	% OF LAND UNDER FOREST COVER
1961	27,362,850	53.33
1973	22,170,700	43.21
1976	19,842,000	38.67
1978	17,522,400	34.15
1982	15,660,000	30.52
1985	14,905,300	29.05

(Source: Hurst 1990:46)

The causes of deforestation in Thailand lie partly in excessive logging but primarily in large scale, illegal clearance of forest land for conversion to agricultural purposes (Hurst 1990: 218; Hirsch 1988:359). The two factors are inter-related and both have contributed to the rapid pace of economic development experienced by Thailand in recent decades.

The campaign to prevent forest encroachment in Thailand has a long and largely unsuccessful record which pre-dates the concerns raised by UNCED (Leungaramsri & Rajesh 1992: 32). In the mid 1980s, efforts to stop illegal logging activities were stepped up but without great success, as the activities of illegal loggers only became more sophisticated in response (Sricharatchanya 17/9/1987: 86). Tensions came to a head in November 1988 when flash floods in southern Thailand killed 350 people. The Government responded by suspending logging activities in the southern region and subsequently banning logging throughout Thailand (Wishart 1989: 13; Sricharatchanya 12/1/1989: 40). This action won popular support and was therefore legally entrenched, despite the opposition of vested logging interests (Sricharatchanya 2/2/1989: 26; Tuntawiroon 1983: 86-91). The Government was able to deal with this opposition by making a controversial deal with Burma allowing the import of logs from that country to supply Thai saw mills (McDonald 22/2/1990: 16.

Official figures indicate that, after the logging ban, the rate of forest encroachment dropped by 83.59% (Leungaramsri & Rajesh 1992:33). Pursuant to the ban, enforcement activities were stepped up. In 1990, 19,051 illegal operations were uncovered and 11,684 arrests of suspected illegal loggers were made. In addition, 188 saw mills were forced to close down in the immediate aftermath of the ban. It is estimated that more than 1.9 million cubic metres of Thai timber have been saved by the ban (Leungaramsri & Rajesh 1992:33-34)

Despite these impressive figures, the logging ban does not provide a comprehensive solution to problems of deforestation and conservation. Leungaramsri and Rajesh provide evidence that illegal logging in Thai forests persists and has simply taken on more surreptitious forms (1992: 39-41). In addition, imports of timber from

Table 2:

Imports of Timber into Thailand From Neighbouring Countries, 1987-1988

COUNTRY	IMPORTS IN 1987 1,000 m³	IMPORTS IN 1988 1,000 m³	% INCREASE
MALAYSIA	636	1,595	151%
INDONESIA	180	320	78%
BURMA	124	303	144%

(Source: The Department of Business Economics in Leungaramsri & Rajesh 1992:42)

neighbouring countries were increasing rapidly at the time of the logging ban, as the figures in Table 2 show, and they have accelerated since with legal and illegal imports also from Laos and Cambodia.

The increased volume of logging traffic from the border areas allows illegally cut timber on the Thai side of its international borders to be easily mixed with foreign timber. At the same time, state development projects have provided opportunities for occasional logging licences to be granted, sometimes over vast areas (Leungaramsri & Rajesh 1992: 43). Each of these factors impairs the efficacy of the logging ban. Furthermore, the environmental benefits of the ban are questionable. While the slowing pace of deforestation in Thailand is welcome, it is clear that this trend had set in before the ban partly in response to the declining areas of forest land available and partly because of the draw of new employment opportunities in urban centres (Thailand National Report 1992: 66). The decline in numbers of saw mills has not been matched by any decline in the number of furniture and wood craft businesses (Leungaramsri & Rajesh 1992: 41). Most disturbing, however, is the rapid expansion of timber imports from neighbouring countries. At the end of the day, the logging ban has done very little to halt deforestation; it has simply passed on the problem to the region as a whole, a solution patently inadequate in global terms.

The New Partnership with NGOs

One of the most notable themes of Thailand's Seventh National Economic and Social Development Plan (1991-1996) is that of promoting a new partnership between the Government and NGOs:

"It is neither fair nor realistic to expect the Government to bear the burden of generating most of the revenues necessary for environmental rehabilitation . . . ambitious plans call for contributions from all sectors of the economy." (1992: 20)

In line with this new approach to Government-NGO cooperation, NGO representatives were invited to sit on the National Preparatory and Co-ordinating Committee (NPCC) which, among other things, prepared the National Report to UNCED and was invited to contribute to the discussion of forest policy. The grass roots representatives, for example, are responsible for the statement in the Thailand National Report that:

"More emphasis needs to be given to aspects such as conservation and protection, redefinition of degraded forests, forest regeneration instead of plantation establishment, people's rights to land and forest, recognition of local knowledge and wider access to the planning process." (1992: 84)

The National Report pays special attention to the roles of NGO actors in reforestation activities. It is clear that in Thailand, contributions are expected from NGO actors of two different kinds – grass roots community organisations and private business organisations. The former are invited to play a greater role in community forestry projects, the latter to participate in commercial plantations. These policies are drawn directly from the Seventh Plan and the Master Plan for the Forest Sector (ibid. 1992: 68-70).

Importantly, both the National Report to UNCED and the Seventh Plan embrace a wider definition of NGOs than one confined to grass roots, community based organisations. The firm commitment of the Thai Government to cooperation with business as well as community organisations is illustrated by the membership of the then Prime Minister, Anand Panyarachun, on the Business Council for Sustainable Development (BCSD), a voluntary council composed of government and business representatives established under the umbrella of UNCED preparatory negotiations to promote sustainable development in industry (McCoy & McCully 1993: 88). In July 1991, the Federation of Thai Industries organised an ASEAN Regional Forum on Business and Environment in Bangkok. These developments show the broadening of social responsibility for environmental issues, a development which also characterised the international negotiations, and the increasing reliance of the Thai Government on commercially inspired reforestation programs.

Grass roots, community organisations have been actively involved in environmental campaigns, including community forest projects, for several years in Thailand (Leungaramsri & Rajesh, 1992: 11). One example is the World Wildlife Fund (Thailand) sponsored project in communities bordering the Khao Yai National Park. This project is based on the premise that forest protection and rural development are inter-related. The project sponsors credit, education and collective business ventures in villages bordering the Park. A co-operative credit society, the Environmental Protection Society, has been formed and villagers who agree to abide by the *National Park Regulations*, which prohibit farming encroachments in the Park, are eligible to receive credit from the Society. In addition, there has been work created for some villagers in low key tourism developments. The project has stalled some forest encroachment and is regarded as successful. The greatest challenge, however, is to replicate the project, with its demanding resource requirements, in other areas (Brockelman 1988: 91-93) and to reconcile conservation objectives with the needs of farmers already in illegal occupation of forest land. The fact that 29% or less of the total land area remains under forest cover demonstrates that, however successful anti-encroachment projects are, they do not offer a complete solution for the reforestation of agricultural land.

At first sight, the shortage of funds to replicate successful forest projects in Thailand, and the great demand for them, is further evidence that Thailand's viewpoint at UNCED was incongruous.

Given the belated offer of the United States to increase overseas aid for forest projects in developing countries, why was the Thai Government not persuaded to break away from the hard line espoused by the Group of 77? Leaving aside the international diplomatic repercussions that such a change in position would most probably have incurred, there are convincing reasons in the domestic sphere which also help to explain the Thai position. These reasons relate to the reforestation programmes which the Thai Government was actively pursuing at the time of UNCED.

Reservation, Resettlement and Reforestation

Various attempts have been made to reserve and protect the remaining forest in Thailand. Since the 1960s, the Royal Forestry Department (RFD) has pursued an active programme of reservation despite the rapid pace of deforestation. In 1985, the area of forest reserves extended to 42% of all Thailand, despite the reduction of actual natural forest cover to between 22% and 29% (Hirsch 1990:168). It is estimated that 1.2 million families, approximately 20% of Thai farmers, are in illegal occupation of land in forest reserves (Hirsch 1990: 168). Attempts by RFD to reclaim the land compulsorily have led to outbreaks of violence in affected communities because many farmers simply have nowhere else to go (Handley 31/10/1991: 15).

The National Forest Policy, 1985, set an ambitious goal of attaining 40% actual permanent forest cover, of which 15% was to be completely protected and 25% was to be classified as productive forest (Dugan: 7). Under the Seventh Plan, the targeted proportion of conservation forest was raised to 25% and the area of commercial forest reduced to 15%. (Thailand National Report: 65) In the National Report, reforestation is presented as one activity which will help the Thai Government to stabilise its carbon dioxide emissions under the *Convention on Global Warming*. The National Report estimated that, for Thailand to stabilise its carbon dioxide emissions from all sources at the 1991 level, the state should ensure that a minimum of 33% of its area is kept permanently under forest cover. (National Report: 68)

The emphasis since the 1980s has been on commercial reforestation involving, primarily, eucalyptus plantations (Dugan:19). A facilitative legal framework and considerable fiscal incentives have been set up to support this policy objective (Puntasen et al. 1992: 190), in line with the Government's "new partnership" with business. Plantation forests, however, have led to local riots (Handley 31/10/1991: 15). This is because farmers without title to land in forest reserves can, at any time, have their land requisitioned by RFD for re-allocation to commercial enterprises and influential landowners for plantation forests. Even when compensation is payable, the rate is only one half to one third of the market price (Puntasen et al. 1992: 190). At the time of UNCED, the army was actively engaged in implementing plans to move 1.25 million people to release their farm land for reforestation (Handley 31/10/1991: 15).This was despite the protests of environmentalists, farmers and the King, who opposed the eucalyptus plantations on environmental grounds (Puntasen et al. 1992: 201).

Puntasen, Siripachai and Punyasavatsut trace the international and national commercial and military interests which have influenced the policy of promoting industrial plantations at the expense of local communities' well being (1991: 191). It is clear that these interests have constrained government policy even when environmental issues have been perceived as a vote winner. With the direct involvement of the military in reforestation programs, the Government at the time of UNCED was under pressure from both sides of the political spectrum – the military, who have successively intervened in politics to overthrow civilian regimes and safeguard their own interests, and the pro-democracy business community who are a valuable ally in expensive electoral campaigns.

The political situation at the time of UNCED is particularly illustrative of the power of these interest groups. In February 1991, the elected government of Chatichai Choonhavan was ousted in a military coup. The military swiftly appointed an interim government under Anand Panyarachan to lead the country into elections under a new constitution. Elections in February 1992 led to victory for a coalition government involving a top military leader, Suchinda Kraprayoon as unelected Prime Minister, but resentment at the continuing military role triggered public rioting in May 1992. The riots were crushed by dramatic military intervention which left at least 50 dead and hundreds wounded Tasker (20/8/92: 33). Fresh elections were called for September 1992 and Anand was re-installed in the interim. As a respected businessman, a member of the international BCSD, and an appointee of the military, Mr. Anand was particularly sensitive to both the interest groups which favour plantation forestry (Handley 31/10/1991: 16). In reality, he was holding the reins, attempting to broker a political compromise between these interests (Girling 1994: 307).

The reasons why Thailand was not tempted to abandon the Group of 77's hard line on forestry at Rio are now clear. Because forestry is such a sensitive issue in domestic politics, the internationalisation of forestry issues, particularly the call for a binding international treaty, was naturally resisted. The past record of deforestation in Thailand did not place the Government in a strong position to advocate forest conservation. Understandably, the Government did not wish to expose itself to adverse publicity regarding the impact of the eucalyptus plantation programme. The turbulent political events of 1992 help to further explain the Thai contribution at Rio. Anand was serving only a temporary period in office and this factor, combined with the difficult political situation at home, prevailed against an overtly political presence at the Rio Conference.

The reforestation programme is yet to show results. By 1989, only 697,000 hectares had been replanted with forest trees, a small area when compared to the 13 million hectares of forest cover lost to agriculture over the past three decades (Thailand National Report: 136). Commercial plantations have been stalled in the face of persistent opposition from communities settled in officially gazetted forest reserves (Anon 19/1/95: 1). Caught between the demands of these communities and the business sector, RFD has been unable to release land for plantation forestry in anything like the amount required. Whatever the good intentions of the Seventh Plan, the Master Plan for the Forest Sector and the National Report to UNCED, the reality is once again a lack of any real consensus on the balance to be struck between the commercial interests of plantation forestry and the needs of farming communities illegally settled in forest reserves. The irony is that while some of these communities may now be favoured with community focussed forestry projects, others remain at risk of forcible eviction from their land to make way for commercial plantations.

CONCLUSION

The UNCED proceedings aroused great interest in Thailand and helped to raise environmental awareness to new heights. In the same month that UNCED took place, the interim government passed the *Environment Protection and Conservation Act, 1992* (BE 2535) This makes provision for environmental policy-making at a high level in government while recognising the role of provincial and local level authorities in implementing environmental projects (Chapter 1). The Act establishes an Environment Fund (Chapter 2) and encourages public participation by recognising the right to greater freedom of information and the role of NGOs in protecting the environment (s.6). The Act is evidence of the real commitment to achieving environmental goals in Thailand. However, the Act does not address the issue of forest conservation, and the institutions established under the Act have no special authority on forestry matters which continue to fall solely within the jurisdiction of RFD. The Act is ample evidence that, while Thailand is ready to take up the environmental challenge generally, and to address the problems of pollution in particular, the forest issue remains shrouded in controversy.

The underlying reason for the lack of progress on forest policy at the international and national level is the failure to resolve the conflicting interests which lie at the heart of forest issues. In Thailand, the conflict is between two rival forms of exploitation, that of plantation forestry and small holder, cash crop agriculture. These groups embrace different models of conservation and/or reforestation, but in both cases environmental imperatives are subsumed by over-riding human concerns with production and consumption. At the international level, the conflict is even more evidently one between exploitation and conservation. Moreover, the notion of sustainable exploitation, embraced wholeheartedly in the *Statement of Forest Principles*, is one that has not worked in practice, as evidenced by Thailand's history of excessive logging in forests reserves prior to the ban. The failure of sustainable exploitation policies throughout the world (Shiva 1993: 84) makes even more clear the need to address the basic conflict between conservation and exploitation which lies at the heart of forest policy.

It is because forest issues raise so sharply this basic conflict of interests that so little progress is in evidence either at the national or the international level. While at both these levels, environmental awareness has increased dramatically in the 1990s and measures which strengthen environmental protection are being adopted, the forest issue demonstrates that this new environmental consciousness is not yet so strong that it can successfully address the more fundamental conflicts which lie at the heart of the major environmental problems challenging the world today.

REFERENCES

Anon, 1995 "Reforestation Target Won't Be Met", *Bangkok Post*, 19/1/95, 1

Brockelman, W., 1988, "Protection and Development in and About Khao Yai Park, Thailand", in Gradwohl, J & Greenberg, R *Saving the Tropical Forests*, Earthscan Publications, London, pp 91-93.

Chulabhorn Mahidol , 1992 , "Statement to Rio Conference" 22(4) *Environmental Policy and Law*, p 236.

Dugan et al., *Rehabilitation of Logged over Forests in Asia /Pacific Region: Country Studies: Annex V, Thailand*, Draft Report, ITTO, p 7.

Girling, J., 1994, "Twin Peaks, Disturbing Shadows", *Southeast Asian Affairs*, pp 305-319.

Handley, P., 1991, "The Land Wars", *Far Eastern Economic Review*, 31/10/1991, 15.

Hirsch, P., 1988, "Spontaneous Land Settlement and Deforestation in Thailand", in Dargavel,J & Dixon,K, *Changing Tropical Forests*, Centre for Resource and Environmental Studies, Canberra, pp 359-376.

Hirsch, P., 1990, "Forests, Forest Reserve and Forest Land in Thailand", 156(2) *The Geographical Journal*, p 166.

Hurst, P., *1990, Rainforest Politics*, 1990, Zed Books, London.

Johnson, S., 1993, *The Earth Summit: The United Nations Conference on Environment and Development*,Graham & Trotman, London.

Kindall, M., "Talking Past Each Other at the Summit" (1993) 4 *Columbia Journal of International Environmental Law and Policy,* pp 69-79.

Kuala Lumpur Declaration on Environment and Development, April 1992, GA Doc A/47/203, Cl.15-17.

Laungaramsri, P. & Rajesh, N., 1992, *The Future of People and Forests in Thailand After the Logging Ban*, Bangkok.

McCoy, M. & McCully, P., 1993, *The Road From Rio*, International Books WISE, Netherlands.

McDonald, H., "Partners in Plunder", *Far Eastern Economic Review*, 22/2/1990, p 16.

Minister of Justice, "UNCED – The Thai Response", a speech to the *Conference on Environment and Development: An Asian-Pacific Response to UNCED*, 30/4/-4/5/93.

Non Legally Binding Authoritative Statement of Principles for a Global Consensus on the Management, Conservation and Sustainable Development of All Types of Forest, A/CONF.152/6/Rev.1, 13/6/1992.

Pallemaerts, M., "International Environmental Law From Stockholm to Rio: Back to the Future?" in Sands, P, *Greening International Law*, 1993, Earthscan, London, pp 1-19.

Panjabi, K., 1992, "The South and the Earth Summit: the Development /Environment Dichotomy 11(1) *Dickson Journal of International Law,* pp 77-138.

Porras, I., 1993, "The Rio Declaration: A New Basis for International Cooperation" in Sands, P, *Greening International Law*, Earthscan, London, pp 20-34.

Puntasen, A. et al., 1992, "Political Economy of Eucalyptus: Business, Bureaucracy and the Thai Government" 22(2) *Journal of Contemporary Asia*, 187.

Shiva, V., "International Controversy Over Sustainable Forestry" in Bergesen & Parmann *Green Globe Yearbook*, 1993 Fridtjof Nansen Institute, OUP, Oxford.

Sricharatchanya, P., "Jungle Warfare", *Far Eastern Economic Review*, 17/9/1987, p 86.

Sricharatchanya, P., "Too Little, Too Late", *Far Eastern Economic Review*, 12/1/1989, p 40.

Sricharatchanya, P., "Getting Lumbered", *Far Eastern Economic Review*, 2/2/1989, p 26.

Tasker, R., 1992, "Voters' Second Chance", *Far Eastern Economic Review*, 20/8/92, p 33.

Thailand National Report to UNCED, 1992, Bangkok.

Tuntawiroon, N., 1983, "Public Perception of Tropical Rainforest and Its Future in Thailand", in, *Environment-Development Natural Resource Crisis in Asia and the*

Pacific: Proceedings of the Symposium Organised by Sahabat Alam Malaysia, Sahabat Alam Malaysia, Penang, Malaysia, pp 86-91.

United Nations Convention on Biological Diversity, UNCED, 5/6/1992, Rio de Janeiro.

United Nations Framework Convention on Climate Change, UNCED, 9/5/1992, Rio de Janeiro.

Wishart, F., "Thai Logging Ban Offers Message of Hope", (1989) *Habitat Australia*, p 13.

THE TAMBON COUNCIL AND COMMUNITY FOREST MANAGEMENT

Apichai Puntasen

INTRODUCTION

The rapid deterioration of global forest resources is quite a recent phenomenon. In the case of Thailand, a 1961 aerial survey of land use indicated that 53.3 percent of the total land area was under forests (Arbhabhirama 1987). In 1985 official figures revealed that only 89.9 million *rai*,[1] or 28 percent of the total land area, was forested. The two major historical factors responsible for this situation have been the reform of the bureaucracy in 1892, resulting in the establishment of strong, centralised state control, and the direction of government development policy since 1961 through a process of 'modernisation'.

The latter, with its development of the country along a Western model of industrialisation, has contributed far more towards the rapid disappearance of Thailand's forest resources. While there is an indication of some reduction in the forest cover from the period 1892 to 1961, the pace of deforestation was far slower during this period than the latter period of 'modernisation', i.e. 1961 to 1985. Development strategies influenced by 'modernisation' have stressed rapid increases in material production with the main objective being to 'catch up' with developed nations without much consideration for resource or environmental costs. The need to expand resource use came primarily through the requirements of industrialisation.

---

[1] 6.25 *rai* = 1 hectare.

As forest land became state land, control over forest management was bureaucratised and centralised. Centralisation contributed to deforestation through inefficiencies in resource management as a result of a long line of bureaucratic controls on policies, together with inflexible top-down rules and regulations without adequate feed-back from the 'bottom', or local level.

The only way in which to slow down or possibly even reverse such detrimental trends of resource utilisation is by breaking this catastrophic combination of centralisation and modernisation, either by redirecting the country's development policy away from modernisation or by opting for decentralisation. Considering the strong influence of processes of globalisation it is inconceivable that the modernisation tendency can be easily halted or redirected. On the other hand, decentralisation has emerged as a contemporary global trend, compatible with the process of globalisation, as it reflects the increasing influence of democratic values across the world, as well as an increasing recognition of economic, resource and environmental gains obtained through the decentralisation of resource management.

Thailand is also moving along this path. The defeat of the late dictatorial regime during the people's uprising in May 1992 points towards the democratic aspirations of the people. The contemporary demand by democratic forces for the Thai government to hasten the country's pace of decentralisation aims to preempt any potential assault on democratic principles. Increased participation of people at the grassroots, or communal level also reduces the undesirable consequences of centralised control and motivates people to become more involved in activities directly related to them.

Effective enactment of the Tambon Council and Tambon Administrative Unit Bill since March 1995 can be considered as one of the major changes of direction toward decentralisation in Thailand. Among many other responsibilities, the Bill delegates the tambon (sub-district) council (TC) with authority to manage its own resources, including its forests. This is a major shift in resource management policy away from central control to a far more decentralised level. This study examines the emerging composition and form of the TC and its potential for managing its own resources.

For present purposes, the focus is specifically on forest resources, as they are one of the most important natural resources in Thailand today.

THE TAMBON COUNCIL AS A PEOPLE'S ORGANISATION

Although the TC was originally created in the late 1950s in principle to serve as the smallest administrative unit in order to propagate democracy at a grass-roots level, in practice it was dominated by regional government officials to serve various policies dictated by the central government. Nevertheless, there has been a long struggle by a series of democratic forces since its inception calling for increasing autonomy of the TC. The passing of the Tambon Council and Tambon Administrative Unit Bill by the end of 1994, and its full enactment by March 1995, indicates the gradual transformation of the TC as a state organisation into more of a people's organisation after a long struggle of almost 40 years. The TC in its present form is still far from being an ideal form of people's organisation. The *kamnan* (tambon chief) and *phu yai baan* (village heads) are ex-officio members of the TC. These people are in turn under the direct command of the District Officer (a centrally appointed government official). As well the TC is still very far from achieving financial autonomy. However, current trends clearly point in the direction of eventual fiscal and political autonomy for the TC, and it has moved substantially in that direction since Prime Minister General Prem Tinsulanonda first officially proclaimed the TC as a people's organisation in 1981. With regard to this trend of development, the current study thus considers the TC as a form of people's organisation.

In this study a people's organisation is identified as an association established to undertake certain tasks or responsibilities seen by the community to address their specific problems, and to be most useful for them. It may be either a formal or an informal organisation. In the case of the TC it is a formal organisation, established and recognised by the government but also representing the interests of people at the village level. This latter aspect can be used to justify the TC as a 'people's organisation'.

The TC has been selected for this purpose because it has the potential to manage its own forest resources, like other kinds of people's organisation such as Buddhist monks working toward forest protection (see Taylor in this volume). Apart form being fully recognised by the government and well funded, the 1995 Act accorded the TC status as 'juridicial person'. The granting of this status means that TCs are given the same legal status as individuals under Thai law, that is the right to own and operate property and to enter into legally binding contractual relationships. This status enables the councils to manage their affairs with greater flexibility, and perhaps, also with greater responsibility. In a tambon where people actively and closely monitor the council's activities, it cannot do otherwise than act responsibly.

The TC consists of the *kamnan*, the village heads of that tambon, the health officer of the tambon, one 'knowledgeable' person per village, and secretary of the council. The *kamnan* or tambon chief is elected by people of the tambon usually from amongst one of the existing village chiefs. The village chiefs are elected by the villagers. Whereas previously the *kamnan* and village chiefs were elected for life (until retirement at 60), new rules stipulate fixed terms of four years. Each village also elects a knowledgeable person or elder/wise person to serve as its representative on the council. In the past the central government tried to exert its policy at the tambon level through the *kamnan*, who is also part of the regional bureaucracy.

The Act terminates all traditional practices and allows the TC to design its own policies as well as to control the use of its own funds, and to have autonomy in entering into any contractual relationship to ensure that the money allocated will be used in the most effective and efficient way. A TC which is seen to be capable of managing its own financial affairs, by raising a regular annual income over a three year period with an annual average of 150,000 baht, will be raised to the new status of "Tambon Administrative Unit", a full-fledged form of local government, which will be allowed to collect its own taxes, legally own land, pass rules and regulations, charge and collect fines and so on. Moreover, the TC being one of the few formal people's organisations recognised by the Thai government, and receiving substantial amounts of financial support from the government, should actually be in a position to look after its own forest resources, if the council has a resolution to do so.

The aspect of formal recognition by the government of the TC is crucial for the role of managing community forests, especially when most community forests existing in Thailand in the past have been reserved forests. By being "reserved", the forests are theoretically protected by officially authorised bodies. No one is allowed to settle or to collect any forest products there. It would be inconsistent for any organisation that does not receive official recognition to manage community forests located in reserved forests.

The newly restructured TC and tambon administrative unit are given two major responsibilities amongst many others: training and job promotion, and the conservation of natural resources and the environment. The focus here on the latter specifically looks at the case of community forest management by the TC.

COMMUNITY FORESTS: DEFINITION AND RELATED OBSERVATIONS

A community forest can be defined as an area where people from local communities agree to protect and grow trees, and collectively to maintain these trees and the other flora and fauna that they support. A traditional community forest is organised to conserve and sustainably manage the forest area. The organisation has full authority to decide on the rules and regulations for common users. The forest land area is clearly demarcated, and this is acknowledged by all other communities living in the vicinity. The main purpose of this kind of forest management is to respond fairly to the needs for survival of members of each community. Resources are therefore expected to be managed efficiently and sustainably.

Community forests have existed throughout the history of village settlement in Thailand. New settlers normally agreed to set aside some existing forest lands or grazing lands for communal uses. While in the past the community was entitled to make its own rules and regulations regarding the use of communal property, especially community forests, the introduction of a Western legal system to

Thailand in 1892 removed such communal rights in favour of private and state ownership. Since the tambon was formally created in 1914, it has been recognised as manager of these public lands. This allocation has been normally acknowledged by the Royal Forest Department (RFD), and documented by the Lands Department. However, the land still remains under the ownership of the state and the RFD has the freedom to resume this land whenever it chooses, if the tambon is located in reserved forest. Otherwise, any confiscation by the state must receive approval by the related TC.

Traditionally, villages in the northeastern region have allocated communal land as burial grounds, and as areas for the village guardian. In the Northeast some communities have also allocated forest land as communal woodlots. However, the South and Central Plains have not had such a tradition. In the South trees have been a part of the livelihood of communities and central to their lives, and thus certain forest areas were not specifically demarcated as community forests. The rice growing areas of the Chaophraya floodplain in central Thailand have no strong traditions of protecting forests.

Community forests are clearly not solely for the purpose of conservation of natural resources. More importantly, their main purpose is for forest resources to be used fairly and efficiently by members of the community. Thus utilisation goes hand-in-hand with conservation. Otherwise incentives for members of the community to conserve these forests will not be sufficiently strong or attractive. In economic terms, communal property with clear rules and regulations observed by members of the community for mutual and equitable benefit is the most appropriate way in which to manage public resources where the usual price mechanism would fail to function efficiently. This is because one normally cannot attach an appropriate price for the utilisation of public property, because by definition this property belongs to everyone and is not owned by any specific individual. The most effective way to manage this form of property is to allow all a fair use of the property, with agreed rules for sustainable usage being strictly observed. Moreover, in the case of community forests the general public also benefits from what are known as 'external economies'. As larger areas of forests are protected, the public will gain from the more balanced environment as well as from the potentially larger supply of forest products.

The main criterion for the community to be able to look after its own forests is its ability to formulate rules which members of the community must observe. These include helping to police the forests. Such practice is a more efficient and effective way of conserving forest areas than if done through government officials. Since government officials do not share the benefits which the community gets in the long-run, it is far easier for them to neglect their responsibilities or to grant illegal concessions for short-term but substantial economic gains, especially when the costs of punishment are not too great or the chances of being 'discovered' are remote.

A study by Saneh Chamarik and Yos Santasombat (1992) outlines eight conditions in order for a community to be able to look after its own forest resources. First, there must be a strong sense of community within the kinship group. This may involve some form of mutual assistance amongst relatives and neighbors, sometimes based on an exchange of labor, and a sharing of common beliefs and traditional practices. Second, there should be mutual benefits for the common users of forest, water and land resources. These resources must be a vital part of the inputs of the production process, and require the mutual conservation of forests. Such common benefits include a common ideology or culture such as forests for burial sites of forests for ancestor spirits. Third, the forest, water and land resources need to be well preserved through maintenance of the community forests. Such maintenance is an integral part of a sustainable agricultural system. Fourth, the community requires a strong leader with wisdom and vision to adopt existing local practices to the changing nature of the socio-economic and political situation.

Fifth, there must already exist some forms of people's organisation in the community, such as village or people's committees for forest conservation, or other related organisations such as irrigation control organisations, TCs, village committees or a committee for forest patrol. Sixth, there must have been a long tradition in recognising some resources, such as forest resources, as the collective property of the community. These resources must be managed by the community to provide mutual benefits for, and fair distribution to, all members. Seventh, the community must be in a state of permanent settlement with certain criteria of social composition and levels of resource use. Despite possible differences in social composition, different members must feel that they belong to the same community. In terms of resource use, resources must not be rapidly exploited to the point that their use cannot continue at the same level in the future. Eighth, the community must have a prevailing resource utilisation network of its own.

The criteria listed above are useful for detecting whether the tambon is capable of looking after its own community forests. While it is not necessary for communities at the tambon level to share all such characteristics, they are important for communities at the sub-tambon level. This is particularly true regarding the sense of belonging to the same community, the desire to share mutual benefits, the availability of forest, water and land resources in sufficient quantities, the existence of strong leadership with vision and wisdom, and a tradition of recognising communal ownership of some important resources, as well as managing them for collective benefits.

At the tambon level one cannot expect much of a sense of belonging to the 'community' because the unit of reference for each individual is at the village level. One can generally expect a conflict of economic interest, especially in resource management at the tambon level. There are often political conflicts at the tambon level, resulting from such conflicts of economic interest. However, tambon members cannot afford to resolve such conflicts through confrontation because they must coexist in the same area. The only way to resolve such conflicts is through compromise and persuasion. If there is any deadlock in the conflict, the TC needs time to resolve this.

Since one cannot expect members within a tambon to share a sense of belonging to the same community, the only way a tambon can share common interests is by satisfying the second condition outlined above. The resources used by the tambon members must be a vital part of the communal production process, and must require the collective conservation of forest. If there are still conflicting interests between different groups within the tambon this must be settled over a period of time.

From the above discussion it can be seen that the TC is in some position of disadvantage in looking after its community forests as compared to other kinds of people's organisations that are less formally organised but have the main purpose of conserving the community forest. On the other hand, the TC's strength lies in the fact that its status is formally recognised by the government.

In the analysis below, after surveying existing TCs in Thailand, case studies will be used to argue that the TC can play a supportive role to other people's organisations, under certain conditions, in conserving community forests.

PROFILE OF TAMBONS' LAND AND FOREST RESOURCES

A survey in 1993 of 174 Tambons across Thailand covered 22 Tambons in the North, 40 in the Northeast, 29 in the South and 83 in the Central Plain.[2] The area covered in the study was sufficiently wide to allow for a regional comparison. In the absence of comprehensive government figures, the survey gives at best a rough indication of land use for tambons in Thailand. The results are summarised in Table 1 below.

On average, the survey shows that the total land area of the tambons in the various regions ranges from 300,000 to 600,000 *rai*. The tambons in the South have a larger average land area than in any other part of the country, while the average land area of

---

[2]   This survey was conducted by the author and Apichart Stitniramai, and Duangmanee Laowakul (see Puntasen et al 1993a) from March-May 1993 in order to study the potential of TCs in protecting their forest resources. The survey was by informal but systematic observation. The provinces covered by the survey in the North are Chiang Rai, Lamphun, Mae Hong Son and Phayao; in the Northeast they are Surin, Kalasin, Buri Ram, Roi Et Ubon Ratchathani, Nakhon Ratchasima and Khon Kaen; in the South they are Trang, Krabi, Phatthalung, Songkhla, Satun, Surat Thani, Nakon Sri Thammarat, Phangnga, Yala and Pattani; in the Central Plain they include Phra Nakhon Sri Ayutthaya, Supanburi, Ang Thong, Saraburi, Chon Buri, Rayaong, Chanthaburi, Nakorn Pathom, Nakon Nayok, Rachaburi, Samut Sakhon and Chachoengsao.

Table 1:
Land Use by an Average Tambon by Region - 1993

LAND USE	North	Northeast	South	Central	Average
Reserved Forests and Mountains	10,548.0	1,554.3	2,926.0	832.9	2,272.0
Community Forests (outside reserved forests)	141.4	881.9	550.3	20.2	315.5
Privately Owned Forests	10,016.1	674.5	1,994.8	138.0	631.8
Public Water Area	26.7	494.4	41.0	44.0	153.0
Natural Streams and Public Canals (length in meters)	(90000.0)	(8,372.2)	(8,233.4)	(5,603.0)	(7,087.6)
Public Grazing Land	0	1,517.9	448.2	44.3	435.8
Other Public Land	144.2	2,183.9	288.9	66.5	619.6
Total Land Area of Tambons	333,613.3	345,290.6	630,537.3	463,503.8	447,653.2

(unbracketed figures in *rai*)

Source : Apichai Puntasen, et al. 1993 (a)

tambons in the North is the smallest. However, tambons in the North have more area under reserved forests (and mountains) than any other region. The North has less cultivable land per tambon than other regions in the country.

In order to maintain the farm lands in the North, there is a need for a good irrigation system and a need to protect the existing forests, especially those in the watershed areas. In fact, the North has a long tradition of organising an indigenous irrigation system, known as *meuang faai*. This has been in existence for the past 700 years. The TCs in the North are also quite active in conserving the community forests.

The area under community forests given in Table 1 represents only that area which belongs to the community and does not include areas under national reserve forests. The Northeast, it is seen, has the largest area under community forests. Despite differences in criteria applied, these findings are consistent with figures compiled by the Royal Forest Department in 1991, showing that from a total area of 1,731,447 *rai* under community forest in Thailand, as much as 1,079,826 *rai* is in the Northeastern region.[3] The existence of such large areas under community forests in the Northeast also indicates a strong tradition of protecting these community forests, for common use, including use for cultural and traditional practices.

The Central region only has a small area under either community or reserve forests. In the North the small area under community forests is offset by a significant area under reserved as well as conserved forests (and mountains). This forested area is critical for agricultural activities, as it helps retain water thus maintaining soil moisture content, and keeping the area fertile. The South, on the other hand, has more area under privately owned forests than any other part of the country. Traditionally, people in the South have earned their living from cultivating fruits and natural rubber, and more recently coffee and palm oil. As a result families work intensively on their own private plots of land, and do not have much time to work with other members of the community. Their ways of life are quite unlike the rice farmers in other parts of the country, or even the commercial dryland smallholders of the North and Northeast who grow tobacco, maize, cassava, sugar cane and other cash crops. Such farming practices have, in the past, involved labour exchanges during the cultivating and harvesting seasons, and this has required close association and strong communal ties. More recently, this system has been superseded by wage labouring.

From the survey of the tambons' land resources, it is seen that the major part of the tambon forest resources are in fact in reserved forests. However, this area still only accounts for about 0.5 percent of the total land area of each tambon. The other categories of land available in each tambon which can be converted into forest land are 'public grazing lands' and 'other public lands'. These two total an

---

[3]   There is slightly different definition between the figures given by the RFD and this study in that the RFD's definition only includes forests looked after by communities and already acknowledged by the RFD. Strictly speaking all these community forests can not be part of the conserved forest areas, while the definition in this study is much broader. For sources of figures, please see Royal Forest Department 1991.

area of 1,055.4 *rai* or 0.2 percent of the average tambon's total land area (see Table 1). The total area under community forests, public grazing lands and other public lands is still less than 1 percent of the total area of the tambons selected. However, if the tambons were allowed to own all reserved forests outside specially protected areas, the average total area held under forests for each Tambon would be at least 12 percent.[4]

It thus becomes clear that for viable community forest management, the area under so-called "community forests" which are under the jurisdiction of the TC should include reserved forests. For without this, the tambon will simply not have enough land under forests. Further, by putting both reserved and community forests under the care of the tambons they will be better protected than if under the protection of government officials, or no one at all.

In the meantime, without a general transfer of reserved forest lands from RFD to TC control, then an average tambon only has to take care of only about one percent of its total land area even if this includes reserved forests within its jurisdiction. In principle, therefore, the average tambon should not encounter any problems in overseeing this "community forest" land. Whether a tambon can, or will, actually do this will be discussed in the next section.

The figure of one percent discussed above is the physical upper limit of the area under "community forests" that an average tambon can have. Actual distribution indicates that this area is slightly larger for the North and Northeast than the national average, as the North has a large area of land under 'reserved forests', while the Northeast has additional areas under 'public grazing land' and 'other public lands'.

Since the amount of available land that can be developed into community forests by each tambon is relatively small, it was proposed by one of the TC members in the survey that each Tambon

---

[4]   According to government figures in 1985 the total forested area was 28 percent - 13 percent under reserved forests and 15 percent under conserved forests (Conserved forest areas are 'absolutely'protected. They include national parks, wildlife sanctuaries and critical watershed areas). Using a process of deduction we can assume that if all reserved forests are distributed to the tambons (which cover the entire country except for the municipalities and sanitation districts) the average reserved forest land per Tambon will be close to 13 percent.

must allocate at least 10,000 *rai* as community forest land. This land can then be distributed amongst various villages within the tambon. In any tambon where the physical upper limit is less than 10,000 *rai*, the government should purchase land from individual villagers in order to make up the difference. The proposed 10,000 *rai* should be considered to be the lower limit for the total amount of land in a Tambon under "community forests". This proposed amount of 10,000 *rai* under community forests actually amounts to only 2.2 percent of an average tambon's total land area. If the government plans to achieve its recently targeted forest area of 40 percent of Thailand's total land area (25 percent conserved and 15 percent economic forests), the most effective way in which to do this would be by allocating 2.2 percent of each TC's land area for community forests. These can also serve as "buffer zones" for the protection of state owned "conserved forests" where no encroachments will be permitted. This proposal is an essential element for establishing community forests. Nevertheless the proposal is not intended to be a standardised prescription. The more significant issue is whether the TC in question is capable and willing to do so under its own existing conditions.

THE POTENTIAL OF TCS IN MANAGING COMMUNITY FORESTS

Saneh Chamarik and Yos Santasombat's 1992 study on community forests in the North of Thailand points out that of a total of 153 community forests surveyed in Chiang Mai, Chiang Rai, Nan, Phayao, Mae Hong Son, Lampang and Lamphun provinces, 16 were under the direct care of various TCs, while 89 forests were being looked after by different village committees. The remaining 48 were under the care of other peoples' organisations, such as the 'irrigation community' (or *meuang faai*), the 'community forest committee', the 'committee of elders' and 'conservation groups' in various villages in different provinces.

Village committees are sub-organisations of the TC at the village level. However, the village committee does not have the status of a juridical person. Legally it may not own forests. With the TC and

Tambon Administrative Units Bill passed in the late 1994, it will become legal for a TC to own community forests within the area of that tambon. The tambon will then be able to delegate the power of managing these forests to its various village committees. Thus under such legislation, of the 153 community forests surveyed in the above study, 105 forests, or almost 70 percent of all the surveyed forests, could actually be managed, directly or indirectly, by TCs.

Among the eight conditions discussed above for a community to protect its own forest, the most important one is the need for the community's members to gain long term mutual benefits from these forests. For this to be possible, there must, however, not be strong conflict of economic interest within the tambon or at the village level in question. This latter condition is crucial for the TC to be able to manage its forest resources. Further, the management and conservation of community forests must be directly relevant to the occupational activities and way of life within the tambon.

Other than the above conditions, the state must also acknowledge the rights of the community over its forest resources. The Tambon Council and Administrative Units Act has not given any assurance on this last right. There is a need for the Act to not only acknowledge communal rights over the community forests, but also to honour the rules and regulations given by the communities to conserve these forests. The Act stipulates that if the TC has been upgraded to the status of the tambon administrative unit, it is entitled to make rules and regulations with a maximum fine of 500 baht. This rate of penalty is still much less than the maximum penalty unofficially but formally imposed by many existing committees.

Further, it is necessary that those residing within the tambon also have legal titles and deeds for their agricultural land holdings. It is estimated that less than 40 percent of people living in Thailand have legal titles to their land. Such conditions of insecurity will make it additionally difficult for people to cooperate with the TCs in maintaining their community forests. For, without legal land titles, and with the fear of eviction at any time, there will be less of an incentive for people to settle permanently or even to till 'their' land, and thus less of an incentive for them to be interested in protecting the forests in the vicinity.

CONCLUSIONS

This study has brought to light some of the conditions required in order for TCs to play a more significant role in managing their forest resources. The maintenance of forest resources by TCs is crucial for the maintenance of forests in the entire country, especially if these community forests are located in buffer zones created for the protection of conserved forests.

Various conditions necessary for TCs to be more effective in managing their own community forests have been outlined. Among these are the need for people living in the tambon to derive mutual economic benefits from the community's forest resources, and there must not be major conflicts of economic interest among tambon residents. Equally important is the need for the state to acknowledge the right of the TC to manage its own forest resources. The state also needs to acknowledge existing rules and regulations framed by the community to conserve its own forests. In order to do this, there is a need for legislation other than that dealing with TCs and the tambon administrative units, notably a new bill on Community Forests. The new Community Forest Law needs to include two important clauses. These are first, to allow communities to use the forests on a sustainable basis; and second, to acknowledge rules and regulations framed by officially recognised committees in order to conserve community forests. The granting of legal land titles and deeds to those living within the tambons, as mentioned above, is also a necessary condition for the tambon to be able to manage its resources more effectively. Further, it has also been proposed that there is a need for each tambon to allocate a nominal minimum of 10,000 *rai* of land towards community forests.

Empirical evidence indicates that TCs in the North are most active in managing and protecting their community forests, particularly from destruction or encroachment by outsiders (Chamarik and Santasombat 1992 and Tangsikabutry et. al 1993). Those forests around watershed areas whose survival is critical for the farming activities of people living in the tambon are particularly well protected.

In the Northeast, as has already been pointed out, people have a long tradition of conserving their community forests. However, such activities have been carried out more at the village level than by the TC. Nevertheless, with a long tradition of forest conservation, together with the new Act on TCs and Tambon Administrative units, it is expected that TCs in the Northeast will participate to a greater extent in the management of their community forests.

In the South, the more individualised lifestyles and agricultural practices of the people makes it a little more difficult for TCs to be as active in forest management as those councils in the North and Northeast of the country. As Table 1 shows, the area under privately owned forests in the South for the average tambon is much larger than under community forests. Perhaps the best way to conserve forests in the South is for TCs to encourage individuals, or a group of individuals, within the tambon to grow forests under their own private initiative.

The situation in the Central Plains area is far more discouraging because most forest areas have already disappeared and have been replaced by agricultural holdings cultivating rice and dryland crops such as sugar-cane, corn and cassava. Industrial estates and commercial complexes have also occupied some of this former forest land. It is therefore extremely difficult, if not altogether impossible at present, for the TC in this region to promote reforestation and forest conservation policies. The most that the TCs in this region can do is to help manage and maintain the existing forest cover, primarily under reserved forests, at the present average of 832.9 *rai* per tambon. It is almost inconceivable that the proposal of tambons ensuring a minimum area of 10,000 *rai* under community forests will succeed in the Central Plain region. There has been such a diversification of land use in the region that the maintenance of community forests is no longer seen by the people as being a necessity. However, the current situation of severe drought as well as very serious flooding in the Chao Phraya basin in the Central Plain region is making people realise the need for forests to help maintain a stable water supply and retain soil moisture. As a result there may be a demand to have a larger area under forests in the future. By that time the TCs in the region may play a more active role in reforestation and in managing community forests.

REFERENCES

Arbhabhirama, Anat, et al., 1987, *Thailand Natural Resources Profile,* Bangkok, Thailand Development Research Institute (TDRI).

Chamarik, Saneh and Santasombat, Yos, 1992, *Community Forests in Thailand: Directions for Development, Vol.2 Community Forests in the North,* Bangkok: Local Development Institute (LDI) Foundation.

International Land Development Consultants (Ilaco) and Netherlands Engineering Consultants (Nedeco), 1971, 1973, *Land Consolidation Project in the Central Plain of Thailand,* unpublished report.

Ingram, James C., 1971, *Economic Change in Thailand,* 1850-1970, Stanford University Press.

Puntasen, Apichai, Stitniramai, Apichart & Laowakul Duangmanee, 1993(a), "Study of the Potential of People's Organisations in Conserving and Protecting Their Natural Resources and Environment: the case of the TC", in Nicro, S., (ed.), *Environment '93: A call for People's Participation in Environmental Management,* proceedings of the Fare 93 Seminar, Dec. 1993. 4th Meeting (in Thai), Bangkok Thailand Environment Institute (TEI).

Puntasen, Apichai, 1993 (b), "The Condition of Soil, Water and Forests in 1993: a Demand for Action", in Nicro, S., (ed.), Environment '93: *A call for People's Participation in Environmental Management,* proceedings of the Fare '93 seminar, Dec. 1993, 4th Meeting (in Thai), Bangkok, Thailand Environment Institute (TEI).

Royal Forestry Department, 1991, *Report on Data on Community Forests in Thailand,* Bangkok, Division of Communal Forests.

Tangsikabutre, P., et al., 1993, "Natural Resources and Environmental Management in the North", in Nicro, S., (ed.), Environment '93: *A Call for People's Participation in Environmental Management,* proceedings of the Fare'93 seminar, Dec., 1993, 4th Meeting (in Thai), Bangkok, Thailand Environment Institute (TEI).

COMPETITION OVER RESOURCES AND LOCAL ENVIRONMENT: THE ROLE OF THAI NGOS*

Rapin Quinn

INTRODUCTION

Since the mid-1980s, the role of Thai NGOs in the development process has been widely recognised by the public, government and international agencies largely for their efforts to deliver social services to the marginal poor (e.g. wage workers both in rural and urban areas as well as small-scale peasantry) and to encourage participatory development. In the early 1980s, the general attention of NGOs was given to promotion of agricultural development in favour of the poor. Although the NGOs have been aware of environmental degradation resulting from the increase of agricultural commercialisation, the environment as such did not become a focus of attention until the late 1980s. This chapter aims to investigate the roles played by NGOs in response to competition over resource use between villagers, officials and private entrepreneurs. It also looks at the impact of this competition on village livelihood and local environment as a consequence of the significant agrarian change[1] taking place in Thailand during the 1980s.

*   This paper is based on the data collection in Mae Rim District, Chiang Mai Province during my fieldwork in January 1993. I am grateful to the villagers of Ban Suksawaeng and NGO workers of the Foundation for Education and Development of Rural Areas (FEDRA), Appropriate Technology Association (ATA), Chiang Mai Diocesan Social Action Centre (CM-DISAC) and Project for Ecological Recovery (PER) for their help and openness with me about their work and difficulties.

The chapter focuses on the development work of four NGOs in a forest-fringe village of Northern Thailand during the 1980s. It begins with a general description of the background and nature of Thai NGOs working in the context of Thai rural development. Next, the activities of four NGOs in a Northern Thai village are examined with attention to competition over resources, environmental issues and the use of "people's participation" and "community culture" by the NGOs in formulating their responses. Finally, the NGO roles in response to competition over natural resources and to the emergence of an environmental movement in this area are discussed. The main argument is that the NGO understanding of local situations and culture in accordance with current changes in the political economy of rural Thailand becomes a key factor in successfully formulating a plan of environmental resource management in this area.

THAI NGOS

There is a wide range of different sorts of Thai NGOs, generally made up of socially conscious educated middle class people. They have emerged as independent organisations since the political "uprising" in 1973 (Prudhisan 1987) and during the period of experimentation with democracy in the 1980s. The origins and ideology of many such organisations can be traced to the students and intellectuals who went to remote areas to experience the life of the rural poor from the late 1960s and to campaign for their development. The rural development NGOs which emerged in the early 1980s have sought to introduce "alternative development" approaches, emphasising not only economic development, but also social, political and cultural dimensions to counter what they see as the negative impact on the marginal poor resulting from government

---

[1]   Based on Norton (1984: Ch. 8), who categorises land use for agriculture into four stages of change: 1) land clearing and early agriculture; 2) the subsistence to commercial transition; 3) the spread of commercial agriculture; and 4) the occurrence of "alternative agriculture" along with the commercial agriculture. Agrarian change incorporates change in social relations of production alongside land use change.

development policies and practices. These Thai NGOs usually see themselves as undertaking "participatory development" whereby they encourage people to work together in identifying their problems, designing their own projects and solving their own development problems [Jon 1986: 15]. They claim that their methods are flexible and their plans and activities can be adapted in response to people's changing needs in different situations. The NGOs range from grass-roots supporting organisations (GSOs) (Carroll 1992), which are organised only at the local level, to organisations which have regional or national structures. They are nearly all linked through networking activities which facilitate the flow of information and support between them.

Thai NGOs thus owe their origin to middle class opposition to authoritarian governments of the 1970s. They generally disagreed with the government's single-minded promotion of economic growth strategy which, they said, neglected the human dimension of development. They consider that the double digit economic growth in Thailand has been achieved at the expense of the traditional agricultural sector and of Thailand's natural resources. By the 1980s, one of the key concepts in Thai NGO thinking was that of "community culture" as a means to help people strengthen themselves in the "politics of alternative development" (Friedman 1992). By community culture, the Thai NGOs refer to every aspect of people's social life, especially in relation to the production process through which the people learn the methods of production, social relations and values, methods of decision making and exercising their power. The aim in understanding community culture lies in a belief that it can be "reproduced" in response to the increasing agrarian change produced by the "capitalist" economy and culture. As Fr. Niphot Thienwihan, the Director of Chiang Mai Diocesan Social Action Centre (DISAC) argues:

A community by nature is dynamic and its ideology has been reproduced continuously. This appears in not only a village which has yet to be influenced by capitalism but also in a village which has already been penetrated by the capitalist culture. In the so-called traditional, semi-traditional and urban-culture-oriented villages, there has been cultural and ideological reproduction in counterbalance with the capitalist culture (Bunthien 1988: 91).

At various times, four "participatory-development" NGOs conducted development programmes in the watershed area where Ban Suksawaeng,[2] the village under study, is located. The NGOs were the Chiang Mai Diocesan Social Action Centre (DISAC), the Foundation for Education and Development of Rural Areas (FEDRA), the Appropriate Technology Association (ATA) and the Project for Ecological Recovery (PER). Two (FEDRA and ATA) were still active in January 1993 when I conducted fieldwork in the village.

DISAC is an independent diocesan Catholic NGO which has links with similar organisations in other diocese, with the Catholic "headquarters" in Bangkok and with Catholic organisations overseas. It was set up in 1974 by the Catholic Council of Thailand for Development (CCTD) and has been important in generating much of the early discussion about community culture as one of the NGO alternative development approaches. It has been supported by local donations and Catholic overseas funding agencies (CUSRI, SRI and RDI 1990). The Foundation for Education and Development of Rural Areas (FEDRA), a medium sized Buddhist NGO was set up in 1974 and run by a senior monk in Chiang Mai. Its development objective has been to maintain and improve the economic and social status of the farmers. The monk's development idea and actions received support from the public, both in cash and kind.

Around the mid-1980s, villagers and FEDRA invited ATA and PER to work in this watershed area. ATA is an appropriate-technology NGO which was set up in 1982 by a group of academics in engineering and sociology. PER is an environmental NGO which was set up in 1986 by a group of social activists with the encouragement of some young forestry officials. The local ATA and PER projects were in principle set up only with the approval and support of their Bangkok headquarters. However, the field workers considered

---

[2]   This is a fictitious name used for the purposes of this article, as are the names of village persons and officials.

themselves relatively free to conduct their rural development activities independently in connection with the local communities.

NGO workers from FEDRA, ATA and PER were active in the Northern Development Workers' Association (NDWA), a regional-networking NGO, which provides a hub for NGO workers in Chiang Mai and other Northern provinces where they could share experiences and discuss work difficulties. The organisations NGO, NGO and NGO were members of the NGO-Co-ordinating Organisations of Rural Development (NGO) which acts as a co-ordinating body for over 200 Thai NGOs working in development throughout rural Thailand. Hence, ATA and PER have a horizontal link with FEDRA at the village level and vertical links with their mother organisations and NGO-CORD at the regional and national levels.

NGO INVOLVEMENT AND ACTIVITIES
IN A FOREST-FRINGE VILLAGE

In the following discussion, I trace the NGO activities and roles in Ban Suksawaeng and the projects they have introduced in response to changing demands of the people as they became increasingly involved in agricultural commercialisation. As a consequence of this growing involvement, there has been increased competition over resources which has meant that greater pressure has been put on local livelihood, production and environment. Many villagers have recognised environmental degradation in their village and sought to respond through their "community culture", which has catalysed an environmental movement in this watershed area. Support for environmental concern has also been evident in the work of NGOs, whose "alternative development" approaches have re-oriented and moved from cultural to environmental movements, as has occurred in many parts of rural Thailand and overseas.

Village context

Ban Suksawaeng is located about 40 km North of Chiang Mai. It was settled by a small group of villagers from different lowland villages in 1963 but officially recognised as a village in 1982. The village is at an altitude of about 500 to 600 metres and lies in a small valley surrounded by degraded forest. Access to the village is by a rough laterite feeder road linked to the Chiang Mai-Fang highway. The road is difficult for vehicles to negotiate, especially in the rainy season. The village is about five kilometres from a Lua village higher up the mountain which, villagers claim, has been occupied continuously for over 200 years.

In the early 1990s, Ban Suksawaeng had a population of about 100 people made up of about 30 households sitting along the village road. There had been about 20 households in the early 1980s. The villagers farm about 200 *rai* of land, one quarter of which is in small lowland parcels in the valley floor while the rest is on steep and forest land. All the land is in the Mae Rim Conservation Forest, which was declared under the Ministerial Rule No. 12 of the 1964 Forest Conservation Act and classified as a watershed area.

The site of Ban Suksawaeng was once a camp for the employees of Thai Phatthana Logging Company. *Lung* Singha, the village founder, was a former worker of the Company, which had received a concession to cut timber in this forest in 1954. After finishing his contract with the firm, he came back to this area in 1963, cleared and occupied about 3 *rai* of low fertile land and about 30 *rai* of highland and initiated the settlement of this village. He urged relatives and friends from lowland villages nearby to come and settle with him. In 1965, six peasants who had either insufficient land to cultivate for household consumption or had lost their lands for various reasons, moved up to occupy land in the new "village". In the 1970s, settlers came from other provinces such as Udon Thani, Buriram, Chachoengsao and Suphanburi through various village connections. Such migration is common in Thailand, especially from the 1960s when land resources began to be squeezed by the population growth and the expansion of agricultural commercialisation (see also Hirsch 1990; Hafner and Yaowalak 1990) which forced or encouraged rural populations to seek new land for cultivation. In the mid 1980s, settlers also came from other districts of Chiang Mai and included a hilltribe group who sold their land cheaply for quick cash and moved from Mae Eye District to Ban Suksawaeng.

The new settlers had close relations with the Lua village mentioned above, which was recognised by forestry officials as *"phuenthi kan ook"* or an "excised area" with special land rights because the village had existed long before the 1964 Forest Conservation Act was issued. Besides learning productive skills and techniques of highland agriculture from the Lua, the new settlers shared environmental resources (especially forest and water) with them. Before Ban Suksawaeng was declared an independent village in 1982, the Lua Village headman had been asked by the District Head to administer and deliver social services (e.g. health and education) to the settlers. There appeared during this period harmony between the villages over the use of natural and social resources.

Villagers who settled in Ban Suksawaeng since 1965 told me that the forest had only become depleted after the separation from the Lua village in 1982. *Lung* Singha argued that the village settlement was not the main reason for forest depletion, as the new settlers were peasants who did not have powerful equipment to chop down trees. Rather, the forest was degraded by the careless misuse of forest resources by logging companies and the negligence of forestry officials who did not ensure that regulations were followed. He recalled that:

From 1965 to 1975 the forest was not yet degraded. . . Forestry officials initially came to mark the trees which they allowed to be cut down. Capitalists [literally translated from *nai thun*] came after to supposedly cut down the marked trees. Without any inspection by the officials, the capitalists cut other trees, including teaks which were not marked. Illegal loggers also brought in outsiders to cut and saw timber. By the time the village was [officially] established in the early 1980s, the forest was completely degraded.

However, the main problem facing the settlers during the early agricultural period was the shortage of rice for year-round consumption. This was not as a result of land shortage, the forest degradation or other environmental problems. *Lung* Singha claimed that even though the land was fertile, rice farming was difficult and not productive for lowland migrants:

> Our crops appeared with uncertain results. Some years were good. Some years were bad. We could not leave our farm to earn money elsewhere. We had to do weeding many times a year in the wet-rice fields and plant other crops to ensure our food sufficiency.

This situation, which is typical for new rice land, continued into the late 1970s. Some villagers had to borrow paddy to meet their consumption needs from nearby lowland villagers at high interest rates of up to 100 percent. *Lung* Singha was afraid that if villagers had to continue borrowing rice from lowland farmers with such a high interest rate, the villagers might sell their land to pay off accumulating debt as he had seen examples occurring in many lowland villages. He therefore sought a way to solve the villagers' rice shortage problem by setting up a "rice bank", of which he had heard from a travelling monk *(phra thudong)*. After trying to contact many organisations, DISAC agreed to support the project.

Linking handouts to participatory development

DISAC undertook a village-economic survey while organising rice for villagers to set up the rice bank project. According to the DISAC survey report, 13 out of 21 households occupied 2-3 *rai* of wet-rice fields, which produced insufficient rice for year-round consumption. Villagers sought cash income for buying food and clothes by selling sugar banana, jackfruit and chilli grown on the steep land. They also sold firewood and charcoal. DISAC saw environmental degradation likely to be increased in this village due to the fact that:

> Every household which had young labour was engaged in cutting timber (illegally) to subsidise their cash income. Often, they sawed

timber to pay off their debt because they had no cash in hand
(Niphot, n.d.: 8-9 and 10).

DISAC, nonetheless, had to respond to the urgent problem of rice
shortage faced by villagers. DISAC tried to apply a "people's
participation" concept[3] in its development work but was unsure how
to bring this concept to the people. In line with practice elsewhere in
other villages, it offered 11 sacks (or 220 kg) of rice to start the rice
project. 10 families were reluctant to join DISAC activities due to
rumours of "communist rice", influenced by the government's
propaganda against the expansion of communism in rural areas to
prevent peasants from supporting non-official persons and groups.
11 poor families decided to become involved in the rice project. From
its past experience in working with poor peasants, DISAC was aware
that the villagers might await economic handouts. It therefore asked
the villagers to make some contribution. The 11 villagers agreed to
give either 2 *tang* of paddy or 60 baht cash, which was used to buy
70-80 tang of paddy for the rice bank from the Lua village. At the
first meeting, the villagers agreed to establish a village development
committee of four members, chaired by *Lung* Singha, the village
founder, to oversee the rice bank activities. This is a different body
from the Village Committee appointed by the government. What
DISAC did here was to link handouts with "participatory
development" in the sense of getting people to be responsible to a
development project run by the village development committee.
DISAC, therefore, played the role of poverty alleviation. However,
there were some obstacles which drew some people away from
participating in the DISAC project. One was a conflict between
village leaders. The other was the political suspicion between the
government and NGOs.

While *Lung* Singha, the village founder, chaired the NGO project,
his opponent for village leadership, Win, sought to enhance his
position through the government channel. Before the village was

---

[3] Beyond the Thai NGO understanding of the term (Jon 1986: 15), Turton (1987: 3)
defines the notion of "people's participation" as "organised efforts to increase control
over resources and regulative institutions in given social situations, on the part of
groups and movements of those hitherto excluded from such control'.

legally recognised in 1982, he was elected as an acting "village head" with the support of local officials. Both customary and legal village leaders sought to win the villagers' support by seeking outside patrons. While Win sought patrons from the authorities who would support his position to establish control over the village, *Lung* Singha, who was over the 60 year age limit for formal headship set by the Local Administration Act, invited NGOs, academics and university students to help develop the village. After a group of Chiang Mai University students came to the village in 1982 and helped build a school, the villagers went to the District Office and asked the District Head to send a teacher to teach their children. The "development" activities of villagers, students and NGO workers were of concern to officials due to allegations of communist infiltration in rural areas. The District Head therefore allowed Ban Suksawaeng to be legally established in 1982 even though the number of houses was less than half the requirement (40 houses) for a village settlement. Win became the first Village Head (locally called *Pholuang* or *Kaeban*) because there was no outstanding competitor.

The rivalry between two village leaders discouraged villagers from participating in the rice bank project and caused difficulties for DISAC to continue its presence in this village. As the Chair, *Lung* Singha did not allow *Pholuang* Win, who had insufficient rice for his family consumption, to join the DISAC rice bank but allowed his relatives and friends to borrow rice, regardless of the agreement that only the members could do so. Eventually, *Lung* Singha's management of the rice bank came under the scrutiny of members and this aggravated the existing tensions among the villagers who, as migrants from different places, were subject to on-going village factionalism. DISAC was quick to recognise this problem and tried to solve it with villagers. At the same time, however, DISAC was facing severe financial problems which paralysed its engagement in further activities.

During this turbulent time, DISAC discovered that "community culture" had revived in response to village disputes. The spirit of *Chaopho Khaeo* occupied a female villager's body and through her condemned the disunity among villagers and called for a change in their behaviour. The tension between villagers reduced after the spirit expressed its concern. Unfortunately, the spirit accused DISAC of causing the dispute. Although DISAC appreciated theoretically the reproduction of community culture responding to village controversy, it realised the suspicion of some Buddhists who feared that villagers might become Catholic if DISAC continued working in this village. Moreover, an incident in which villagers demanded social welfare from the local government while student camps and DISAC were present in this village activated the "mistrust" between the local officials and social activists, including DISAC. The DISAC Director therefore invited FEDRA to take over the village rice bank in 1982.

Because of the political mistrust between the government and NGOs at this time, access to natural resources and local environment were not the focus of NGO activities. However, there was an increasing awareness among NGOs that the potential economic support from outside could aggravate environmental problems, which would affect village livelihood.

Attempting to help maintain village settlement in the forest

FEDRA's main development principles were to help farmers and promote their agricultural occupation with the expectation that they would maintain Buddhism and develop their local community (see Vanpen 1988 and Darlington 1990). In practice, FEDRA encouraged "participatory development" and "community culture" as its approaches to development in the belief that these approaches could help villagers to better their lives in harmony with the environment. FEDRA wanted to ensure too that the villages stayed intact and the villagers were not forced off their land to become labourers in the city. To avoid this the villagers had to be able to meet their immediate needs, to which end FEDRA continued the DISAC rice bank project. At a village meeting in 1983, the FEDRA Chairperson explained the Foundation's main principles and projects such as the rice banks, buffalo banks and revolving funds (cf Vanpen 1988) and asked villagers why they only grew one crop a year. The villagers replied that their lands were far away from village streams, resulting in water shortage during the dry season, but they could solve the water supply problem by building a traditional irrigation system *(muang fai)* if they had financial resources. FEDRA subsequently allowed ten villagers to borrow 2,000 baht each from FEDRA's revolving fund project to build a weir *(fai)* and dig a water channel *(lam muang)* passing through their land. Knowing that FEDRA had a special budget to assist peasants who did not have capital for investment in agriculture, all villagers (including some villagers who were involved in the waterway construction), also asked to borrow 1,000 baht each from FEDRA's revolving fund project to expand their cash crop production such as soya bean, peanut, chilli and *rai*sing pigs for sale. FEDRA met these loans with the agreement that the loan interest would be fed back into a village fund to be run by a new village development committee which FEDRA would help to set up.

Some critical remarks concerning the ways in which FEDRA conducted its development activities in this village reveal a gap between ideals and reality. A young FEDRA worker responsible for the village development activities noted that as FEDRA had already designed the projects which the villagers were urged to join, this could not be called "participatory development" in a real sense. He also noted that although the revolving fund project prevented many villagers from falling into large debt because of its low interest rate (e.g. 10 percent per year as compared to 60 percent required by money lenders), the project became a factor to influence the villagers to encroach on the conservation forest to grow cash crops, a move not expected by FEDRA (Prayat 1985). This was the "power structure of the community *(khrongsang amnat khong chumchon)*" that DISAC had warned FEDRA in its survey report to watch out for. That is, without an understanding of village leaders, factions, local culture and the influence from outside, FEDRA's development activities could become a catalyst for promoting the market-oriented economy (Niphot, n.d.: 25).

To counter the tide of market economy emerging in Ban Suksaweang, Phithak – a FEDRA worker – tried to convince villagers to maintain their own "community culture" as he perceived it. He brought a loom to the village in the hope that female villagers would spend some time after their work in the field to do weaving for domestic uses and reduce the need for cash. He was disappointed when he saw the loom was kept under a villager's house instead of being used. In this case, Phithak re-assessed his belief in community culture against the reality in which villagers were struggling to keep up with increasing household expenditure needs (education, health, consumer goods and transport, together with agricultural investment), already about 10,000 to 12,000 baht (A$ 500 to 600) per month in 1985 for a five-member household located on the forest frontier (Prayat 1985).

While most NGOs focused their work until the mid-1980s on the promotion of agricultural production to enhance people's control over resources, they were also concerned about the environment, but it was not their explicit focus of attention. They tried to restrict the forest encroachment by villagers with a simple solution, that if the villagers could maximise income from their production without being "exploited" by local traders, the people would stop encroaching on the forest for fear of environmental degradation. ATA, an appropriate-technology NGO, came to help FEDRA and villagers undertake a soya bean experiment in 1985 to maximise yield, thereby limiting the amount of land clearance. In 1986, ATA proposed to set up a small hydropower plant to generate electricity in Ban Suksawaeng. The ATA proposal included the establishment of a village rice mill for villagers to reduce the cost of milling and transportation to have the rice milled outside the village; and an electric oven for villagers to dry soya beans so that they could be preserved in bags for sale when the price was good. The NGO workers (FEDRA and ATA) discussed with the villagers the ways in which they could reduce their expenditure with the expectation that the logging in Mae Rim Conservation Forest could be reduced too. Over a year, the villagers took turns to help two ATA engineers construct the small hypropower plant. This practice was regarded by the ATA as a "people's participation" approach. However, not long after the electricity was first used, salesmen from towns came to promote various kinds of consumer goods such as television, videos and stereos which the villagers began to buy on credit. As a result, they required substantial income to afford the goods and pay off debts. This in turn placed more pressure on existing forest resources.

The competition over land and forest resources in Ban Suksawaeng was increasingly intense by the late 1980s, when government policies stimulated economic growth through tourism and agro-business. Local brokers and private entrepreneurs from both Bangkok and Chiang Mai sought to buy land in this village for creating agro-business ventures and building holiday houses. In exchange for commission, *Pholuang* Win and some local middlemen convinced villagers to sell their lands. Local forestry officials saw the potential for rapid forest encroachment if villagers sold land to outsiders. They therefore tried to implement a government land title directive of 1985 which allowed only 15 *rai* of lowlands to be legally registered to a single household head. This failed, however, because the villagers refused to register their land and protested against the directive for fear that at the same time as registering their lowlands, they would lose their rights over their upland plots. Several villagers, unsure about the future of their settlement in Ban Suksawaeng, jointly sold their rights over both lowlands and uplands (over 100 *rai* at about 400 baht per *rai*) to a Bangkok doctor and his friend in January and February 1988. While the doctor's friend used 50 *rai* of land to grow sweet tamarind, coconut and mango for the local market, the doctor left his land idle.

After the attempt to impose land registration on the villagers of Ban Suksaweng failed, local forestry officials sought another alternative to consolidate their claim on the state forest. They expanded the Forestry Department teak plantations in degraded areas, thereby establishing government control over the land and achieving reforestation. At the same time, they employed villagers as wage workers (55 baht a day), which they believed would reduce their need to cut timber for cash. They also forbade any further forest encroachment and land transactions to private entrepreneurs, with the threat that if these continued the villagers would have to be re-located out of the forest altogether.

In response to the forestry officials' threat of re-location, village leaders and NGO workers invited in the Project for Ecological Recovery (PER), an environmental NGO which was interested in working in this forest-fringe village. Three NGOs (FEDRA, PER and ATA) tried to find a way in which the villagers could continue to live and survive in this village without damaging the forest environment. They wished to demonstrate to the forest officials that the villagers could help conserve the forest and should not be seen simply as agents of destruction. To do this first of all, three NGOs had to re-orient their development activities from the focus of their expertise and interests to the focus on environmental issues which became the village's main problem in the late 1980s.

It can be seen from the above that the NGOs attempted to help villagers maintain their settlement in this forest-fringe village by applying their perceptions of "people's participation" and "community culture". Guided by their philanthropic ideology, the NGOs used their development resources and expertise to support village agriculture so that the villagers would have their basic necessities. FEDRA focused its work on economic and social aspects; ATA on appropriate technology to enhance the village economy while PER addressed the balance of economic and ecological dimensions. The three NGOs expected that the villagers would be able to help themselves when the NGOs moved out of the village all together. But the NGOs paid little attention to analysis of changing situations and attitudes. The NGO activities had a reverse effect and became forces which exacerbated a move to promote commercial agriculture and incursion into the forest areas. This was not what the NGOs had anticipated. In the next section, I will explain the ways in which the three NGOs (FEDRA, ATA and PER) discussed their development perceptions and re-oriented their approaches and activities in the hope of finding a methodology which was more suitable to the locality, situation and culture than that which they had applied in the past.

Facilitating environmental resource management

After working in this village for a number of years, the NGOs had learnt from past experience about the shortcomings of their development approaches in response to agrarian change. They began to understand that their practice of working separately by focusing on their respective organisational philosophies did not work, because all aspects of development – social, economic, political and environmental – are interwoven. As an ATA worker argued, "it is unrealistic that one NGO undertakes technological activities and waits for the other to raise people's consciousness". A PER worker also argued that most NGOs played only a minimal intervention role as development educator because they believed too much in the "people's capacity" or the belief that the people could understand their own situations and development better than outsiders:

> The common belief among NGOs in working with villagers is to let people obtain a self-learning process. That is to say, allowing villagers to think, understand and act by themselves. These NGOs are inclined to refuse any kind of guidance *(kan chi nam)*, arguing that development workers should not think on behalf of the people.
>
> The situation of forest degradation in this area does not allow those NGOs not to take any action. If a villager continues or allows others to chop trees, the drought would certainly appear in this area as a consequence. Or if the people ceased to cut timber altogether, where would they obtain their income? This problem had to be solved by trying a new alternative (PER Monthly Report, 1987).

The NGO workers from the three organisations working in Ban Suksawaeng therefore agreed to work hand in hand in response to the competition over resource use between villagers, local forestry officials and private entrepreneurs, and to tackle environmental degradation in the area of this village.

The threat by officials to re-locate the village put the NGOs in a strong position to convince villagers to pay attention to environmental issues. PER, with the help of FEDRA and ATA workers, undertook a historical study of the forest depletion in both Ban Suksawaeng and the Lua village. While collecting data to write their report, the discourse between villagers and NGO workers helped the villagers construct social knowledge of how village labour had been expropriated by timber producers at the expense of local environment and village production. At the same time, the NGOs tried to convince the villagers to change their agricultural practice from intensification and commercialisation to alley-cropping and mixed farming methods as "alternative agriculture", to prevent soil erosion and nutrient deficiency as well as create a sustainable land use system.

Some villagers were reluctant to follow the NGO techniques. A young peasant who had just started up a family said that he could not afford the risk if NGOs' new techniques failed. He therefore waited to see whether the "alternative agriculture" worked before making a decision to follow the NGO methods. In addition, the village founder claimed that the methods were "suitable for dry-land agriculture as in the Northeast" rather than Ban Suksawaeng where FEDRA lent the money to the villagers to construct a *muang fai*. Being motivated by self-interest to maintain their lands in the forest, a few middle income villagers, however, adopted the NGO conservation techniques on approximately one-third of their holdings to show the local forestry officials their environmental concern.

The local forestry officials saw that the NGO activities were helpful to their work, especially as the official annual budget for forest management was small and their human resources were inadequate for patrolling a vast forest area. They agreed with the NGOs to introduce villagers to agricultural techniques which were friendly to the forest. The forestry officials believed that the environmental degradation would be reduced if the NGO proposal of "alternative agriculture" (such as alley cropping, mixed farming and biological pest control) was successful. More importantly, the officials expected the NGOs to organise villagers not to chop down trees and to help protect the forest from encroachment by private entrepreneurs, who allegedly organised to have land in the conservation forest registered corruptly through their political links. The invasion of the forest by these influential people went beyond the control of local, low-ranking forestry officials.

As we have seen in the previous section, the ATA hydro-electricity project was initiated to help villagers generate income and improve their living conditions. Before the project was started, FEDRA, ATA and villagers had discussed the impact of the project on environmental resources, especially the use of water for agriculture (ATA Report, n.d.: 22). When ATA finished installing a hydropower plant for generating electricity in the Lua village in March 1987, the workers from three NGOs (PER, ATA and FEDRA) discussed with the

Lua the possibility of participation in an environmental resource management plan in which other villages, including Ban Suksawaeng, would participate. The ATA workers explained to the villagers that the electricity was generated from the water resource, which depended on an intact forest. They asked villagers to observe the electrical power in relation to the water level. During my fieldwork, I heard villagers complaining about the hydro-electricity power fluctuating, causing short circuits and damaging their electrical equipment. They knew that this happened because there was extensive use of water for commercial agriculture, especially in the dry season. In addition, villagers noted that when the rain fell heavily on the mountains, there was flooding in lowland villages and little water remaining in the high land. This, they said, had never happened before. It was likely that NGO activities encouraged villagers to recognise the negative impact of environmental degradation and the need for forest protection. The villagers and NGO workers, therefore, agreed to organise an opening ceremony for the hydro-power plant in which local officials (including the District Head, Forest Superintendent, Sub-district Head and eight Village Headmen responsible for eight villages located in the watershed area including Ban Suksawaeng) were invited to participate and to help map out the environmental resource management project.

Unlike the Lua village, Ban Suksawaeng had neither a long history of settlement nor a leader who was able to unite village factions to initiate a resource management plan. The NGO workers, therefore, decided to initiate the plan in the Lua village where some traditional leaders still remembered the village history and culture, especially in upland production. Clearing forest land, for instance, was very important to the Lua and there were certain restraints. Before farming upland rice, a Lua leader had to perform a ritual to ask permission from the "lord of land" *(chaothi chaotang)*. They avoided cutting big trees by choosing an open area with few trees for fear that the "lord of forest" *(chaopa)* living in the big trees would harm them. Based on the Lua's culture of upland cultivation, the NGOs identified what they called a "community forest" approach referring to a culture in which human beings were able to live in harmony with their environment.

Over a month before the opening ceremony was held, the villagers and NGOs prepared a proposal for land and forest management in order to negotiate with local officials about the future settlement in the forest. The proposal was processed with the advice of a leader from Thung Yao Village, Lamphun Province. PER invited him to discuss the experience of forest protection in his village and how this had helped reduce the negative impact which resulted from economic-oriented development. The proposal included the discussion of forest boundaries between villages and of forest classification in each village. Similar activities were also conducted in Ban Suksawaeng, where the land and forest resources were divided into two categories. One was the "conservation forest" *(pa anurak)* in which the watershed and evergreen forest were located. The villagers set up rules forbidding anybody to chop trees in the "conservation forest". The other was the "utility forest" *(pa chaisoi)* where the forest was relatively degraded. The villagers agreed to cut only some kinds of trees in the "utility forest" for use within the village community (PER 1987b).

After the religious ceremony held in March 1987 to open the hydropower plant in the Lua village had finished, a Lua leader proposed the land and forest management plan to a meeting attended by the district head, forest superintendent, Sub-district Head and village headmen from each of the eight villages in the sub-distict *(tambon)*. The presentation began with an outline of the situation of forest degradation and its consequences, notably soil erosion and the water shortage which affected all 8 villages. Then, the proposed land and forest management plan was presented and followed by the sets of rules for forest protection which had been agreed by the villagers themselves. The district head, however, was concerned by a forest protection rule which referred to legal action being taken against a forest encroacher. The rule said that if a villager encroached the forest, his village headman would be punished by law. In this case, the district head pointed out that legal action could not be pursued against the village head because he himself did not break the laws. Thus, the discussion between villagers and local officials helped ensure that the forest protection rules were pragmatic and the plan was accepted, in principle, by the meeting attendants.

The details of the plan in each village were subsequently pursued by the villagers themselves. About a year later, PER helped the villagers of the Lua village and Ban Suksawaeng to conduct their forest survey and classification. In 1988, after PER workers withdrew from this area all together, Bun (an ATA worker) with the help of Chai (a FEDRA worker) took on the further task of forest management activities in addition to their regular tasks. As Mae Lo stream was the main stream used by five villages in the watershed area, Bun helped organise the village leaders of those five villages to draw a sketch map which indicated their forest boundaries, because local forest officials did not have a detailed map of the area. Then, the village representatives discussed their village boundaries. Moreover, Bun and a group of villagers (about 10 people) patrolled the forest areas around Mae Lo stream every fortnight. In addition, both NGO workers from FEDRA and ATA encouraged the continuing co-operation between villagers and local forestry officials. Later, they also sought the support of other NGOs from Chiang Mai and Bangkok in the forest management activities to counter external pressure on the forest. Those agencies included the Multi-Cropping Centre, Chiang Mai University; Sam Mun Highland Development Project; the Royal Forestry Department and the NGO-CORD. While forest management activities started in 1992, Bun was uncertain how long he would be able to conduct these activities with villagers. This was because financial support was now difficult to obtain as funding agencies had shifted their support to fund environmental campaign activities at the national rather than community-based level.

In summary, NGOs have encouraged villagers to develop a co-operative plan for land and forest management. It commenced with the Lua, who still recognised their culture of forest settlement, and it extended to other villages around the Mae Lo stream. The motivation of villagers to be involved in resource management was supported by PER, FEDRA and ATA, and was accepted by local officials. While the villagers wanted to maintain their settlement in the forest fringe, the officials wanted the villagers to help them protect the forest from being destroyed by illegal loggers and private entrepreneurs who had both economic and political influence.

NGO ROLES IN COMPETITION OVER RESOURCES AND ENVIRONMENTAL CONCERN

Competition over resources and environmental problems are not new issues in Thai rural development. However, these issues had been obscured by the political conflicts between "Right" (such as military and royalists) and "Left" (such as student activists, socially-concerned NGOs and politicians) for over two decades of the Thai development history (Hirsch 1993). Over the period, there have been changes in the Thai political economy from military-dominated regimes to the "economic rationalism" which was highlighted by the Chatchai government (1988-1991). The competition over resource use between villagers, officials and private entrepreneurs became prominent in the late 1980s and, in many areas of rural Thailand, developed into conflicts. The Ban Suksawaeng case illustrates the issues of competition over resources and local environment covering the period mentioned. However, in this case, both issues were handled in a moderate way compared to other rural areas because of the collaboration between villagers, NGOs and local officials. The co-operation arose from the NGO roles which were accepted by other development actors.

Throughout the 1980s, four NGOs tried to help the villagers of Ban Suksawaeng control their own productive resources (e.g. land, capital and skill) so that they would be able to afford their basic minimum needs (e.g. food, clothes, shelter and medicine). Despite the rumour of "communist rice", the early settlers appreciated DISAC for helping them set up a rice bank at the time when they faced rice shortage. The FEDRA revolving fund project allowed the poor to obtain capital investment at a low interest rate. Moreover, the villagers were generally able to have access to the village fund, which accumulated and was available for further investment by the villagers. The ATA soya bean experiment project helped villagers to learn new techniques to maximise the yield per *rai*. The ATA small hydropower plant project supplied electricity which allowed villagers to undertake new ventures. The PER mixed farming and alley-cropping techniques promoted the balance of ecological and economic systems with the aim of ensuring the village would be allowed by the forestry officials to remain in the Mae Rim Conservation Forest.

In their role as poverty alleviators, the NGOs disagreed with the handout approach because it did not support villagers in the long run once the handout was finished. They therefore provided an initial donation and encouraged the villagers to participate in managing their own productive resources through the village representatives or development committees elected by villagers themselves. For example, Phithak (a FEDRA worker) helped the village development committee members, who had a little formal education, by teaching them how to manage development projects, conduct village meetings and do book keeping. However, after Phithak left FEDRA, the village development committee could not handle the development projects on their own. Villagers said that they did not trust the committee for fear of corruption and asked the committee to sell paddy in the rice bank and pay out to them in cash. The FEDRA revolving fund was also set back because villagers did not want to pursue it further.

A number of factors could be drawn upon to explain the failure. First, the people's participation approach introduced by NGOs came as a new concept to most rural poor who were accustomed to alms giving and philanthropic activities. Second, the successful implementation of people's participation was difficult because it was time-consuming and area-limited. That is to say the approach highlights the need for development education for people to learn how to control their development under the influence of external forces. This has to be done with respect to locality and culture. Third, Ban Suksawaeng was a new village where the settlers came from different places and stayed in the same village. A PER worker called it *"Ban Kaengho"*, a Northern Thai dish which has a mixture of many kinds of vegetables and meats, due to the frustration in successfully implementing the people's participation approach in this village.

There were changing needs as the rural people became more incorporated into and dependent upon the cash economy. While NGO projects had already been designed by the NGO headquarters, most villagers chose to get involved (not "participate" in the real sense) in the project or organisation which was likely to benefit them most. Moreover, some villagers helped shape activities which, they believed, would enhance their income. The weir digging and hydro-electricity projects were cases in point of where FEDRA and ATA conducted development activities responding to people's needs along the lines of a market-oriented economy. Chai, a FEDRA worker after Phithak, considered the NGO role in economic and technological aspects of development in this village as catalytic of agrarian change. He concluded that:

> We can not claim that the influence of economic change comes only from official conduct. While solving economic problems along with the villagers, the NGOs in fact play a significant role in the process of change as well. We support agricultural intensification and commercialisation financially; organise trips for villagers to see various kinds of agricultural innovation; and adopt the techniques without the understanding of the concept behind those techniques. We (both villagers and NGOs) are still struggling for the betterment in the state's framework and mechanism.

Chai's statement coincided with the opinion of the Sub-district extension officer, who told me that NGO economic and technological activities supported his work greatly. The NGOs, the extension officer argued, helped change the farmers' values from subsistence to commercial economy by offering not only the financial assistance but also new agricultural techniques. In particular, they encouraged farmers to be confident in agricultural innovation. From the opinion of both GO and NGO organisers, it appears that the NGOs were effective agents of agrarian transformation consistent with the aim of government agencies.

One might argue that the poverty alleviation and income generating activities go hand in glove because the people generate their income to alleviate their poverty. Such an argument is countered by the evidence shown in Ban Suksawaeng, where the village income generating activities did not eliminate poverty. That is because the more villagers earned, the more they spent on various kinds of consumer goods, and the more environmental problems arose. In this regard, the poverty alleviation and income generating activities have to be done in accordance with development education to promote people's understanding of their situation and of the impact of environmental problems on their livelihood.

Using "community culture" proved a difficult process. A FEDRA worker tried to solve the problem of local environment and maintain the village settlement by bringing in the notion of "community culture" to the people. He brought a loom for the female villagers and a teacher to teach them how to weave their clothes for domestic use to reduce the need for cash. He was distressed when the female villagers ignored his initiative. The community culture approach did not work in this situation because it was used to serve a return to the past rather than to fit into the present. However, the community culture approach was used successfully by PER workers, who promoted Lua culture to argue a place for village settlement in the forest and to seek the co-operation between villagers and officials to protect the local environment from being destroyed by timber producers and private entrepreneurs. As we can see, the Lua ability to live in relative harmony with nature was brought out by the NGOs from the past to serve the present problems of competition over resources and local environment degradation. The formation of the land and forest resource management project by villagers and NGOs showed that the NGOs understood the local situation and culture and how they could respond to changes in the political economy of rural Thailand. As a result, they played not only a development education role, but also served as intermediaries between villagers and officials through supporting the people's environmental movement.

CONCLUSION

This chapter has shown, through a local case study, how several indigenous Thai NGOs have responded to the problems affecting villagers as a result of agrarian change, which has produced conflict and competition over resources and local environmental problems throughout the 1980s. The competition over resources in Ban Suksawaeng reflects events which occurred in rural Thailand in two periods. In the period to the mid-1980s, there was economic competition between the state, community and business (logging companies and money lenders) over forest resources in the forms of concessions, declaration of conservation forest and high interest rates. But at that time, the issue of competition over resources was dominated by the "ideological" conflict – from the nation down to the village – between the authorities, villagers, university students and academics who were involved in the villages and grass-roots NGOs. The second period was from the mid-1980s, when the ideological conflict began to decline and the competition over resources became more prominent, involving villagers, officials and, in this period, private entrepreneurs who had purchased, often illegally with the help of corrupt officials, large plots of land in the Mae Rim Conservation Forest. While the entrepreneurs began to break the law and infringe regulations in attempts to gain control over land in Ban Suksawaeng, the local forestry officials tried to stop the forest encroachment by seeking the co-operation of villagers and NGOs to protect the forest.

Looking more widely, the NGOs emerged during a period of political uprising outside bureaucratic and / or business control. They were influenced by "human development" or "alternative development" concepts in the mid-1970s, which opposed the government's economic growth strategies. NGOs also adopted an anti-capitalist position, while intending to work with and on behalf of the poor in remote areas. Through trial-and-error experiences, the NGOs attempted to implement a "people's participation" and "community culture" approach to their work. NGO responses to the people's problems have moved from the strong ideological orientation of the 1970s to a more realistic understanding of empirical situations and the various development actors competing for control over resources and affecting the local environment. Although they were seen as an agent for agrarian change by local officials, the NGOs also played a critical role as poverty alleviators, development educators and mediators for moderating competition over resources and formulating a plan of environmental resource management in this area.

REFERENCES

Appropriate Technology Association (ATA), n.d., *"Raingan khan samruat saphab setthakit lae sangkhom Ban Muangka, Tambon Saluang, Amphoe Mae Rim, Changwat Chiang Mai"* (The Socio-Economic Survey Report of Muangka Village, Saluang Sub-district, Mae Rim District, Chiang Mai Province), Roneo.

Bunthien Thongprasan, 1988 [2531], *Naeokit watthanatham chumchon nai ngan phatthana* [The Concept of Community Culture in Development Work], (in Thai), Bangkok: Catholic Council for Thai Development (CCTD).

Carroll, T. F., 1992, *Intermediary NGOs: The Supporting Link in Grassroots Development*, West Hartford: Kumarian Press.

Chulalongkorn University Social Research Institute (CUSRI), Social Research Institute (SRI-Chiang Mai University) and Rural Development Institute (RDI-Khon Khaen University), 1990, *Directory of Public Interest Non-Government Organisations in Thailand*, Bangkok: Chulalongkorn University Publishing House

Darlington, S. M., 1990, "Buddhism, Morality and Change: The Local Response to Development in Northern Thailand", Ph.D. Thesis (Anthropology), University of Michigan, Ann Arbor.

Friedman, J., 1992, *Empowerment: The Politics of Alternative Development*, Cambridge (Mass): Blackwell Publishers.

Hafner, J. A. and Yaowalak Apichatvallop, 1990, "Migrant Farmers and the Shrinking Forests of Northeast Thailand", in Poffenberger, M., (ed.), *Keepers of the Forest: Land Management Alternatives in Southeast Asia*, West Hartford: Kumarin Press: 64-94.

Hirsch, P., 1990, *Development Dilemmas in Rural Thailand*, Singapore: Oxford University Press.

Hirsch, P., 1993, "Competition and Conflict over Resources: Internationalisation of Thailand's Rural Economy?", Paper presented at Thai Studies Group Annual Conference on "The Globalisation of Thailand", ANU.

Jon Ungphakhon, 1986 [2529], "Khabuankhan ongkan phattana ekkachon nai prathet Thai" [The Movement of the Non-Government Organisations (NGOs) in Thailand], *Pacharayasan* , [in Thai], 13(5): 13-20.

Niphot Thienwihan, n.d., *"Prasopkan thamngan phattana khong soon sangkhom phattana sapha Khatholic: Korani suksa Ban Huay Somsuk, Chiang Mai"* [Development Experiences of the Diocesan Social Action Centre: A Case Study of Ban Huay Somsuk, Chiang Mai], (in Thai), Catholic Council of Thailand for Development (CCTD).

Norton, W., 1984, *Historical Analysis in Geography*, London: Longman.

PER Monthly Report, 1987a [2530].

PER Report of Forest Survey, 1987b [2530].

Prayat Chaturaphonphithakkul, 1985 [2528], *"Botrien chak ngoen thun mun wien: Suksa chapo korani: Kan dam noen ngan muban samachik"* [Lesson learnt from the Revolving Fund Project: Case Study of a (FEDRA's) Village Member], Report presented to the Thai Volunteer Service (TVS), (in Thai).

Prudhisan Jumbala, 1987, "Interest and Pressure Groups", in Somsakdi Xuto, (ed.) *Government and Politics of Thailand*, London: Oxford University Press, pp 110-167.

Social Research Institute (SRI), 1986 [2528], *Khomun pheunthan radup muban Amphoe Mae Rim, Changwat Chiang Mai* [Basic Data at the Village Level, Mae Rim District, Chiang Mai Province], Research Report, Social Research Institute (SRI), Chiang Mai University.

Vanpen Surarueks, 1988, "Issues and Experiences in the Use of Community Participation by NGO in Rural Development Programs in Thailand: An Analysis and Evaluation of the Foundation for Education and Development of Rural Areas (FEDRA)", in *Thi ra-ruek 72 pi Phra Thepkawi* [The Commemoration of 72nd Birthday of Phra Thepkawi], Chiang Mai: FEDRA.

COMMUNITY FORESTRY AND WATERSHED NETWORKS IN NORTHERN THAILAND

Pratuang Narintarangkul Na Ayuthaya[1]

INTRODUCTION

One of the main issues concerning rural society in northern Thailand is competition over resources that form the basic means of production. Competition is between the state and communities, between communities, between individuals and the state and between individuals within communities. Conflict over resources is manifested in many forms, and social movements have emerged to articulate interests of disadvantaged groups. One of the most significant movements in recent years is the emergence of community forest networks, which have organised on a watershed basis in several northern Thai watersheds. These networks have mobilised at several levels, from grassroots activism to influence in the policy arena.

This essay aims to reflect on certain contradictions that have emerged in state-led natural resource management over time. Resulting problems are numerous, and include issues of income distribution, ecological balance and social conflict. At the same time, there is an accumulated experience of grassroots approaches to solving some of these problems, to the extent that such efforts have become part of the local way of life and culture. In the following account, the experience of the Mae Wang watershed is presented. It is shown how cultural adaptation to changing conditions has given local people proficiency and confidence as resource managers. Local

---

[1]   Translated by Philip Hirsch and Prue Borthwick

mobilisation here is an example of both promising efforts and obstacles faced by the people's movement that calls itself the "Mae Wang Watershed Network". This network has expanded to encompass several other watersheds and taken on the abbreviated name of "*Nuai Neua*: Northern Unit".

CHANGE IN MAE WANG WATERSHED

The Mae Wang Watershed Network is a people's organisation located in the forested Mae Wang watershed. Mae Wang is a branch of the Ping River, which is the major tributary of the Chaophraya. Mae Wang watershed is located entirely within Chiang Mai Province in northern Thailand. The watershed can be divided into upper and lower sections, which represent quite distinct human ecological features. Those living in the upper watershed are referred to colloquially as "*muu khon doi*: uplanders". More than half are Karen, and the remainder are northern Thai (*khonmeuang*, also referred to as *Tai-Yuan*) and Hmong. Those living in the lower part are known locally as "*muu khon pheun lum*: lowlanders" and are mainly *khonmeuang*, although there is also one Hmong village that comprises less than one percent of the population. Cultivation in most of the lower section is of wet rice land, at altitudes between 300 and 700 metres above sea level. The upper section is cultivated as wet rice terraces and rotational swidden fields at altitudes mainly between 700 and 1500 metres.

Most communities in the upper section use water from tributaries of the Mae Wang for cultivation and domestic purposes. Only a small number of farmers use water from the Mae Wang river itself. The river nevertheless provides an important source of protein in the form of fish, which are also sometimes sold in order to provide a cash income for purchasing rice and other necessities. Rice from the limited area of terraced fields and swiddens is often short toward the end of the wet season. Non-timber forest products are also sold for cash income. However, such sources of income have declined as state-led development initiatives have brought new forms of cultivation into the upper watershed area, notably cultivation of new crops such as wheat and barley, together with cool climate vegetables and perennials such as apples, *buai* (*Myrica nagi*) and *thoo* (*Prunus persica*). Contract farming has also made inroads, mainly to serve industries such as beer breweries and tomato canning.

These agricultural developments have had a widespread impact on the way of life of the uplanders in Mae Wang. In particular, the subsistence economy has been partially destroyed as forests have been cleared for planting of cool climate crops. Those with access to capital have prospered further, while those depending more directly on forest or wet rice farming have found their sources of sustenance threatened by the new developments. Moreover, the water itself has become toxic as new crops with low resistance to pests and disease have required heavy application of pesticides over approximately 700 hectares in 17 villages, estimated to total 5 tonnes of undiluted chemicals per year over the whole area.

The loss of traditional subsistence livelihoods has forced some of the poorer families to move further up into the forest to clear land for cultivation. In other cases, they have hired themselves out as labourers in illicit timber felling controlled by urban traders. Some have responded to new developments by enlarging their areas under cultivation. These responses have simply exacerbated environmental degradation and hastened destruction of the subsistence economy. At the same time, the state has gained greater legitimacy in its accusation that local people are destroying the nation's forests. It has also thereby lent more weight to programs to move people out of the watershed area or to squeeze livelihoods such that people will move of their own accord, including through forest plantation schemes.

The pressure exerted by state authorities is one reason for the establishment of *Nuai Neua* in the Mae Wang watershed. In addition to trying to resolve problems of destruction of environment and subsistence economy, *Nuai Neua* has been concerned with trying to deal with problems emanating from state activities in the area, and more widely at a policy level.

Those living in the lower section of the watershed use the Mae Wang River more directly for wet rice cultivation. 11 traditional *meuang faai* irrigation schemes irrigate some 8,000 to 11,000 hectares. Three crops per year are grown in many areas, and agriculture is commercialised. Intensification has been occurring since the 1960s in line with the government's policy of export-oriented production. The area is Thailand's main source of onions for export, producing about 24,000 tonnes per annum. There are several annual rotation systems, including wet season rice and dry season rice separated by cultivation of onions or soya beans.

Intensification of agriculture has led to intensification of water demand, while the dry season supply has diminished. As a result, water conflicts have arisen within *meuang faai* irrigation societies. Most attribute reduced stream flow to destruction of forest in the upper watershed, and irrigation leaders have discussed the problem with leaders in upper watershed communities. Forest protection and regeneration have also been discussed. The interests and activities of *Nuai Neua* have thus extended to the lower section of Mae Wang watershed. Uplanders and lowlanders have joined forces in an attempt to manage resources jointly and work toward a more sustainable pattern of resource use. Nevertheless, there are also many lowlanders who blame uplanders for forest destruction, in line with the official attitude that environmental degradation is caused primarily by those living in the upper watershed area (often referred to as *Chaokhao*, or hilltribes, with the negative connotation of not being Thai - see Anan's Chapter 11 in this volume). They also concur with the government policy of relocating uplanders to lowland areas, and this issue has become an important topic with which *Nuai Neua* has to deal.

CULTURE, PRODUCTION AND EMERGENT COMMUNITY MOBILISATION

Before the formal establishment of *Nuai Neua* in October 1993, the movement had taken root in emergent form in several upland villages. These roots were to be found in existing community structures, for example the *meuang faai*, community forest and forest protection committees, and also village committees. These groups had formed and gained experience in managing the existing resource base. Such management was based both on exisiting knowledge and livelihoods, and on knowledge and experience gained from outside. For example, non-governmental organisations (NGOs) and academic researchers working in the area provided experience, and some local people were invited to participate in seminars and workshops elsewhere. Knowledge gained was combined with local practical experience to increase the confidence of local leaders, who mobilised to establish a network on the basis that problems faced could not be solved within the confines of single communities in isolation. Emergent community mobilisation was based on a number of elements, set out below.

Approach to problem solving

The key problems in the upper Mae Wang watershed are connected with environmental degradation and associated decline in the subsistence resource base, notably land, water and forest resources. This has led state authorities to plan eviction of communities resident in the watershed in the name of conservation, leading to a variety of community responses. Responses by the communities of Mae Sapock and Nong Tao have served as models for many other villages in the watershed.

Raising the issue of who destroys and who preserves the forest is one of the means by which community leaders raise the interest and awareness of fellow villagers. This issue is also used to respond to allegations that local people are primarily to blame for forest destruction. The reality as discussed locally is more complex, and it is concluded that the state, business interests and villagers are all in fact "forest thieves". The blame should not be put on one party or another; more important is to find means of conserving what remains.

The explanation of forest degradation is not used merely as a justification for continued residence close to the forest. It is also a reminder to community members of the need for all to play a role in forest protection. Decline in water in the Mae Sapock stream is explained as an outcome of the need for villagers to replace loss of subsistence income by serving as labourers for illicit logging operators, in order to purchase food or pay off debts. Alternatively, the need to pay off loans while agricultural productivity is low is seen as a cause for forest encroachment to increase income.

This local analysis of the problems at Mae Sapock was applied in establishing an organisation whose aim was to reduce the need to work for illicit loggers rather than directly to guide resource and environmental management. The issues concerning most were illicit logging, drying up of streams and forest plantations on land currently used for agriculture.

Solution of the problem of loans was seen to rest with the setting up of a savings fund, with loans allotted on the principle of prior need. Special priority is given to those depending on wage labouring for illicit loggers. Cooperation is needed in a number of areas, including accumulation of funds, accounting, taking part in group activities, and generating capital by joint agricultural production and sale of non-timber forest products. The main objective is to reduce dependency on high-interest loans and timber labouring.

The savings group was the first non-state forum for discussion of common problems. This forum led to discussion of the need to conserve forest close to the village and in the upper watershed of Mae Sapock stream. Both these forest areas hold great importance for local livelihoods. Forest close to the village is important as a source of food and firewood, and also as a wind break during the wet season. It also serves as a buffer against fire during the dry season burning of fields. The need for rules to govern and control forest exploitation was seen to apply in the case both of Mae Sapock villagers and those from elsewhere, who may not otherwise be aware of the village's forest management agreements. Management of forest close to the village thus became an issue to be dealt with more widely than just within the savings group, as it concerns all villagers and needs to be recognised by surrounding communities also.

The upper watershed forest, known as *"paa khun Huai Mae Sapock"*, needs to be conserved and protected from agricultural conversion as it is the source area of the stream on which the community depends for agricultural production. However, this forest is located in Nong Tao village, which means that conservation requires cooperation between the two villages. Leaders from Mae Sapock thus negotiated with leaders from Nong Tao.

The establishment of rules in the village of Mae Sapock included restrictions placed on villagers from surrounding communities, which in turn has led these communities to set their own rules. Each community has tried to delimit those with rights to use particular areas of forest. Agreement between neighbouring communities started from 1989 after Mae Sapock and Mae Muud agreed on demarcation of their neighbouring forest areas used for collection of various forest products. Also at this time, an agreement was reached between Mae Sapock and Nong Tao, in this case resulting from a request by the lower village not to cut swiddens in the upper stream area. These agreements led to inclusion of many other upper Mae Wang communities in bilateral or trilateral agreements on joint forest management, and in some cases also to unilateral rules that villagers from neighbouring communities were expected to respect. This set of agreements can be seen as the embryonic development of what was to become *Nuai Neua*.

Culture, belief and land classification

Despite differences of approach in explaining the cause of local environmental degradation and differences in means of forest conservation, most villages have established organisational means to protect land, water and forest resources. These means are based on a variety of objectives and beliefs. For example, the village of Khun Puai is concerned with establishing a written agreement for protection of the upper watershed. Other areas of forest are protected according to traditional beliefs and customs. For example, Karen communities protect forest through a traditional practice of hanging the umbilical cord of newborn infants on particular trees, which become sacred as the source of the 37 "soul components" of that individual. Any harm that befalls the tree will lead to illness or death both of the "soul sibling" of that tree and of the person responsible for its destruction. There are thus concrete and more abstract bases for organisational approaches to forest management in Mae Wang. However, a common understanding among all villagers is that culture is the basis for resource management, and cultural conservation is integral to environmental conservation. This means that it is important to maintain livelihoods that are not reduced to dependency on wage labouring or production of industrial raw materials for lowland factories, as the thrust of government policy tends to support. Culture has thereby become a core element in the articulation of community rights in resource management.

The system of land classification for use and conservation is an important cultural component of the body of applied local knowledge in the upper Mae Wang watershed. This knowledge is applied in resource and environmental conservation for the purpose of improving the sustainability of resource use in support of local livelihoods. The details of land classification in each locality reflect longstanding traditions of resource use and understanding of local ecology, based on particular world views. At the same time, such classification changes with changing ecological, social, economic and political circumstances. Land classification is related to use rights and conditions, to property rights over resources, and also to sufficiency of subsistence-based livelihood.

Traditional land classification in the absence of state influence in Mae Wang can be classified broadly into four types: forest, rotational rice swiddens, wet rice terraces and household compounds. All four have a direct relationship with subsistence based production.

Forest land

Forest land is the basis for subsistence livelihood. It is the source of forest foods, in the form of wild vegetables, wildlife, herbal medicine, firewood, and timber for house construction. Forested land is also seen as important for protection of stream sources, which are intimately connected with patterns of settlement. 15 of the 17 villages of upper watershed are located on tributaries of the Mae Wang river (Figure 1). The importance of forest in providing sustenance and protecting streams has long been recognised and is reflected in customary beliefs, proverbs, traditional teachings, lullabies, funeral rites and other forms that reinforce and transfer knowledge and ideas from one generation to the next.

Table 1:
Karen forest types in Mae Wang Watershed

FOREST TYPE	CHARACTERISTIC
Village forest	Forest close to the village, used for various subsistence uses.
Moist forest	Moist forest is described as being in the form of "a green frog incubating its eggs", in Karen known as "*dae meu boe*". Such forest is surrounded by mountains, and protrudes at the centre somewhat like the back of a turtle or an incubating frog. Land underlying such forest is fertile with year-round moisture. Water seeps out at the edge of this forest to form springs and small pools, serving as the source of streams. Karen believe that the spirits of such forests are particularly fierce, and few dare establish settlements or fields in these areas.
Head of springs	Forest at the head of springs known as "*naa u lu*". This is similar in many ways to the first type of forest, moist and cool. As in the first case, few dare touch it due to fear of resident spirits.
Head of fields	Forest at the head of swiddens and wet rice fields, known as "*thii chaa thii*". This forest is protected by the owners of adjacent fields, who see its value in preventing soil erosion damaging to cultivation. It is also seen as the residence of water spirits, whose departure with cutting of the trees would lead to drying up of water sources needed for farming.
Surrounding salt licks	Forests surrounding salt licks, known as "*mopuu*". This forest also has a resident water spirit, with areas of standing water year-round. It usually contains large trees and is home to much wildlife. Karen are also afraid of spirits in this type of forest and prefer to leave it intact.
Village burial area	Burial forests are reserved as a serene resting place for the dead. Any disturbance of such forest is believed to cause trouble for the spirit of the dead, and also to their descendants living close by. As a result, this forest is carefully conserved.
Mountain pass forest	This forest is known as "*taa de do*". Located in mountain passes, such forest is believed to be a pathway for spirits and is hence left alone.

Study of Karen wisdom in forest conservation in the Mae Wang watershed has shown that forest conservation by villagers is related to a way of life based on interdependence between people and nature. Karen classify forest into many types in close relation to livelihoods, and the classifications vary by village according to the ecology of settlement. Seven forest types are identified in Table 1.

Beliefs affecting forest use and classification are an important basis for forest management in the Mae Wang watershed. They are thus also an important foundation for Karen people locally and *Nuai Neua* more widely in building self confidence and in explaining to outsiders the role of local people as managers and conservers, rather than as destroyers of forest.

While Karen communities classify forest according to many criteria, broadly they can be categorised into protection forest and use forest types. These classifications sit uneasily with official watershed classification systems of the Royal Forestry Department and the National Environment Board, who use biophysical criteria such as slope and soil type to indicate which areas are suited to protection from human interference, which are suited to commercial exploitation and so on. Differences between official and local systems can lead to conflict, particularly when eviction of longstanding communities is proposed (see Santita's Chapter 13 in this volume).

According to local classification, conservation forest is not separated from livelihood needs. For example, upper watershed forest is the source of many types of herbal medicines and food, such as mushrooms, bamboo shoots, wild vegetables and fish from streams. In some cases, these non-timber forest products are also sold to lowlanders. Knowledge of the forest and its uses is a science acquired through practical experience over a long period of time. Such practical knowledge requires close association with the forest, for example in knowing which mushrooms are edible and which are poisonous. Thus, local conservation does not rest with the protection of one tree species or another, but rather with the way of life and associated knowledge of those who live with and from the forest. Maintenance of this way of life and preventing alienation of people from their surroundings is a key aspect of such conservation. In the words of Karen village headman Joni Odochao:

'Us hill people can live only with intact forest. Intact forest must have seven layers. These include four layers above ground. A tree in the intact forest must be like this always: the large tree is at the centre; saplings and bushes surround this tree. These are the living quarters of birds and insects. Above the bushes and saplings are trees next down from that at the centre, trying to catch up with their "fathers" and "mothers". There are orchids attached to branches, eating off the trees. At the lowest level are grasses and mushrooms. As for the layers below the surface, there are roots, tubers, worms, snakes; there are sweet potatoes, taros. It's like this everywhere. But if one element is missing, the system is degraded, we cannot survive' (interview 1994).

Swiddens

Swidden land is another production area important to the livelihood of residents of upper Mae Wang. Because of the limited area of flat land, making a living cannot rely on a single type of production. Technologies of production are thus diverse, each part having contributed to subsistence from the past up to the present. Swidden cultivation is part of the production system practiced by all three main ethnic groups in the upper watershed.

A study of the history of settlement at Mae Sapock shows that swidden cultivation predates wet rice farming. Present day rice terraces were originally cleared and farmed as swiddens. It was only after the second world war that weirs and irrigation channels were dug during the agricultural off-season to support construction of wet rice terraces. Other communities in the watershed show a similar pattern of intensification.

Swidden farming has been the basic technology of production since the upper Mae Wang valley was first settled several generations ago. In the past, swidden land was common property within the community. Land was not designated on a permanent basis to individual households. Rather, claims were recognised on a use basis through placing of markers for areas to be cleared, burned and cultivated. Rights to the land ended with the harvest. After a period of several years' fallow, the land might then be cultivated by the same or by a different household. In the case of rice terraces, however, those who cleared, leveled and developed the terrace established a permanent customary right to it, which might be passed on to kin.

Before the widespread development of rice terraces, each community had several areas of swidden fields. Mae Sapock, for example, had five: *Tong Phaa Mon, Tong Mae Sapock Tai, Tong Mae Sapock Neua, Tong Huai Jakhrai* and *Tong Wang Uu* (*Tong* means field). Each area was farmed for a single year, with the whole community working the same area. The following year this area would be left fallow, on a five year cycle as all households moved to the next area, to return on a five year rotation. During the fallow, some of the land would be converted to rice terraces, subject to the labour potential of each kinship group. This process can be seen as the start of a move from community-based common property to kinship-based common property.

The area used for swidden is not irrigable by traditional or state-managed irrigation systems. This may either be because it is too elevated, or because water diversions have not yet been constructed. Rainfed rice swiddening involves a number of stages of land preparation, including staking land claims, negotiating with prior users if necessary, and clearing of the larger trees to remove shade while leaving the stumps. Not all the trees are cut, and a windbreak is maintained at the edge of each field. Clearing is carried out during the dry season to allow for burning, and it is then left until the start of the rains. Various subsistence and marketable crops are planted at the start of the wet season. While dry rice is the traditional staple, other crops and forest products would often be sold to lowlanders at Ban Kaad or elsewhere in lowland Sanpatong District where there is a surplus, to make up for shortfalls in upper Mae Wang. More recently, wet rice has become the staple, with dry rice grown in swiddens serving as a supplement. In a few cases, dry season rice grown as a second crop in irrigable wet rice fields has taken the place of this supplement, and vegetables grown on swidden land are also an important dietary component.

Reciprocal labour sharing is used for swidden cultivation. The temporary user of the plot decides on what is to be grown, timing of planting, inputs, labour mobilisation, pest control and maintenance of soil cover by various means, including allowing certain existing plants and trees to continue to grow. This allows the plot to continue as a source of natural forest foods. Neighbours or kinfolk provide extra labour as needed.

Swidden farming is an intricate agricultural system, in terms of both the restoration of the soil cover and the prevention of crop disease and pests through natural techniques. The plot may lie fallow for up to five years before it is used for cultivation again. Various plant species are conserved in order to preserve the balance of the natural ecosystem or to use as a local food source. Not only rice is to be found growing in these plots but also many other useful plants, including vegetables planted in among the rice and edible wild plants, herbal medicines or windbreaks. Wild plants are also conserved and tended by the user of the plot. The seeds of different plants are selected and collected to ensure their propagation in future years.

This ongoing selective propagation of species is generally accepted by agriculturists as an excellent method of genetic preservation. It is more effective than storing the gene species in laboratories as the seeds propagated through laboratories have a higher risk of failure to germinate. The natural cultivation methods, the conservation technologies and the rotational swidden farming system of the Mae Wang Catchment area constitutes a model of conservation of edible plant species. Just how many hundreds or thousands of edible plant species there are in the Mae Wang Catchment area has not been investigated to date. More important is the research already conducted by the uplanders into which varieties of plants are edible and which are not. The results of this research are stored carefully in the seed banks known as "rotational swidden fields", which the government and townsfolk stigmatise as *"rai leuan loi*: literally, mobile, floating fields" and claim are the principal cause of the destruction of the forests.

Cultivation in swidden areas has changed in many ways, from the objectives and techniques of cultivation through to patterns of land tenure. These changes are due to the process of government intervention and development. Pressure has been applied to communities in a number of areas.

Swidden farming in many places has begun to be replaced by cash crops. In particular, this has occurred in Hmong rotational swidden farming areas. Lowlanders who had migrated to higher ground have introduced many modern crops and·integrated agriculture through state-led development initiatives and through contract farming for investors from private enterprise. These new crops include the planting of soybeans during the rainy season in Ban Huai Youak, Ban Sopwin, Ban Huai Pong; cabbage and barley grown at Ban Kon Wang, Huai Hoi, Mae Hae and cut flowers at Ban Nong Tao, Mae Sapock, Ban Mai Wang Pha Poon. Producing the new cash crops has necessitated changes in cultivation methods such as monoculture. The new crops required the soil to be loosened and soil tilled, often destroying topsoil.

The area available for swidden farming has been reduced by the proclamation of state forest reserves, bans on rotational swidden farming and the "carving up" of land through adoption of modern inheritance practices. Traditional cultivation techniques have had to change as successive years' crops must now be cultivated on the same spot. This has meant that the depleted soil has to be replenished through the use of chemical fertilizers and crops protected through pesticides. In turn this creates a dependence on outside forces, for example state agencies and other organisations promoting initiatives such as integrated fruit farming.

There have also been changes to the traditional property system governng swidden land. While traditionally, swidden land was common property within the community, with households having rights to the land that they cleared, burned and cultivated, these households are now establishing a permanent customary right to this land. This is because swidden lands are no longer the main production site for the community, but rather a supplement to the main production from wet rice farming.

The traditional reciprocal labour sharing in cultivation of swidden land is no longer possible, and this in turn has affected the community base of production and land management. Only households who have insufficient wet rice fields are still cultivating swidden fields. They, too, have been affected by changes in the community's labour organisation. These few households are forced to choose locations in which produce can be harvested and transported using only their own labour.

Swidden fields are most usually located at the upper extremity of the wet rice fields belonging to each household. These scattered patches now replace the traditional continuous field of dry rice cultivation. Although there may be no clear agreement as to whether these patches of land belong to the community or to the householder, repeated cultivation of rice fields leads farmers to claim permanent rights to land, including full rights to pass it on to someone else without having to be accountable to the community. This is most clearly demonstrated when these plots are sold to people from outside the community, as has been the case increasingly since the late 1980s.

Terraced wet rice fields

Terraced wet rice fields have also been an important cultivation area for communities. Progress in irrigation technologies using weirs and channels has led to the development of terraced wet rice fields by communities in the Mae Wang catchment area. There are no clear documents or oral historical evidence to say when land was first cleared for wet rice farming or in which community. But it is estimated that this occured before the second world war, possibly during the early years of the the Kawila dynasty when the laws were changed to allow payment of taxes in money instead of by provision of corvee labour.

Oral history reports of the establishment of the lowland villages of Sopwin, Mae Moot, Mai Wang Poon and Huai Pong claim that their ancestors were variously "Four Baht Tax Evaders" from San Pa Tong and members of the Khamu ethnic group who had come to the area as timber workers for British timber companies. Over time they cleared the land, dug irrigation channels and built weirs, with some buying additional land from the Karen people and assimilating as Northern Thais.

However, the establishment of terraced wet rice fields began in earnest after the second world war when more people came into the area and began forming communities which provided a suffcient labour force to mobilise for digging irrigation channels and constructing weirs. For instance, in Mae Sapock, the community began to build the Pa Toop irrigation channel, which is the longest channel bearing water from the Mae Wang river to the village, just after the end of Japanese occupation under the leadership of the grandfather of Headman To Koh who was the *"sicro"* (traditional leader) of the village at that time. This enabled the water to be brought to irrigate the area now known as Tong Mae Sapock Tai which is the biggest wet rice field of the village, no less than 200 *rai* in area.

For the Karen and the Northern Thai in the Mae Wang Catchment area, the wet rice terraces were central to the establishment of a permanent community. Farmers no longer had to move every year or two in order to have the labour force close to the fields under cultivation. By the late 1950s this form of migration had ceased entirely. Even though dry rice or swidden fields are still cultivated, the modern methods of rotational swidden farming have changed, and the swidden fields are now not sufficiently important to require the population to move around after them.

In Mae Sapock, the area of intensive study, the last community migration of this kind occurred in 1959, after the clearing of land for wet rice farming by Headman To Koh and his neighbours at Tong Pha Mon by the Mae Wang river. This was the last area cleared in the Mae Sapock catchment area. The community of Ban Pah Mon was the last to migrate from Ban Mae Sapock Neua Tai.

The terraced wet rice fields thus became central to the cohesion of the community. For these communities, the wet rice fields came to have a depth of meaning beyond that of a production site for subsistence farming or cash crops. The wet rice fields came to be a centre of culture and cohesion bound up with the notion of a permanent community for wet rice cultivators of the highlands. These farmers had the wisdom and ability to adapt their life style as best they could to changing political and economic circumstances in the same way that the lowlanders did.

The system of land tenure of the wet rice terraces is currently in a state of confusion due to the move from community based property to individual property, a move forced on communities largely through the the vast expansion of intensive cash crop cultivation which requires higher capital investment. Traditionally, wet rice fields were communal property with individual household and kinship groups' rights to land established on a use basis, with those who cleared the land earning a permanent customary right able to be passed on to kin. The claims to land had to be accepted and legitimised through due community processes, whereby the community considered claims in light of who cleared the land, who cultivated it and to whom the former owner of the land had passed it on. The cultivation process for wet rice meant that a large labour force had to be mobilised to maintain irrigation channels and weirs. No individual farmer could do this alone. Reciprocal labour sharing with family or kin was needed at many stages of cultivation. The sharing of information as to cultivation, organisation of labour and rest periods was conducted through a convivial drinking circle. These activities were held in the fields, so that although there were no aerial maps to prove whose land was whose, no signatures from the state to prove that the holder of the title deed was the real owner, farmers in Mae Wang Catchment area were able to cultivate their own fields, knowing through more organic methods who held tenure to the land based on the farming activities of each household.

The move from community based property to individual property took place during a period when land became a commodity which could be pawned, mortgaged, sold or ownership transferred. The need for clear inheritance rights became more pressing after the intensification of commercial cultivation from the 1970s onwards. This coincided with demands on the government to recognise rights to land according to the 1954 land law, so that such land could be used as collateral for investment monies or as surety in court cases.

The government began to respond to these demands, first attending to the needs of the lowland communities. SK1 title deeds were issued to citizens in 1954 as initial proof of claim to the land in the upper Mae Wang catchment area, in Ban Sopwin, Mai Wang Pha Poon, Huai Pong, Mae Moot, eventually having to be changed to NS3 and full title. However, not many households actually had the SK1 documents, so only a few were able to otain full title deeds. Those who did obtain titles tended to be the wealthy farmers and village leaders who were close to the government officials and had more opportunities than most villagers. Hmong and Karen were particularly disadvantaged, since they were generally granted fewer citizenship rights than the Northen Thai (see Anan Ganjanapan in this volume).

In 1954 when the SK1 documents were first issued, many Karen and Hmong from Mae Win Sub-district had not yet obtained citizenship. Moreover their only method of transport to the San Pa Tong District was walking, with the closest village being 40 kilometers away. Only a year after the introduction of SK1 the government put a stop to further issuing of these forms of title. Thus, when the government announced that title deeds were to be changed from SK1 to full titles after 1970, only a few highlanders even heard about the new proclamation. Further, in 1965 the government declared this area of forest a National Forest Reserve in accordance with the National Forest Reserve Act of 1964. As for those who did manage to obtain the necessary documentation to exempt their land from the reserve, the deeds only covered wet rice fields and the home site, while the land of those without deeds was declared forest reserve.

The inequities in issuing of documents became a significant tool in the hands of some wealthy farmers.They seized the opportunty to borrow money fom the banks, using their title deeds as guarantees, and then lent out this money at high rates to those who were unable to borrow capital for investment themselves. This led to class differentiation and an exploitative patronage system among the villagers. Those in debt to the wealthy merchants had to work for the patron to repay their debts, including allowing the patron to decide what the debtor's land would be used for, leading to an informal type of contract farming. These events occured wherever commercial crops were grown in the upper Mae Wang catchment area. Some farrmers solved their debt problems by selling their fields to the patron. In times when land prices were high, farmers were pressured into repaying their debts by "selling" the land, even though the land had never had a legal title deed.

Despite all this, the communal system of land tenure in Mae Wang Catchment area is still used by the community, under certain conditions, namely that land has not changed hands and been sold outside the community or been passed on through modern inheritance. The remaining land is still subject to the traditional system of community tenure and management, which is discussed in more detail below.

Whenever land comes under state-sanctioned title, the communal property system is inevitably weakened. When land passes outside the community, the use of that land is often a source of conflict for the community. This conflict may be in the area of water use, for example where the new owner does not conform with custom in participating in labour sharing to maintain irrigation channels, but rather hires labour instead or pays an annual fee for water. Where kin and community traditionally mobilised to harvest crops, hired labour may be used, thus sending up the price of labour beyond communities' means. This has also worked to reduce the traditional importance and value given to reciprocal labour sharing in the eyes of the community and replaced it with wage labour.

Another effect of the adoption of state land titling systems is the sub-division of land holdings into smaller and smaller plots until they are insufficient for subsistence farming and can only be of value if further rises in the price of land mean they can be sold off. Today, the modern inheritance system and the sale of land to outsiders has caused these smallholdings to be further sub-divided to the point where some people inherit plots that are too small to farm and leave them untended.

Wet rice fields are generally in smallholdings of 1-5 rai per family. Household claims over these smallholdings have existed since the first forest land was cleared for wet rice planting. Owing to the nature of the terrain, land to be cleared for wet rice cultivation had to be selected according to its irrigability. Today there is virtually no land left suitable for wet rice cultivation. Such land that remains is located in headwater forest areas, which are important as they are the water source of streams feeding existing irrigation systems. Villagers protect these and do not allow them to be further cleared.

The attempts to solve these problems of shifting cultivation by the government also had a significant impact in the wet rice areas. The construction of roads linking village and town and the commencement of the Royal Project which sought to develop commercial agriculture in the highlands after 1977 marked the start of more intensive cultivation using modern production technologies in response to market demand. As well as the Royal Project and government development agencies, village merchants had an important role in promoting commercial crop cultivation, through the exploitation of farmers' debts as described above. Cash crop cultivation began with native crops for lowlanders' use, like garlic and onions to use as seedstock, and the planting of chillies and cabbage after the rice. But the intensive use of wet rice fields for a second crop began with the promotion of soybean cultivation by local village merchants in response to the government call for domestic cultivation to replace the import of soybeans for production of animal feeds.

Villages in the Mae Win sub-district responded in a big way, with almost every cultivation area, no matter how remote, growing soybean crops. This was because villagers saw that soybeans required only a small initial investment, were easy to grow and did not require the level of inputs needed for the vegetables promoted by the Royal Project. All that soybeans required was to cut straw, drop in the seed, retain water in the field for a day, and except for occasional watering and pest elimination, that was all until harvest time. The lack of complication and the similarity to rice growing was another reason that villagers chose this crop in preference to those encouraged by the Royal Project.

The move to growing a second crop afer the wet season rice affected production techniques in the wet rice fields as well. Cultivation of soybeans normally took four months, which meant the farmers risked the beans getting moist and mouldy and thus selling for less. To fit in two crops before the rainy season, they had to cut a month off the usual cultivation time. This was done by changing to non-light sensitive varieties of rice which grew more quickly. Along with changes to rice varieties, villagers adopted other changes to technology such as use of mechanised ploughing and the use of hired labour to increase efficiency in production and meet market demands.

There were other reasons for these changes, too. For instance, the change to mechanised ploughing was also caused by the loss of grazing land to cultivation, so that buffaloes and oxen sometimes destroyed villagers' crops, causing strife within the village; or when water levels rose and fell rapidly and it was feared that there would not be enough water for crops, or for reasons to do with availabilty of labour as young people migrated to the city for work, then machines or hired labour made farming quicker and easier.

Even though these changes have brought upland communities more fully within the market economy, with associated increase in risk, most have managed to survive as smallholders despite the pressures faced. This has been due to several aspects of flexibility in traditional resource management in all four areas of production: from forest products; from rotational shifting cultivation; from rice cultivation; and from cottage industry. In the case of rice cultivation, subsistence production continues to take precedence over commercial cultivation, so that labour and land demands of commercial cropping are normally secondary to the main task of producing rice sufficient for survival. This is despite pressure from various governmental development agencies and traders to move toward a pattern of commercial monocropping. Commercial cropping in rice terraces and swiddens thus remains a secondary activity. Whenever there is a threat to basic subsistence production, farmers in the upper Mae Wang watershed have managed – sometimes against the odds – to adapt and maintain their subsistence livelihood.

Household compounds

The household compound is also important for production. Although small in area, such land is held as undisputed property by the household and used carefully and intensively for subsistence. Other than serving as a site for various domestic activities, as a meeting place and for ceremonial purposes, the compound is also a site for older women to pass on skills such as weaving of cloth, or for men to pass on skills in bamboo weaving of field implements. Even though there is a decline in such activity, it is likely to be replaced by other cottage industry.

Nearby the house there is usually a garden planted to vegetables and edible herbs. Often medicinal herbs are also planted, as are flowers that are used for both decorative and ceremonial purposes. The underside of houses is used to keep agricultural implements and to raise chickens, cows and buffalo. These domestic animals are sources of food, draught power and are used in ceremonial activities.

In summary, there are four main production systems that depend closely on traditional environmental knowledge. However, over time these production systems have been adapted through indigenous processes of technological change in such a way that the subsistence economy of Mae Wang has survived. Yet the communities under discussion do not exist in isolation from the state and the wider economy of which they are increasingly a part. Dependence on outsiders for goods that cannot be produced locally started with exhange of forest products for goods supplied by lowlanders. Later this developed into cash cropping on dry season rice terraces and in swiddens. This move toward a market orientation was externally driven by a state less concerned with local people's welfare than with opium eradication, driving out communist influence and prohibiting shifting cultivation. The means by which communities have subsequently been exposed to the risks associated with market-oriented production and integration within the capitalist economy are the subject of the following analysis.

STATE AND CAPITAL INVOLVEMENT IN MAE WANG WATERSHED

The role of state involvement has been alluded to with regard to various aspects of changing ways of thinking about land use, decision making, tenure patterns and economic structures at a community level. This section describes the impact of such involvement, the pressures it has created and the unprecedented response by local people.

Pressure on community forests

Pressure on community forest lands has occurred over three interlocking periods. Each has elicited a response by local people, culminating in the emergence and leadership of *Nuai Neua*.

The first period of pressure commenced with the gazetting of the upper Mae Wang watershed as national forest reserve in 1965. This was despite the fact that most communities had already developed permanent rice terraces. There was no proper survey. Forestry officials informed local people through the *kamnan* (sub-district chief) that the area was now forest reserve. The former *kamnan* says that people were told that if they had any objections, they were to report them to the Sanpatong District Office. However, only a few lowlanders who had SK1 land certificates were able to make such objections. The majority of people in the area not only had no certificates, but as ethnic minorities they did not hold Thai citizenship and had no identity cards so were unable to report. The result was to turn the settlements of the upper watershed into illegal squatter communities. Further pressures were exerted with the granting of logging concessions to outside companies. Between 1969 and 1985, the area was logged for timber that was initially used for railway sleepers and electricity poles, and later to supply processing mills.

Granting of concessions led not only to the cutting of forest, but also to construction of logging tracks. What had previously been an isolated area was now opened up. This led both to an influx of new settlers and to incursion on the forest by commercial interests such as the Thai-am Tobacco Company which needed wood for its kilns in the lower part of the watershed. There followed a rapid decline in timber availability in the area, which was further exacerbated by influential local people's poaching of timber in league with Sanpatong sawmillers. These illegal operations actually preceded the logging concessions, but increased rapidly with ease of access provided by the logging tracks. The Mae Wang river was used to float logs downstream. Initially, the logging operations did not cause any great hardship for local people, as the forests were still plentiful. Indeed, many local people benefited from opportunities to work as wage labourers in logging operations, either working in extraction helping to cut the trees, drag the logs with elephants and float them downriver, or working with forestry officials in marking trees eligible for cutting. Similarly, the declaration of forest reserve did not immediately lead to any great hardship, as local people saw it as a prerogative of the state that did not have any real influence on their lives, which they carried on as normal.

The pressure of state forestry interests commenced with the establishment of a forest protection and plantation unit in the area from 1975. Officials started to claim that local people were responsible for degradation in the condition of local forests. One of the principal ways in which the unit showed results was to arrest local people caught clearing forest for swiddens. Shifting cultivation gradually became the primary scapegoat for forest loss, and the weight of such allegations was only increased by the arrest of Hmong settlers in Ban Mon Ya, Khun Wang and Ban Mae Hae who were caught growing opium. This was despite previous acceptance and even encouragement of opium cultivation during the period that General Pao Sriyaynon was director of the Police Department during the 1950s.

Pressure from state forestry authorities was a significant factor in the support given by many communities in the area to the Communist Party of Thailand. During the 1970s, the upper Mae Wang watershed became an important area of agitation and support for those opposed to the government.

The second main period of pressure commenced with plantation forestry and alienation of villagers' land as part of a campaign to eliminate shifting cultivation. The campaign was based on the assumption that local people and their rotational farming practices were the major culprits in forest loss. Following expiry of the logging concession in 1985, RFD began a program of forest restoration through plantations and stipulated that farming had to occur in permanent plots.

RFD was responsible for demarcating between state forestry land and villagers' agricultural land. The intention was to "stabilise" the farming practices of *"khon doi"*, or "mountain people". This forestry policy was the driving force behind other agencies that brought projects into the area, for example the Land Development Department, the Royal Projects Division and the Agricutural Extension Department.

Division between state forestry land and village land was at the discretion of RFD, who marked out land to be set aside for conservation and restoration of forest. Each village was allocated an area in which farming could occur, but only under permanent cultivation. The right bank of the Mae Wang River was largely set aside for forestry, while areas on the left bank were allocated for cultivation. However, neither formal title nor alternative documentation of tenure rights were given for such land.

Some villages were able to accommodate and accept this situation. Others, notably those on the right bank of the Mae Wang River, had little permanent rice land and depended substantially on shifting cultivation. Confiscation of swiddens for forest plantation thus caused considerable hardship to these communities, for example Ban Khun Puai, Nong Monthaa and Khun Wang. The ill-feeling that resulted from hardships associated with constrained livelihoods was exacerbated by token arrests of local people on grounds of encroaching on state forest land. Pent-up resentment has lasted and has been a significant factor in the support for activism culminating in *Nuai Neua*.

The third and most intense period of pressure came with declaration of parts of the watershed as national park land, within the Khun Khan and Doi Inthanon National Parks. Since 1992, the government has had a policy of extending conservation forest to 25 percent of the total land area of Thailand, within which Mae Wang was designated a target area. Occupation of national parks is strictly prohibited, implying that resettlement of existing communities would be required. This threat was the sparking point for a 48 kilometre march by *Nuai Neua*, demanding a change in policy and a return of forest management rights to the community.

Promotion of cash cropping by state and capital interests

Another source of pressure on agricultural land came with promotion of cash cropping. From the point of view of the state, there were two main reasons for such promotion. First was the desire to draw local people away from the influence of the Communist Party of Thailand. Second was an attempt to eradicate shifting agriculture, notably opium cultivation. State agencies put their faith in market-oriented monocropping as a means of poverty eradication, and of stabilising shifting cultivation and forest encroachment.

From the late 1970s onward, the increase of commercial agriculture started to place many pressures on resource use in the upper Mae Wang watershed. These pressures were associated with state and private initiatives. Most were based on the notion that traditional agriculture was backward and incapable of supporting local people. Shifting agriculture was seen by outsiders as both inefficient and environmentally destructive. In its place, permanent agriculture was supported through assistance given by the Land Development Department (LDD) in creation of new terraces, and by the Royal Projects Division for planting flowers for sale and planting various cool season annuals and perennials, notably fruit trees.

These changes led to a rapid increase in dependence on the market and concomitant decline in self-sufficiency. Problems were exacerbated by limitations in the programs described above. The terraces cleared by bulldozer were not suitable for rice cultivation as they were too high to irrigate, and much of the topsoil was removed during the clearing process. Moreover, many areas were sold to outsiders buying up land for recreation and *"suan kaset"*, or hobby farms. As LDD completed terracing in a particular area, the remaining surrounding forest was declared off-limits by RFD both for swidden cultivation and for collection of forest products. Thus, both forest land and swiddens were lost to local people for subsistence purposes.

The constraints imposed led to dependence on the limited area of rice terraces and small areas of land previously farmed as swiddens that now had to be put under permanent cultivation. Intensification of land use has thus been rapid, and has necessitated production that is market oriented – in marked contrast to traditional self-sufficiency. Furthermore, the monocropping that has been a feature of the new market-based cultivation system has led to a significant loss of diversity in cultivars, with farmers now dependent on a few crops grown from purchased seed rather than on the wide range of rice strains and other crops previously grown in a pattern of intercropping.

The new pattern of market-based cropping has had important impacts on local people, notably in their need for credit. This commenced with the arrival of private traders, but has intensified as contract farming has developed. The dependence of farmers under this system is exacerbated by their lack of title, and this has served as another source of support for *Nuai Neua*, which has been active in demanding security of tenure for farmers in the upper watershed.

NUAI NEUA

The problems faced locally are seen by leaders of the Mae Wang Watershed Network to be closely related to forest loss, whether in terms of drying up of irrigation channels, rainfall decline or pressure from a state that regards local people as squatters. These problems have accumulated over a long period of time. After many meetings, local leaders of the Network have ultimately come to the conclusion that there are numerous issues that cannot be solved in isolation and that a broader cooperative framework is required.

The idea of establishing an organisational framework for mobilisation beyond a single watershed that involves alliances with groups other than fellow villagers came to fruition from early 1994. Several parties were involved, including northern non-governmental development organisations, Chiengmai University Social Research Institute, and the Mae Wang Watershed Network. A meeting was held to review past strategies, obstacles and achievements and to discuss the best way forward for diverse and scattered groups with common interests.

Four main conclusions emerged from this meeting regarding mobilisation strategy. First, a common approach among people's organisations in northern Thailand is required to give strength in unity. The group named itself the Northern Farmers' Development Network (NFDN), also known as *Nuai Neua*. Second, two main issues will receive attention in the decade to come, in order to respond to the problems of constituent organisations. These are marketing and production problems with agricultural commodities, and problems regarding land, water and forest resources. The third conclusion was the need to develop a clear mobilisation strategy based on the urgent local needs of member organisations. Fourth was the need to seek alliances beyond existing membership, first and foremost from local people's organisations elsewhere, but also from NGOs and the academic community. The aim would not be to achieve "victory" over anyone, but rather to fight for justice.

Following the setting of this strategy, the Committee of *Nuai Neua* investigated the key common issues being faced in several localities. Of most concern were the implications of expanding protected areas to cover 25 percent of the country's territory. Of this 25 per cent, more than half is located in the North, and it overlaps with upland swiddens, rice terraces and orchards being worked by local people, particularly ethnic minorities. State policy is to resettle these hill dwellers to lowland areas. Already many villages have been relocated, for example Pha Cho and Wang Neua villages in Lampang province and Hmong villages in Khlong Lan District of Kamphaengphet province. Elsewhere, data collected by the Department of Land Development is used as a basis for resettlement. Taking advantage of information supplied by NGOs, *Nuai Neua* decided to use the issue of resettlement out of protected areas as a focus for an unprecedented mobilisation strategy. Three levels of mobilisation were developed as part of the *Nuai Neua* framework: the level of the village community, level of the watershed network and the policy and legal level.

At the level of the village community, two main activities serve as the basis of mobilisation by *Nuai Neua* and local leaders. First is to inform the community of state policy and its local implications, notably the expansion of protected areas. Information supplied by NGOs is critical in communicating such details. Second is to establish conservation groups to systematise use of natural resources and to prevent environmental destruction. Using the experience of Mae Wang, three zones are marked out to establish forest use and protection: conservation forest, village woodlots and agricultural land including swiddens, rice terraces and household compounds.

This local zonation is used for negotiating with state authorities, as a conflict management tool locally within the community, and also to establish a local resource management plan.

Activities in each community are also supportive of the development of watershed networks. In particular, demarcation and zonation requires cooperation between villages that ultimately leads to watershed-level cooperation. Nevertheless, formal establishment of watershed level networks is important for mobilisation and coordination at this level. It also facilitates action at the policy level.

Policy level mobilisation occurs simultaneously with activities at the first two levels. Attention is given to informing watershed networks of state policy initiatives and implementation plans. Communities are also encouraged to negotiate or place demands with local state officials in order to hone bargaining skills and inform themselves which local state agencies are responsible for what aspects of policy.

Beyond the level of local government, there is cooperation with national level NGOs such as NGO-COORD, Project for Ecological Recovery and with sympathetic academics, notably with Chiengmai University Social Research Institute. These allies of *Nuai Neua* occasionally help facilitate negotiation with high level officials. Such negotiation may be an outcome of petitions submitted to the Prime Minister or of meetings requested with a particular minister, notably the Minister of Agriculture and Forestry. The media have been sympathetic allies in pressing for such negotiation. Academics have helped by informing the groups of the travel itineraries of particular Ministers in advance. The outcome of negotiations depends in part on the weight of local feeling expressed, and recognition of this was behind the regular demonstrations held during 1994-5. Virtually every time the Prime Minister visited the North to open a project or officiate in some other capacity, he was met with no fewer than 100 petitioners.

Each petition is refined through meetings between village leaders, NGOs and academics. Each time, a common position has been rehearsed and acceptable negotiating compromises agreed internally in advance. In the early stages, virtually every negotiation ended with appointment of local officials to deal with the issues, but these officials hold no authority to change policy or laws. Thus, despite support from large groups of villagers, little was achieved from these negotiations in 1994. Only political decisions could effect a real outcome. While village leaders were aware of these limitations, they went along with them as a strategic means of showing the mass of villagers where real power lies.

The experience during 1994 led *Nuai Neua* to establish a policy of not negotiating with local officials, but rather to target the Minister of Agriculture and Forestry for future negotiations over the protected areas issues. A 48 kilometre march took place in April 1995, involving some 20,000 villagers from about 50 upland communities. The march drew inspiration from the Northeastern Small Farmers Network, which has organised mass marches on Bangkok over various issues facing that region. Marching South from Chiang Mai, the protest reached Lamphun, where the Minister for Agriculture and Forestry finally agreed to meet with the rally organisers at the Provincial Office. The negotiation took place on 3 May 1995, with five main negotiating points. First was the provision of compensation to those who had already been relocated, including the right to harvest from fields already planted. Second was to cease declaring protected areas where settlement has already occurred. Third was to expedite the drafting of the Community Forest Law. Fourth was to drive out business interests who have encroached on forest land. Finally, it was demanded that a Working Committee be established by Cabinet resolution to deal with the issues, and that the Committee be comprised of village leaders, academics, NGOs and government officials in equal numbers. Ultimately, the negotiations were only able to proceed up to a certain point of agreement, which was crystallised as a Ministerial order. Shortly afterward, the Parliament was dissolved and elections called. Since then, *Nuai Neua* has continued its mobilisation.

CONCLUSION

In summary, *Nuai Neua* has emerged in response to the problems arising from local level changes. Indigenous modes of resource management, including local land classification systems based on traditional practices, have informed and inspired leaders of the movement in their rejection of inappropriate resource management approaches imposed on communities by the state. This contradiction has also conscientised local people and elicited participation in the movement. In particular, it has led to demands for return of resource management rights and powers to local communities. It is recognised that there are limits to individual action that necessitate community organisation, to communities working in isolation hence the need for watershed level organisation, and ultimately to local mobilisation when a forum is needed for national level action. *Nuai Neua* in particular, and networks more generally, provide the bridge that helps give local people a voice in national level decisions that affect their lives, livelihoods and the environment on which all depend.

BANGKOK'S ENVIRONMENTAL PROBLEMS: STAKEHOLDERS AND AVENUES FOR CHANGE

Helen Ross

INTRODUCTION

Bangkok's environmental problems are manifold and ubiquitous. Most residents suffer from the transportation system, air pollution, noise, water pollution, water supply, flooding, subsidence and garbage collection, though they experience them in different ways according to their socioeconomic status, place of residence, and family and community characteristics. Environmental problems threaten health and well-being, and they have impacts on family and community bonds. They now also pose an economic threat.

Environmental experts commonly look to technical solutions to environmental problems. If traffic congestion is the complaint, roads, flyovers, and mass transport are the first options considered. This is treating the symptoms. After outlining the city's main problems, this chapter examines the underlying societal causes of Bangkok's environmental crisis. It goes on to consider the potential sources of reform among the various 'stakeholders' whose actions shape the city – politicians, public servants, business-people and private citizens.

BANGKOK'S ENVIRONMENTAL PROBLEMS

Bangkok's environmental problems are notorious. Traffic in particular is a favourite topic of everyday conversation, people from all classes of society comparing notes on their experiences. The talk-back shows of radio FM100, a station whose sole purpose is traffic news and discussion, provide catharsis for travellers who feel that their experience is not so bad as others' after all. Noise and air pollution are largely a consequence of the traffic. These are experienced worst by those who live and work at street level, and the lower-income commuters who endure long exposure during slow bus rides to and from work. The middle-class and higher income people can live away from the main streets, and cocoon themselves from the worst of the heat, air pollution and noise in air conditioned cars and houses (Anuchat 1991, Anuchat and Ross 1992).

In a survey of 1200 Bangkok residents conducted by our research team late in 1992, 58.2% listed traffic problems among the three worst disadvantages of living in Bangkok. This was followed by air pollution (49.2%) and housing and population issues such as slums and the number of condominiums (16.9%). Priorities for government action were traffic congestion (named by 77.2% of people in their top three suggestions), air pollution (40.7%) water pollution (14.7%), housing and population issues (9.1%) and the cost of living (7%). This emphasis on environmental issues is telling, as the survey included social and economic factors and infrastructure. 13.6% of our respondents found no advantages in living in Bangkok, and a further 49.3% could list only one advantage – most often economic opportunity. Other opportunities mentioned were convenient transportation, closeness to civilization, and good facilities.

Water pollution touches fewer people's lives directly, but has severe impacts on those whose lives are still oriented around *klongs* (canals), and the many slum dwellers who depend on them for domestic purposes (Anuchat and Ross 1992). The water is highly polluted throughout Bangkok, close to biologically dead in the inner and middle zones (Dhiraporn, forthcoming). It seriously affects neighbouring agricultural areas and the provinces downstream. The lack of sewerage in Bangkok – the first systems are only now being built and will serve only a small proportion of the city's population (Kasemsan 1993) – means that 75 percent of Bangkok's water pollution is due to domestic and related sources such as restaurants, markets, hospitals and hotels (TDRI 1988, Thongchai et al 1987). The remaining 25 percent, from industrial sources, should not be overlooked however. By 1990 there were over 25,000 waste-producing factories in the Bangkok Metropolitan Region (TDRI 1993a). Despite recent attempts to concentrate industry in industrial estates, the bulk of Bangkok's industry consists of small, poorly controlled enterprises scattered throughout the metropolitan area. There is little ecological or public health rationale for the location of activities, and poor knowledge of how air and water flows expose the public to the waste products of traffic and industry.

The gradual deterioration of Bangkok's canal and river system, once the cultural and practical focus of the city, is symbolised in the way fewer houses, buildings and activities now orient to canals. The *loy kratong* festival is but a reminder of the days when people thought it important to thank the river for its sustenance and apologise for the necessity of polluting it (Segaller 1979).

Flooding, an ecological feature of the floodplain delta environment, is now largely controlled in central and eastern Bangkok due to flood control engineering works. It is a continuing risk in western Bangkok and the surrounding provinces, to which the waters are diverted. Seasonal floods can linger for months because of the flatness of the land and the weakened drainage system. Canal flow capacities have been reduced by decades of neglect – some filled to provide road space, and many blocked, silted up or narrowed. The increased hard surfaces in the city put more pressure on the canals to handle run-off. The floods are also putrid, owing to water pollution and the filth washed from the streets.

In the three years to 1994, floods were forgotten locally, and water shortage became the talk of the town. Drought had reduced the supply available. Water pressure was low in the pipes, so middle-class people bought pumps to ensure that water reached their houses. This disadvantaged their lower income neighbours all the more. Rural areas were disadvantaged by the competition for water: farmers were instructed to plant only one rice crop. In the 1994 monsoon season, flooding returned. I am not aware of any public education efforts to encourage water conservation by Bangkok households and commercial users. There is a major engineering proposal on the books to divert water from the Meklong River to supply Bangkok (Sopida 1992).

Alternate sources of water are problematic. Bangkok formerly depended much more on underground water, but its use has been blamed for the severe subsidence which afflicts the city and the coast. Parts of Bangkok, only one to one and a half metres above sea level to start with, are subsiding at rates of up to eight centimetres per year (Kasemsan 1993). Large chunks of land have literally fallen into the Gulf of Siam in Samut Sakhon province south west of Bangkok. While there is some debate as to whether the heavy drawing of groundwater really causes the subsidence, there is a strong commitment to reducing dependence on it. Rainwater, stored in enormous jars, is the other source of water for people in the remaining rural parts of the Bangkok Metropolitan Area and surrounding provinces. It is becoming increasingly risky owing to air pollution.

Garbage is the other major environmental problem in Bangkok. Westernisation of consumer tastes has decreased the proportion of biodegradable wastes, and increased the proportions of plastic, glass and metals. Some parts of the city are unserviced by garbage collections (16% in 1989); here residents throw their rubbish into *klongs* or onto vacant land, or have to carry it themselves to a main road for collection. One of the innovations of the Bangkok Governor Chamlong's administration in the late 1980s and early 1990s was special narrow garbage trucks which could penetrate constricted *sois* (lanes) and garbage collecting boats to service the *klong* communities. Traffic congestion impedes the efficiency of garbage collection. In 1989 each truck was taking one and a half to two hours for a trip of 25-45 kilometres to one of the three 'garbage mountains' (National Environment Board 1989). These are vast areas of land where organic waste is separated out to be made into fertiliser or left to decompose naturally. Licensed scavengers who live on site in self-built dwellings separate everything useful from the inorganic wastes for recycling. Households specialise in glass, aluminium, other metals, and plastic bags, which are passed to other informal sector specialists to be hand washed and dried for re-use.

Bangkok's concentration of population and activities, and the rate of domestic and commercial consumption of resources, equally causes environmental problems for rural areas. There is competition for water upstream of the city, and those downstream and on either side suffer the water pollution. Dams, built both for water resources and provision of electricity, have been high points of environmental conflicts (Hirsch 1993). Air pollutants also circulate beyond the city. While the concentrations are reduced, there is high potential for pollutants such as lead to enter food chains through their distribution through air and water into agricultural areas.

HOW DID BANGKOK REACH THIS STATE?

The history of how Bangkok's environment came to be so unfavourable is a complex one. Among the factors are:

1. The history of modernisation since the time of King Rama IV (1851-1868), in which modernisation, or more aptly 'westernisation', became part of a diplomatic strategy to avert colonisation by western powers (as well as a fascination in its own right). Thailand's form of modernisation was highly imitative. Blended with traditional social organisation and ways of doing business, it was not conducive to efficient government decision-making.

2. The resultant conversion of Bangkok from a water-based to a road-based society, through which canals were filled to provide roads, but without a road network sufficiently developed to provide for an efficient transportation system. In the process, the flood plain ecological system has received severe interference.

3. The cumulative neglect of the civic infrastructure needs of a modern and urbanised society, from road networks to sanitation and green spaces. (In village Thailand, waterways provided transport routes and waste disposal, and public green spaces were unnecessary since villagers had access to one another's

privately-owned land and the waterways for recreation and social activity – see below).

4. Cultural factors such as the nature of property rights and land-owning patterns. Bangkok's development of land plots largely follows the outlines of rural property holdings. Traditionally most land was privately owned, but unfenced. The traditional property system allowed rights of way and use to others, so that there was no demand for publicly owned recreational land. Private land is now walled-off, denying thoroughfare (Suwattana Thadaniti, personal communication). There is no commonly-owned land which could remain to provide public parks, and developers have no incentive to set aside such land when converting agricultural land into housing estates.

5. The one-sided national emphasis on economic growth, most of which has been concentrated in Bangkok and its vicinity (48% of GDP in 1989: TDRI 1993). This has led to heavy migration, and high demand on natural resources and existing infrastructure. Investment has been far more readily available for directly productive economic purposes such as national highways and the airport, than for indirect investments in civic infrastructure. Nevertheless, the lack of infrastructure, particularly the road and transport system, is now a threat to economic efficiency.

6. Limitations in political and institutional capacity to rectify these trends.

The last factor is the subject of this chapter.

DECISION-MAKING IN AND ABOUT BANGKOK

No city is completely efficient. However strongly planned, a city evolves from the cumulative effects of countless small decisions and actions by the variety of inhabitants and office bearers pursuing their various goals (Anuchat and Ross 1994, Ross and Anuchat 1994).

Residents build or rent their houses according to the locations and styles they aspire to, or can afford. The choices and lifestyles of surrounding residents affect the social and symbolic desirability of a residential area to other potential members. Small or larger businesses similarly locate their enterprises strategically, from the food hawkers who set up their stalls between transport routes and residential areas, to the owners of shop-houses lining major roads, to major corporations mingling with their kind in 'business districts'. Government departments try to provide the services, or regulate the activities, they have been entrusted with, from water supply to the provision of transport, or traffic management. Planners attempt to coordinate these activities in certain ways, and take a long-term view of the needs for efficiency and equity in city-living. Politicians (or elite decision-makers under previous systems of governance) have overall power of decision-making, at least while in government. In a democratic system, the public service is there to carry out the government's decisions, and the electorate is nominally its master.

A useful way of considering and analysing the roles of the various 'actors' whose interests and decisions shape and reshape the city, is through the concept of 'stakeholders'. The concept of 'stakeholder' is an analytical one, effectively meaning an 'interest group'. On a small scale, the stakeholders in an issue may be individuals. Where larger-scale issues are concerned, 'stakeholders' are people and organisations grouped according to their interests, for instance 'local residents', 'business interests' and 'regulatory authorities'. These may or may not be cohesive groups. Some may operate as organised interests, for instance if slum residents are represented by a community committee or NGO, or business interests by a Chamber of Commerce. Local residents, on the other hand, may have similar concerns but not be organised formally at all.

The concept of 'stakeholder' is used both to 'map' an issue and to identify all types of people whose interests should be represented in a decision-making process. What are the interests, what types of people are interested, and what are their commonalities and conflicts? How should each of these sets of people, or their interests, be represented in a public participation process? In this chapter, I am using a stakeholder analysis to examine the parties to a long-term,

informal process of decision-making which results in transformations of Bangkok (Anuchat, Ross and Wiseman 1995; Ross and
Anuchat 1994).

The diversity of interests active in the formation of Bangkok can
be grouped at the broadest scale as

- political representatives – politicians and political parties
  involved in the elected roles of democratic government, in the
  national parliament and the Bangkok Metropolitan
  Administration

- public service – the corresponding government departments and
  their staff, at national and city levels

- business interests – from large commercial operations to small
  family and informal sector businesses, operating across all
  commercial sectors

- other non-government interests – NGOs, individual opinion
  leaders, local communities, and academics.

These groupings are somewhat arbitrary, and they obscure
complexities within their memberships. For instance, the Thai
military is a powerful player in all national decision-making and has
roles within the political and business categories. These roles do not
appear strong in the shaping of Bangkok, but they have been very
influential in rural development and environmental controversies.
Individual opinion leaders may become politicians for part of their
careers, or work through politicians and public service departments
as well as through NGOs and social movements within the
stakeholder category of other non-government interests.

The role of Thai Buddhism, in its several contemporary variants,
is a mixed one, with some parts serving the status quo but other
parts inspiring public support for a variety of causes and values.
Non-establishment Buddhism is part of the inspiration of two of the
stakeholder groups. The main opinion leaders within the 'other non-
government' stakeholder category appeal strongly to Buddhist

values in their promotion of a new social justice and environmental ethic for Thai society. Fundamentalist sectarian Buddhism was a powerful impetus behind the new "honest" politics. Otherwise, establishment Buddhism has traditionally been highly supportive of conservative government. Local monasteries remain a focal point of many of Bangkok's urban communities, and often they are a rallying point for community action. (Schools and other non-religious community centres have become the focus for a few urban communities, especially where people do not have good rapport with their *Wat*).

The changes which take place in the built environment reflect interactions between the agendas of numerous 'stakeholders', with the interests of the most powerful or effective probably prevailing. If elite interests in car transport prevail, slums and old quarters may be demolished to make way for freeways. If the local residents are well organised, they may resist the freeways being built. If planning departments are strong, they may designate a green belt around the city. If business interests are strong, they may prevent such a policy, or circumvent its enforcement.

The interactions among these stakeholders are complex. For instance, what we think of as 'planning' is not simply a matter of having an effective planning department located somewhere in the public service. It also requires political will to give priority to planning over lobbying by interest groups, and to allow effective enforcement of planning mechanisms. It also requires the non-government stakeholders (business and others) to share the planning goals and comply with them in their own actions. Bangkok is currently witnessing new alliances between some business interests and other non-government interests (key individuals and academics) towards the common goal of improving the city.

The relationships among these four main stakeholder groups are in transition. The current shift in relationships cannot be regarded as linear or constant – it may become as irregular as the many swings and permutations of nominally-democratic and military government over the last few decades.

THE OLD STYLE OF POLITICS

Until the late 1980s, under both democratic and military governments of Thailand, Bangkok had been shaped by a limited set of interests. This pattern continues to a diminishing extent. The running of Bangkok was dominated by the national level of government, with a majority of civic functions in the hands of national departments of government, especially the many departments within the powerful portfolio of the Ministry of Interior. These departments operated in a strongly hierarchical fashion with weak lateral communication with other departments (Jacobs 1971). Coordination of any activity was thus very difficult. the Bangkok Metropolitan Administration (BMA) had (and still has) a very limited and unbalanced set of responsibilities and powers. Most practical tasks it wished to achieve cut across the responsibilities of national government, and required the cooperation of national departments. The BMA was under the control of appointed governors till 1985. National level departments, though nominally under the control of elected or appointed Ministers, operated very autonomously (Chai-Anan 1990, Jacobs 1971). The practical details of managing Bangkok were not high on the national political agenda. Linkages between the national level political and departmental stakeholders appear to have been weak. Ministers were more likely to approve projects generated by their departments than to lead new initiatives.

Linkages between politicians and the business sector ranged from strong to weak, depending on the scale and power of the business, and the particular marital and other social or economic links of its key members into the elite of Thailand's society. Large or rich businesses could have strong and beneficial links both with politicians and public servants, while small and poorer businesses (down to small family businesses and even informal sector operators) managed with lower-level and more localised allegiances or missed out. One variant of this type of relationship was 'money politics', lobbying backed by donation to the individual politician, party coffers or perhaps an agreed cause. This aspect of money politics is probably behind many surprise grantings of building permission, the many pieces of building, environmental and planning legislation which contain deliberate loopholes, and the legislation which looks good on the books but no one expects to be enforced. 'Money politics' should not be viewed purely in western moralistic terms. It has a cultural basis in the so-called patron-client relationships of mutual reliance between leaders and followers, and is also related to rural concepts of democracy and the lack of effective local government in rural areas (Logerfo 1992). Another reason for decisions which promote business but are detrimental to the safety and convenience of other citizens is the cultural trait of willingness to strike compromises to avoid conflicts (Thinapan and Likhit 1989).

The other relationship between business leaders, politicians and senior public servants (including members of the military) is a social one. There is a web of kinship, marital, business and 'old school' or military college relationships bonding the members of Thailand's elite, across these stakeholder groups. Personal familiarity and mutual financial or social interest supports communication and encourages mutual assistance.

Ordinary citizens, for the most part, had weak links with the other stakeholder groups. Political representation was often by the practice of 'vote-buying' (Logerfo 1992), brokered through key individuals, in rural areas often from the business sector. Voters thus enjoyed a temporary financial favour in return for their vote, and had little expectation of their interests being represented by those they had elected (their interests would seldom have been represented under the former system of governance either). Relations with the public service were also bureaucratic, with the focus on procedures and pleasing superiors rather than service to the public (Thinapan and Likhit 1989). Some relatively powerful individuals, opinion leaders and social reformers, often with a non establishment Buddhist ethic, have had influence within this non-government stakeholder group (see below).

The effect of 'old politics' on the growth of Bangkok has been to foster self-interested and laissez-faire development to an extraordinary degree. Almost exclusive national focus on economic growth, without the counterbalance of effective planning and provision of urban infrastructure, led to the burgeoning of Bangkok in an inefficient manner. Limited legislative control and intent to enforce the little legislation available was such that it was easy to get permission to build virtually anything, anywhere. Those with financial power and good political connections shaped the city according to their interests, and the arrangements one would expect to mitigate in the public interest, such as planning, were kept ineffective. Laissez-faire development may also have been in the general interests of less powerful social groups, in that slum communities have been able to form readily on vacant land and have proved hard to evict. There are relatively few reports of dislocation of slum communities in the middle decades of this century to provide space for grand roads and large civic buildings. The Rajdamnoern Avenue area, modelled on Paris boulevardes, is the main example of urban redevelopment requiring massive evictions (interview with former BMA senior planning official, April 1993).

NEW POLITICS

An emerging form of politics has begun to alter these relationships since the late 1980s. Starting with the BMA, whose Governors began to be elected in 1985, more democratic forms are appearing. The administration of Governor Chamlong was pivotal, in making a virtue of honest politics and creating an ambitious electoral platform of urban reform (not all fulfilled). This and subsequent administrations have performed a feat in electoral education, of encouraging voter responsibility and expectations of their elected leaders, who in turn try to respond to electors' wishes. This is a revolution for poorer voters. This trend is extending to the national level of politics, with several parties espousing honest and responsive politics. The efficiency of Bangkok is also becoming a national-level issue, at least with the politicians representing Bangkok.

A new variety of business-people is strongly behind the democratic changes, to the extent of participating, and assisting their workers to participate, in the pro-democracy demonstrations of

April-May 1992. Some use their business roles, such as ownership of newspapers, for reform purposes (Sondhi 1992). Thai newspapers, despite a lack of press freedom, have been vocal on environmental and social equity matters for many years. There is a growing view in the business sector that the inefficiencies of Bangkok are bad for business as well as for society, and that self-interest must be put aside in the common interest (interview with business adviser to Ministry of Interior, 1993).

A different type of change is slowly taking place in the public service. Though reforms to the structure of government are slow, there is increasing recognition of the need for coordination and cooperation between departments, and between the city and national levels of government. Since the departments retain their strong hierarchical structures, with authority concentrated at senior levels, and reorganisation of departments is not common, the means adopted has been committees. Each department concerned with an issue is represented on one or more committees dealing with that issue. The deliberations may be ponderous, but communication is taking place. The efficiency remains to be seen – there are at least 30 committees dealing with traffic (interview with former BMA senior planning official, April 1993). The committee structure does appear to be allowing new initiatives to be considered, such as a school bus system to reduce the amount of traffic devoted to delivering and collecting children from school (up to 30 percent of traffic in some parts of the city) and plans for new towns to be built to relocate the public service and possibly certain other functions from Bangkok.

The new politics is not having a smooth path, though surprisingly it was fostered by the military-appointed government of 1991-1992. The military stated rationale for its 1991 coup was the extent of corruption within the then elected government, and the civilian it appointed as Prime Minister, Anand Panyarachun, was a strong and popular practical reformer. Urban reforms gained strength under the democratic coalition government of Chuan Leekpai after late 1993, despite instability in the coalition. However, vote buying was prevalant in the 1995 election which brought the Chart Thai party into power. The new politics has not replaced the old politics, but it has made considerable inroads.

CONCLUSION: OPPORTUNITIES FOR CHANGE

Despite the conservatism I have described as the 'old politics', there is a creative potential in Thai society to stimulate change from a small base of concerned people. In the witty family planning campaign of the 1970s, condoms and discussion of family planning were made acceptable through stunts appealing to the cultural sense of fun. The organised protests against Nam Choan and Pak Mun dams (Hirsch 1993) involved a coalition of rural people, their monks, city based environmental NGOs, students and some academics. Nam Choan particularly was a turning point in Thai environmental politics (Hirsch 1993). The Magic Eyes campaign against littering, though criticised for its lack of an ecological basis, was begun by an individual from a prominent business family, gained invaluable financial and logistical backing from the business sector, and had wide public appeal (especially to children) through its jingle and media advertisements. Radio FM100, the traffic reporting station, is a different example of Thai ingenuity put to a practical environmental and social purpose.

The emergence of 'honest politics' provides a better than usual political opportunity for change to be initiated. A public sense of crisis about urban issues, shared by the populace, some public servants, business people and politicians, is helping to build political pressure to use this opportunity. Business opinion, and thus receptiveness to urban reforms which will undoubtedly challenge old business prerogatives, is changing. Many business leaders see that an inefficient Bangkok is affecting their productivity and future financial opportunities, and are supporting government in principle in seeking reforms. While the commitment to change is growing, it remains extremely difficult to achieve since planning, the obvious visionary and coordination mechanism in most societies, and the institutional arrangements necessary to support it, are so weak. At present the government and public service commitment to change remains largely directed to single-issue solutions, such as school buses and the set of proposals for new towns (interviews with officers of the Department of Town and Country Planning, National Economic and Social Development Board, business adviser to the Minister of the Interior, and a politician representing Bangkok).

Neither of the government stakeholders in Bangkok – the politicians (political parties) and their public servants – are sufficiently secure in office (in politicians' case) or coordinated to lead and sustain a drive for reform on the scale that Bangkok requires. The exigencies of their roles also mitigate against effective action. Politicians obtain much more electoral visibility from monumental projects, such as freeways, than from systematic reforms to public transport and traffic management. The monumental projects, however, tend to treat symptoms rather than causes, ignore the human behaviour factors in the problems, and often create new problems for other parts of the urban system (Anuchat and Ross 1992). Departments have to focus on their particular responsibilities; only planning branches can have a comprehensive role.

Given the limitations of the government stakeholders, our research team sees the impetus for reform of Bangkok coming from innovators within the other two stakeholder categories. Sub-groups within the non-government (community) category could well form coalitions, as they have through the series of dam protests in the late 1980s and in the alternative agriculture movement (Seri and Bennoun 1988). Initiatives are likely to be led by a few Buddhist intellectuals and reformers, through the human rights and environmental NGOs they have created to promote their vision for a Thai society based on well-being rather than wealth. These individuals have multiple social roles, as authors, independent academics (not necessarily currently employed in a university), Buddhists and NGO leaders. Over at least three decades, these individuals and organisations have been building up public support for their alternate view of an equitable society. They have achieved influence through their writings, public appearances, and capacity to communicate at all levels of the Thai social hierarchy. Their connections have helped protect them from the types of pressure which silenced other critics of government in the past. As they turn their attention from rural to urban environmental issues, they are likely to link with urban neighbourhood community leaders and local monks, slum leaders and the NGOs which serve slum interests, and to motivate a broad spectrum of community interests.

This sub-group already receives support from some of the reformist elements in the business community, who use their talents and business opportunities towards social goals. The press, owned by some democratically motivated people, is a potent force in encouraging political accountability and public participation in the democratic system. The media has been vital in publicly-initiated protest campaigns, and in helping to shape new values in Thai society. One set of business reformers appears motivated by Buddhist and social values, and by democratic ideals learnt through western educational and business contact. They are gaining support from business people whose values are more conventionally economic, but whose business interests are threatened by inefficiency.

While the non-government reformers use public protest where necessary, their main strategies are patient public education, coalition building and direct negotiation with other stakeholders. The scale and complexity of reforms required in Bangkok, especially if they are to be achieved without undue hardship to poorer people, will require cooperation from all stakeholders. All stakeholder groups need a role in any decision-making process, or at least for their basic interests to be satisfied by the outcomes. They must also **want** the reforms to succeed, since any party can undermine any policy through non-compliance. The reformers' skills in cooperative problem-solving, and the climate created by political opportunity and business frustration, could well bring all parties into cooperation.

The Traffic Crisis '94 group shows the type of new approach we might expect from publicly- initiated action. It is a sophisticated coalition of concerned individuals formed in early 1994 to try to find new solutions to Bangkok's traffic problems. The core committee involves people mainly from the community and business sectors, but with connections with the government stakeholder groups. Anand Panyarachun, former Prime Minister and now an NGO leader, is a prominent member, alongside academic and campaigner Prawese Wasi. Their procedure was to hold a series of workshops with selected participants, to try to generate a comprehensive new traffic management plan based on a systems view of the city and its people. Press reports suggest it gained implicit support from the Prime Minister and the Governor of Bangkok early in its process (*Sunday Post*, 16 January 1994).

Western countries are increasingly leaning to public participation to solve the problems which governments cannot solve alone – and especially those which may result in embarrassing and expensive protests if the public is displeased. In Bangkok we are seeing the first signs of a different form of public participation, in which the initiative is taken not by government inviting the public, but by members of the public offering their visions, motivation and talents to the rest of the public and government in a collaborative way.

Acknowledgements

This chapter is based on the research project *Impacts of modernisation and urbanisation in Bangkok: an ecological and biosocial study*, a UNESCO Man and the Biosphere Program Project Area 11 (human settlements) study. It is a collaboration between Mahidol and Chulalongkorn Universities in Bangkok, and the Australian National University, led by Helen Ross, Anuchat Poungsomlee, Krittaya Archavanitkul, Aphichart Chamratrithirong, and Suwattana Thadaniti. Funding bodies are International Development Research Centre (Canada), the major sponsor, with UNESCO, Australian Agency for International Development, and the participating departments.

Other members of our research team from Mahidol and Chulalongkorn Universities have helped to evolve the ideas in this chapter. Suwattana Thadaniti has patiently explained some of the politics and practice of Thai planning to me. Anuchat Poungsomlee, Krittaya Archavanitkul, and Sureeporn Punpuing have also provided me with background on Thai politics and the workings of some of the stakeholder groups. The Thai Studies Group at ANU, through its seminars and visiting speakers, has provided invaluable access to key players in the process I have described.

REFERENCES

Anuchat Poungsomlee 1991, *An integrative study of an urban ecosystem: the case of Bangkok*. PhD thesis, Centre for Resource and Environmental Studies, Australian National University, Canberra.

Anuchat Poungsomlee and Ross, H., 1992, *Impacts of modernisation and urbanisation in Bangkok: preliminary report*, Institute for Population and Social Research, Mahidol University, Bangkok.

Anuchat Poungsomlee and Ross, H., 1994, 'Local capacity towards sustainable development of Bangkok', Paper presented at Global Forum '94 Academic Conference, Manchester, 29 June – 1 July 1994.

Anuchat Poungsomlee, Ross, H, and Wiseman, R., 1995, 'Trouble with traffic' in *Risks and opportunities: managing environmental conflict and change*, eds V. Brown et al, Earthscan, London.

Chai-anan Samudhvanija 1990, 'Administrative reform', in *Thailand on the move: stumbling blocks and breakthroughs*, ed Suchart Prasith-rathsint, Thailand University Research Association, Bangkok.

Dhiraporn Kangagate forthcoming, Figures to be published in the final report of the project *Impacts of modernisation and urbanisation in Bangkok*.

Hirsch, P., 1993, *Political economy of environment in Thailand*, Journal of Contemporary Asia Publishers, Manila.

Jacobs, N., 1971, *Modernisation without development*, Praeger, New York.

Kasemsan Suwarnrat 1993, 'Water resource problems and water pollution in Bangkok', in *Symposium on environment and culture with emphasis on urban issues*, ed Siam Society, Siam Society, Bangkok.

Logerfo, J., 1992, 'Political trade secrets', *The Manager*, no. 48, 36-39.

National Environment Board 1989, *Refuse management in Bangkok and its vicinity*, NEB, Bangkok (in Thai).

Ross, H. and Anuchat Poungsomlee, 1994, 'Summary', 'Analysis of linkages', 'Qualification of human resources', papers presented at Technical Workshop on the Qualification of Human Resources, Teaching and Research for the Planning and Management of the Environment, Curitiba, Brazil, 6-10 June.

Segaller, D., 1979, *Thai ways*, Thai International, Bangkok.

Seri Phongphit and Bennoun, R. (eds.) 1988, *Turning point of Thai farmers*, Thailand Institute for Rural Development, Bangkok.

Sondhi Limthongkul, 1992, 'The Thai State and freedom of information', paper presented at Australian National University Thai Studies Group Conference The State and Civil Society, 18 October 1992.

Sopida Werakultawan, 1992, 'On the water front', *The Manager*, no 43, 34-39.

TDRI 1988, *Development of a framework for water quality management of the Chao Phraya and Thachin Rivers*, Paper prepared for the NEB, TDRI, Bangkok.

TDRI 1993a, National urban development policy framework final report: volume 2, TDRI, Bangkok.

TDRI 1993b, *Thailand economic information kit*, TDRI, Bangkok.

Thinapan Nakata and Likhit Dhiravegin, 1989, 'Social and cultural aspects of the Thai polity', In *Thailand's national development: social and economic background,* ed Suchart Prasith-rathsint, Thai University Research Association, Bangkok.

Thongchai Panswad et al., 1987, *Domestic wastewaters and water pollution problems in Bangkok and its vicinity,* National Environment Board, Bangkok (in Thai).

THE VARIED RESPONSES TO AN ENVIRONMENTAL CRISIS IN THE EXTENDED BANGKOK METROPOLITAN REGION

Charles Greenberg

INTRODUCTION

The large metropolitan areas of Asia are developing in a form that not only blurs the distinctions between rural and urban, but which also extends the ambit of urbanity as far as 100 kilometres from the city's central core (Ginsburg et al, 1991). This process is largely a function of internationalised and industrialised capital, intrinsically geared to expaned spatial forms of capitalist production, engulfing frontiers and hinterlands. As Yeung (1990, xviii) has written, "The Asian landscape is becoming an urban landscape."

The objective of this chapter is to analyze the environmental costs of peri-urban industrial development in the Bangkok Region, and the various forms of environmentalism that have emerged as a response to the consequent ecological deterioration. After a description of industrial growth in the Extended Bangkok Metropolitan Region (EBMR), the chapter examines roots of environmental neglect in Thailand. This is followed by discussion of the eclectic nature of environmentalist responses in the EBMR. Reasons for optimism are given in the conclusion.

THE EXTENDED BANGKOK METROPOLITAN REGION

The EBMR is an area consisting of Bangkok and 13 adjacent provinces; 5 in the inner ring and 8 in the outer ring. The region is loosely contained in a circle 100 kilometres around the centre of

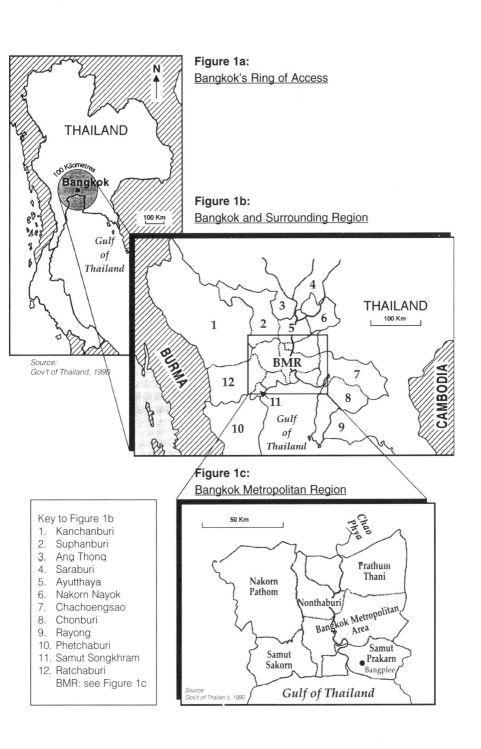

Figure 1a:
Bangkok's Ring of Access

Figure 1b:
Bangkok and Surrounding Region

Source:
Gov't of Thailand, 1990

THAILAND

100 Kilometres
Bangkok

100 Km

Gulf
of
Thailand

4
3
1   2   5   6
BMR
12   7
11   8
10   9
Gulf
of
Thailand

BURMA

CAMBODIA

THAILAND
100 Km

Figure 1c:
Bangkok Metropolitan Region

Key to Figure 1b
1. Kanchanburi
2. Suphanburi
3. Ang Thong
4. Saraburi
5. Ayutthaya
6. Nakorn Nayok
7. Chachoengsao
8. Chonburi
9. Rayong
10. Phetchaburi
11. Samut Songkhram
12. Ratchaburi
    BMR: see Figure 1c

50 Km

Chao
Phya

Prathum
Thani

Nakorn
Pathom

Nonthaburi

Bangkok Metropolitan
Area

Samut
Sakorn

Samut
Prakarn
Bangplee

Source:
Gov't of Thailan 1, 1990

Gulf of Thailand

Bangkok, and is referred to as the "Ring of Access" (Greenberg, 1990) (see Figure 1a). The entire region comprises approximately 54,000 square kilometres, one tenth of the total land area of the whole kingdom of Thailand (Figure 1b). At the outset there are several economic and demographic points concerning the EBMR which are worth mentioning. The official population (1990) of the EBMR was 13.5 million (Thailand Population and Housing Census, 1990). Yet it is well known that this an underestimation as there are hundreds of thousands of workers, some seasonal, as well as many children who are not included in surveys or in the national census.

Given Thailand's size, current industrial activity – if evenly distributed throughout the country – would not in itself present a serious environmental problem. The country's relatively large land area alone should permit an assimilation of pollution loads (Thailand Development Research Institute 1990). The industrial base, however, is highly concentrated in the EBMR, creating an excessive industrial agglomeration effect. Fifty-two percent of industries (76 percent in terms of GDP) are located in the five provinces of the inner ring (Figure 1c) (Department of Industrial Works 1990). The malevolent effects of industrial development are absent in most other parts of the country.

Within the Bangkok region, industrial activities that contribute most to environmental degradation are both highly concentrated in the inner ring (Figure 1c) as well and dispersed throughout the outer ring (Figure 1a), particularly along the east coast. It is important to note that major industrial locations are not necessarily near large urban areas. This is a reflection of a region-based pattern of urbanization that stretches several tens of kilometres from the Bangkok metropolitan area.

It is apposite at this point to record that levels of both GDP and population are growing in the EBMR more quickly than in the Kingdom as a whole. The primacy of this wider region continues to ascend as the primacy of Bangkok city itself is declining. In fact, Bangkok city's GDP and population levels are expanding at a decreasing rate, a clear indication that the focus of growth now lies in the extended region shown in Figure 1a. The inner ring alone now accounts for 50 percent of national GDP and 70 percent of manufacturing output (National Urban Development Policy

Framework [NUDPF], 1991). The total size of the industrial sector in terms of number of factories grew from 631 in 1969 to 51,500 in 1989, and approximately half are considered 'polluters' of water, air or both. (*Business Review*, 1993, 38).

The EBMR's rapidly changing society, uprooted by the unbinding power of technology, is altering its landscape socially, economically, and spatially. Bangkok and its extended environs have been transformed into a boundless urban region of contiguous settlement, invariably characterised by a rich mix of land use and un-precedented land use conversion rates. Aside from the diminishing agricultural land, Bangkok's outer city is a tapestry of disparate land uses; industry, housing, recreation, aquaculture, and shopping malls.

Although economic incentives are the overriding cause of land conversion to nonagricultural uses, pollution is also harming farmland and reducing potential productivity. Emissions from a growing number of automobiles and omnipresent factories have damaging effects on grain crops such as rice, fruit trees, and livestock. Also, brackish toxic waste water from aquaculture (especially prawn farming) and golf courses contaminate agricultural lands in the fertile low lying drainage divides. Data from the Food Control Division of the Ministry of Health show harmful levels of lead, cadmium, and mercury are present in food marketed in the Bangkok region. There is no specific estimate of the amount of agricultural land that has been converted to other uses due to various forms of 'urban' pollution, but farmers (and fishers) throughout the region complain vociferously about insufficient and ineffective environmental protection. As one report stated, ". . . it is obvious that failure to require reasonable environmental controls acts primarily as a subsidy to urban and industrial uses and as a penalty to agricultural uses" (Barasopit et al; 1990, 51).

THE ROOTS OF NEGLECT

Historically, the state's involvement with the environment and resources was restricted to dispensing land parcels to patrons and elites who were connected to the ruling power. As an example, in the late nineteenth century, in what is today's EBMR, the mostly unoccupied lands surrounding Bangkok were to become the granary which would satisfy Bowring Treaty rice quotas. Hence, canals had to be cut through the harsh natural landscape, forming the lattice work of waterways that opened the Central Plain ricebowl. Officials, nobility, royal family members, and occasionally commoners claimed large sections of land along the new banks. This form of patronage by rewarding loyal followers ensured the survival and 'goodstanding' of the regime in power. The resources and environment were critical tools of control and political survival.

Throughout the post-Bowring period, rice production was increased through expanding land, as opposed to improving techniques of production. In the 1930s, Zimmerman discerned that the new canal irrigation schemes, ". . . could support triply its present population, and have higher average income . . ." (1931: 311) if tilling techniques were advanced. Poorly developed agricultural methods, Feeny (1979) would argue, are the result of the Bangkok elites' maintenance of the status quo, which keeps their positions and income secure. Absentee landowners had little motivation to invest in intensification as the existing mode of cultivation drew considerable profits. Higher production was thus achieved through encroaching on marginal lands, mangroves, and forests.

This form of power is merely a continuation of political weaponry used in premodern kingdoms. Agricultural surplus and forest products were siphoned off from the peasants to build opulent palaces and shrines, ensuring political legitimacy and authority. Old practices seem to die hard.

Into the late twentieth century, although land use has changed dramatically with the rise of an industrial landscape, the state still appears to be fundamentally preoccupied with survival and continuity. The state's support and even promotion of large scale commercial tropical deforestation, export-orientated aquaculture, unclean industry, and proliferating golf course development have collectively amounted to a profound environmental challenge to both state and citizen. The state continues to ensure its own survival and maintain loyalty by contributing to the further deterioration of the environment. How the current government chooses to utilize the environment for economic and political legitimacy has a pressing impact on its survival and stability. As time passes, state negligence may, ironically, prove to be the source of its decline.

To illustrate the environmental costs of political and economic legitimation, I would refer to the inherent contradictions between Thailand's current directions toward high economic growth and the environmental degradation in Bangkok's outer city. Thirty-five kilometres southeast of Bangkok, in the heart of what is referred to as the Samut Prakarn provincial industrial belt, lies Bangplee (Figure 1c). This small district is host to a large industrial estate and hundreds of factories. It is also the national centre of Thailand's leather tanning industry, with more than a hundred of such enterprises. The Bangplee tanning industry is very much a globally-orientated production locus, as the chemicals for the process are imported from Japan and Europe, eighty percent of the hides are from China, and final markets are mainly North American and European (Industrial Estate Authority of Thailand, 1991).

The heavy pollution from tanning has catastrophic effects. Chemical wastes are extraordinarily toxic and damaging; streams, canals and rivers near the tanneries are bluish-white and chalky, and aside from humans, there is total absence of living organisms, including vegetation, in the immediate vicinity. A tannery factory manager comments on the toxicity of the chemical waste that is routinely produced: "A drop of this waste water on the leg of the child leaves caustic wounds. If the whole body is covered, there is a life threat in five minutes" (Bangkok Post, World Bank/IMF Special Edition, 1991).

With little regard to this dire situation, in October, 1991, the National Economic and Social Development Board (NESDB) – the premier state run planning agency in Thailand – presented cabinet with the Seventh Five-Year Plan. It was approved and passed immediately. The contents were impressive, reflecting continued and imposing economic progress, and unprecedented rise in GDP, expansion of the industrial base by nearly ten percent, and increase of exports by 14.7 percent per annum in value or nine percent in volume, and enormous per capita income growth. Criticisms of the plan, (identical to those of previous plans) were that quality of life and environmental protection were secondary considerations. Although lip service was paid by the NESDB to environmental issues, positive action through policy initiatives was limited (NUDPF, 1991).

Accordingly, export-oriented industries, such as the leather tannery plants, large or small, will continue to be supported and promoted by state apparatus. The perceived fiscal contribution that the leather tannery offers to the economy (and state stability) rises above and beyond its environmental offences. Thailand, then, appears to be following most developing countries, particularly in east and southeast Asia, that have seen measurable indices of output and wealth soar while the environment has taken second place to production and industrialisation. Environmental priorities are lost in a maze of competing developmental problems.

In terms of industrial policy, present-day environmental negligence can be attributed to the beginning of the current wave of military leaders, the most prominent being Field Marshal Sarit Thanarat, coming to 'absolute power' after a 1957 coup. Sarit encouraged private investment, abolished labor unions, and in 1959 formed the Board of Investment (BOI). It was an industrial strategy augmented by the arrival of the World Bank and the United States as major economic players (and stakeholders), leading to a massive capital penetration that was as much a military operation as a development scheme.

Sarit and his successors also made natural resources available to prospective industrialists at price levels below market value. This trend continues today. Lands for industrial production, golf course developments, and aquaculture are made accessible to developers and investors. Water, forests and power are also being sacrificed at privileged rates and surplus volumes. These arrangements are characterized by both the state and investors paying little heed to demands for conservation and environmental protection.

The case of Samut Prakan

To demonstrate the government's often ineffectual and muddled policy on the environment I would refer to the recent conflict over environmental repair in Samut Prakarn. Of 3,351 factories in this industrial province, 2,180 have been found failing to comply with pollution standards and regulations stated in the National Factory Law of 1992 (*Manager*; 1992, 16). The Industry Ministry, moreover, proposes to relocate up to 500 factories and has selected sites for most in Minburi and Pathum Thani. Others have been told to relocate into the 35 industrial estates scattered through the EBMR.

The government has offered reparation, compensation and three year tax breaks to the firms facing relocation. The relocation policy, under protest, appears to be permanently stalled, as most of the factories, represented by the powerful Samut Prakarn Chamber of Commerce, have refused to submit to the government's demands. The Chamber of Commerce is headed up by Anantachai Kunananthakul, Chief Executive Officer and President of Siam Steel Group, who has his largest production facility in Samut Prakarn and has been identified by the ministry as the province's most threatening environmental perpetrator.

There are three points to draw out from this confrontation. First, it is clear (particularly to those who live or have travelled through Samut Prakarn) that in the past the government has neglected to promote environmental safeguards. The air quality is the worst in the Kingdom, and smog levels are often higher than in Los Angeles (Greenberg 1992). From the early 1980s Samut Prakarn has been the industrial heartland of Thailand's restructured export-orientated economy. For decades the state shirked its responsibility in Samut Prakarn in terms of the environment. Regulation standards for air and water emissions were never enforced or monitored, and subsequently the current confrontation may have been unavoidable.

Second, relocation will disperse the pollution crisis to other parts of the EBMR. Spatial consolidation of the production process leads to more efficient pollution management. This indeed is the philosophical platform of the industrial estates, the panacea the state appears to be promoting.

Third, the State is incapable of enforcing its environmental edicts. Powerful industrialists such as Khun Anantachai are unresponsive to the state's attempt to improve the environment.

As long as industrial capital is in conflict with and overrides state policy, environmental reform will be temporized.

ECLECTIC ENVIRONMENTALISM IN THE EBMR

Within the EBMR, as elsewhere, environmentalism or responses to environmental breakdown are manifested in different forms by diverse and heterogeneous stakeholders. This section, with an optimistic tone, examines the eclectic environmental movement in the EBMR. Most significantly, it demonstrates that the state does not stand alone, nor is it the most influential and constructive player leading the region out of its environmental crisis.

Field surveys conducted by this author between 1991 and 1994 in the lower Central Plain of Thailand revealed that urban and rural populations were concerned with environmental deterioration more than any other issue. Moreover, the people are sensibly and acutely aware that the costs of environmental degradation are rarely distributed to the responsible parties. In this regard they acknowledge that only through their activism will sustainable environmental policy be realized.

Throughout Thailand, but particularly in the EBMR, the integration of both urban and rural populations into mainstream consumer society coincides with an increasing awareness of environmental degradation. Hirsch (1993:15) maintains that a large proportion of the Thai population has recently been affected. Encroaching industrialization presents new environmental challenges that are impossible to disregard, as it profoundly affects people's economic sustenance and personal health.

Public awareness of environmental issues is high. The media has enhanced the visibility of the environmental message and has, to a lesser extent, attracted participation. Thai journalist Ing K's two recent internationally released documentaries, "Thailand For Sale" and "The Green Menace" have stirred up controversy and discourse in terms of environmental change.

Educational programs have been instituted that are beginning to deter the pervasive 'throw away' culture. The role the state plays in shaping a new environmental ethic through public education is unclear, but what is evident is the presence of a perceived need for environmental change among city and rural populations of the EBMR (Greenberg; 1994, 41).

As mentioned above, the EBMR is driven economically by export-orientated industrialization. Increasingly it is becoming clear that continued prosperity of this crucial sector of the economy will be contingent upon environmental quality. The marriage of environment and export-based manufacturing was not present through the booming 1980s. Current trade policy, however, cannot afford to disregard this union.

In the international trade arena, policy has been implemented that encourages or even threatens trading partners to enforce or regulate a set of environmental standards. Grewe (1994, 18) informs us that in the United States, Congress' concern with environmental standards can and will act to curtail trade liberalization with certain countries. Moreover, environmental quality was a critical negotiating point under the Uruguay Round of GATT talks. Thailand's export based tuna canning industry, for example, has been directly influenced by the U.S. Marine Mammal Act. Thai industrialists are aware of the stringent environmental provisions built into NAFTA. This signals a trend that will certainly be part of an ASEAN Free Trade Agreement, and be instrumental in future APEC negotiations.

Several international corporations operating in the EBMR appear to be taking a leading and influential role in shaping industrial environmental policy. 3M Thailand for example, have proven in their newly expanded production facilities in Lad Krabang that 'pollution prevention pays'. Their state of the art plant is equipped with the finest pollution prevention technologies and has demonstrated that corporations that cause minimal environmental impact can reduce production costs and liability exposure.

The National Factory Act of 1992 has in place harsh fines for industrial violators. There is evidence that these will be more stringently enforced in coming years. Private industry has also been responsible for the rapid growth of the pollution control equipment market, which is expecting a 20 - 25 percent annual increase through the 1990s (*Business Review*; 1993, 41). There are currently over 30 firms, mostly European and American, already supplying equipment to industries in the EBMR. Also, as of 1994, the state has put to tender a number of industrial sewage treatment projects for the EBMR (two in Bangkok and one each in Samut Prakan, Pathum Thani, Chonburi, Saraburi, and Rayong – the treatment centres in Chonburi, Saraburi, and Rayong cater specifically to hazardous waste products).

Bang Kachao and local environmentalism in the EBMR

To demonstrate the diversity of the environmental movement, and to illustrate that protest does not just target industrial development, the following example is presented. The mobilization of ordinary citizens at times of environmental stress in Bangkok's outer city was revealed in September 1991 when Thailand's former Prime Minister, Anand Panyarachun unveiled a US$300 million government scheme to develop an extraordinary public park in Phra Pradaeng district of Samut Prakarn province. Named Bang Kachao Park after one of the six *tambons* (sub-districts) where it would be developed, the ambitious 1,500 hectare project would serve as a "lung" for the residents of Bangkok; "trees in the park will help filter tens of thousands of tonnes of toxic dust and carbon monoxide released into the air each year and thus produce more fresh air for the metropolis", said Anand. With a botanical garden, a health park and two zoos, Bang Kachao Park was hailed as an ecological messiah. Government officials at all levels praised the project with optimistic and lavish words (Greenberg, 1993). This would be the contemporary parallel of an opulent palace or shrine to legitimise power during the premodern kingdoms.

Although Anand was intent on detailing a conspicuous public image for his park, the pertinent questions are: who benefits from the park, and who is it for? Certainly not the local residents who will have their land expropriated, and who have practiced and valued conservation for the last century. Local residents did not need another green area, they live in one. In the spirit of urban and elite bias, residents of Bangkok and the ruling power would be the recipients, and local residents would be the victims. It is worth noting that the 24 factories and warehouses in the affected area, almost all absentee owned, were exempt from expropriation.

Exclusive, emblematic, and ceremonial projects such as Bang Kachao, and many of the 150 golf courses throughout the Kingdom, dressed up in 'public' and 'environmentally friendly' verbiage should not be mistaken as development. If completed, Bang Kachao would displace some 35,000 people and draw an estimated five million visitors a year. Local residents perceived the potential urban assault with animosity. Moreover, the compensation promised to the landowners was 500 Baht per square metre, while market value of the land was a minimum 1,250 Baht and as high as 5,000 Baht per square metre, depending on accessibility. Any environmental planning scheme for Bang Kachao should improve income and environmental quality for the local population. The proposed park would eliminate a traditional agricultural lifestyle and replace it with a few paltry service and maintenance jobs, a trade-off which was unable to sway local residents. A state official from the National Environment Board (NEB) is on record as saying that, if local residents do not sell their land to the state, it will eventually fall into the hands of investors and speculators, anyway.

Bang Kachao was expected to be an easy sell for Anand, presumably because of the positive environmental aspect associated with it. Local residents organized a series of protests and rallies, often with over 10,000 activists, fighting successfully to retain their land and halt further park planning. They called on non-government organizations and local academics to support their cause, and even vowed to take their case to His Majesty the King. *Kamnans* from the six affected *tambons* addressed Anand and called on the government to review its decision on land expropriation. Their land, they told Anand:

> "is not a god-send but the outcome of laborious perseverance by the residents and their forefathers. . . . if the state sees the beauty of our hard work then we feel we are being punished because of our own good work, which is unfair" (*Bangkok Post*, 1991).

The protest became a media spectacle and was organized effectively. Its virtue was to give the lie to self-aggrandizement, attempting to legitimise and ensure power.

A handful of other examples drawn from the EBMR under-score the nascent success of local-level environmentalism. Most notably, a Klong Toey citizen's advocate group received positive media exposure and entered the politics of the environment after a 1991 fire and explosion at the nearby port warehouse left five people dead and tens of thousands with indeterminable illness from exposure to toxic chemicals.

These examples speak to a rise and legitimacy for a new pillar of environmental management. A new environmentalism is emerging, which Hirsch (see Chapter 2 this volume) has termed "peripheral environmentalism". This is a movement from below, driven by both despondency and urgency, which has developed a political flavour of activism and protest.

CONCLUSION: RECOVERING THE ENVIRONMENT

The destruction and preservation of the urban environment are no longer the exclusive domain of Bangkok city, but are intrinsically a regional issue. Just as region-based urbanisation now character-izes the settlement system in the EBMR, region-based urban pollution now characterises the environment of the EBMR. Consequently, traditional management of these problems along very local or sectoral lines is no longer adequate. An approach that recognizes the regional nature of these issues is a more logical and rational way to organise environmental information and to implement ameliorative policies.

Policy recommendations and strategies need to be sensitive to the region-based urban space economy of the EBMR as well as sympathetic to current social and political conditions. They need also to be especially cognisant of a society where production, consumption and profit are guiding values.

Three years after the Bang Kachao fiasco, former Prime Minister Anand, referring to the current environmental crisis stated, ". . . every country at a certain stage of development has been through this degradation process and 30, 40 years later they had to wake up. We're waking up too, but this is part of the human evolutionary process" (*The Nation*, 1995).

So Thailand is not alone in allowing the environmental problems to reach a state of crisis before acting. Lessons from the past suggest that catastrophic damage must occur before action is taken. The 1980s would have been the best chance for environmental policy to be enacted in the EBMR. Not surprisingly, the opportunity was passed up. This should not signal a resignation of environmental repair. To the contrary, the time has come to mobilise the heterogeneous voices of concern and piece together an environmental movement. Several studies confirm that as a society broadens its technological base and experiences socio-economic growth, it eventually becomes sensitised to sustainable development. Grossman and Krueger (1992) argue that pollution loads and emissions increase with GDP up to approximately $5000 per capita a year. Beyond that point, pollution allegedly declines. The EBMR is close to reaching this plateau. Harrison (1993, 301) maintains that high levels of industrialization and urbanization lead to an apex in human relations with the environment. Urban based leisure and wide car ownership allow the oft-romanticized countryside to be attainable, leading to pressures for preservation and pollution limitation.

Humans' attitudes to the environment are characterised by a natural bond, not unlike parent-child relationships. Further, the environment is resilient and in many instances responds well to conservation and repair (consider the Thames River in London, or air quality in Pittsburgh). The EBMR's unprecedented rapid industrial growth placed an unnatural strain on the environment, but remedy is imminent.

This leads to a final and crucial point regarding the survival and sustenance of environmentalism. The success of a collective environmentalism depends on the political structures of the state. An autocratic and oppressive state can crush local movements before they are effective and mobilised. As Thailand creeps toward democratisation, the various movements can aspire to greater freedom and flexibility. Environmentalism can not operate in a vacuum, and cooperation from the state will be instrumental. The hopes for prosperity-induced democratisation with an expected political trickledown and hegemonic decentralisation may be the most important factor contributing to a broadened EBMR environmental movement.

REFERENCES

Bangkok Post, World Bank/IMF Special Edition (1991, October 14) How to Stop Pollution and Promote Industry, p 11.

Bangkok Post,1991, "Bang Kachao Land Case may go to King", September 30.

Barasopit Mekivichai et al., 1990, *Urbanization and the Environment: Managing the Conflict*, Bangkok: TDRI Research Report no. 6.

Business Review (1993) "Environment and Business: Striking a Balance?", Bangkok, pp 32-44.

Department of Industrial works (DIW), 1990, *Annual Report*, Bangkok.

Feeny, David, 1979, "Post World War II Thai Agricultural Development Policy: Continuity or Change", *Poverty and Social Change in Southeast Asia*, ed. Ozay Mehnet, Ottawa: University of Ottawa Press.

Ginsburg, N., McGee, T., and Koppel, B. (eds.), 1991, *The Extended Metropolis: Settlement Transition in Asia*, Honolulu: University of Hawaii Press.

Government of Thailand Population and Housing Census, 1990, *Report*, Bangkok.

Greenberg, C., 1990, [with the assistance of T.G. McGee]. *Mega-urban Development: The Extended Metropolitan Region of Bangkok*, Paper presented at the Annual Meeting of the Association of Asian Studies, Chicago, Ill. 5-8 April.

Greenberg, C.,1991, Quo Vadis Bangkok?, *The Nation* (Bangkok), Oct 20.

Greenberg, Charles, 1992, "Angelic Scatter: The Outer Cities of Los Angeles and Bangkok" Paper presented at Canadian Association of Geographers annual meeting, Vancouver, May.

Greenberg, Charles, 1993, *The Grand Illusion*, Canadian Council for Southeast Asian Studies, Toronto.

Greenberg, Charles, 1994, "Environmental Sustainability in the EBMR", *Western Geography*, Vol. 4, pg. 29-44.

Grewe, Maureen, 1994, "Enforcing Environmental Quality: Why Trade Policy isn't the Answer", The Thailand Development Research Institute, *Quarterly Review*, Volume 9, No. 1, pp 16-20.

Grossman, Gene M. and Alan B. Krueger, 1992, "Environmental Impacts of a North American Free Trade Agreement." Discussion Paper No. 158. Princeton University, February.

Harrison, Paul, 1993, *The Third Revolution: Population, Environment and a Sustainable World*, London: Penguin.

Hirsch, Philip, 1993, *Political Economy of Environment in Thailand*, Manila: Journal of Contemporary Asia Publishers.

Industrial Estate Authority of Thailand (IEAT), 1991, Annual Report, Bangkok.

Manager, 1992, "Cleaning up Samut Prakarn", Bangkok, January, pp 16-17.

The Nation, 1995, "A Sense of Duty and of Humour: an Interview with the Former Prime Minister", January 07.

NUDPF (National Urban Development Policy Framework), 1991, Recommended Development Strategies and Investment Programs for the Seventh Plan (1992-1996), Bangkok.

Thailand Development Research Institute. (TDRI), 1990, *Urbanization and Environment; Managing the Conflict,* Research Report, No. 6. Bangkok.

Thailand Development Research Institute (TDRI), 1991, *National Urban Development Policy Framework: Recommended Srategies and Investment Programs for the Seventh Economic and Social Development Plan.* Draft Final Report, Prepared for NESDB, Area No. 7, Bangkok.

Yeung, Yue-Man, 1990, *Changing Cities of Pacific Asia*, Hong Kong: Chinese University Press.

Zimmermann, Carl, 1931, *Siam Rural Economic Survey*, 1930-31.

INDUSTRIAL POLLUTION AND GOVERNMENT POLICY IN THAILAND: RHETORIC VERSUS REALITY[1]

Timothy Forsyth

INTRODUCTION: ENVIRONMENTAL POLITICS AND INDUSTRIALIZATION IN THAILAND

Whilst much environmental concern in Thailand has so far focused on deforestation and dam construction, the impact of industry on environment is an increasingly emotive issue. Thailand has undergone rapid industrialization at the same time that environment has risen to become a topic of local and national concern. Industrialization has not only posed new threats to environment, but has also empowered factory workers and specialists who are willing to challenge government policies concerned with industrialization.

Thailand has encouraged industrialisation since the first five year plan in the early1960s, and foreign investment since the early 1970s. In 1973, the Board of Investment (BOI) was established as the main government agency to promote industrialization. Industrialization was seen by government to be a key route to development, and in 1977 the powers of the BOI were increased by the Industrial Promotion Act.

Early industrialization in Thailand was designed to boost domestic industry and help the country's balance-of-payments by manufacturing goods normally imported from abroad (import-

---

[1] This paper was researched with the help of the Chaiyong Limthongkul Foundation of Thailand and *Asia, Inc.* magazine, Hong Kong. I would like to thank Paul Clements Hunt at Environmental Business Group Co. Ltd., and Qwanrudee Limvorapitak of the Thailand Environment Institute, Bangkok, for sharing their own work on industrial pollution in Thailand.

substituting industrialization). This was combined with a policy of restricting foreign investment to joint ventures with Thai companies, so that some benefit from production could stay with Thailand, and domestic companies could learn from foreign counterparts.

However, since the mid-1980s, Thailand has begun to favour export-oriented industrialization, rather than simply the manufacture of goods normally imported. In addition, an increasing number of factories are totally foreign owned. The BOI claims these changes have enabled Thailand to grow rapidly as an economic power, and become one of Southeast Asia's "tiger" economies. Critics, however, state that today's industrialization has only introduced polluting industries manufacturing goods with no domestic use for Thailand, and which often involve a high degree of risk for workforces. They also say factories only locate in Thailand because of cheap labor and, controversially, in order to avoid locating dirty industries within their own countries.

Environmental legislation is one response to the hazards of industrialization, and this has developed during the period of industrial growth in Thailand. The Industrial Promotion Act (1977) actively encouraged industrialization, but also laid stipulations on the BOI to avoid investment that may lead to environmental damage. In 1992, environmental policy was revamped by the so-called "Environment Act" and associated measures. These created new government agencies aiming to monitor and enforce en-vironmental safeguards. The acts also proposed to limit pollution by designating specific pollution-control zones and by encouraging polluting industries to locate within industrial estates.

Today, the government claims that a political infrastructure exists in order to maximize industrialization whilst also protecting environment. Opponents claim the opposite. Citizen groups, specialist observers, and NCOs claim that the new government agencies lack power within government, and that the industrialization is continuing unabated because the BOI continues to attract investment from export-oriented polluting industries. Furthermore, there is evidence that one new government agency charged with investigating environmental health was closed after challenging the safety record of a major foreign investor.

Environmental policy in Thailand is in the midst of a power struggle within government between the new pro-environment agencies, and the older, pro-industry bodies. Added to this, non-governmental bodies such as factory workers, medical specialists, and citizen groups are voicing their concern for extra environmental protection. The resulting debate is influencing the formulation of environmental policy. In Thailand, industrialization has empower-ed new sectors of society affected by the negative impacts of pollution. Yet, so far, the seat of political power remains with those seeking to increase industrialization.

GOVERNMENT POLICY: STATED AIMS

Attracting foreign investment

In 1973, the Board of Investment (BOI) was established with the aim of bringing import-substituting industries to Thailand. The Industrial Promotion Act (IPA) of 1977 strengthened the incentives the BOI could offer to attract investment "in those activities which are important and beneficial to economic and social development, and security of the country." Table 1 shows the growth of manu-facturing industry in Thailand as a result of foreign investment, and Table 2 indicates how this has impacted on specific industries, in particular the chemicals, metallic and non-metallic, and electrical appliance industries.

Table 1:

Net inflows of inward foreign investment by sector 1970 - 1990

(Billion Baht per year)

Net investment inflow	average 1970-9	average 1980-4	1987	1990
Primary Sector	0.19	1.53	0.48	1.9
Secondary Sector	0.54	2.10	4.75	29.07
Tertiary Sector	0.89	2.87	3.82	31.54

(Source: Bank of Thailand, simplified from EBG, 1993a:10)

Table 2:

Net inflows of inward foreign investment for specified industries 1970-1990

(Billion Baht per year)

Net investment inflow	average 1970-9	average 1980-4	1987	1990
Food	0.06	0.06	0.44	1.95
Textiles	0.20	0.17	1.00	1.76
Metallic, non-metallic	0.03	0.28	0.37	2.84
Electrical appliances	0.12	0.64	1.14	10.83
Chemicals	0.07	0.23	0.87	4.29
Petroleum products	0.02	0.41	-0.02	0.89

(Source: Bank of Thailand, simplified from EBG, 1993a:10)

In terms of location within Thailand, the BOI has attempted to promote investment outside Bangkok since at least 1985. The BOI identifies three zones for investment incentives. The first is Bangkok and the central provinces of Samut Prakan, Samut Sakhon, Nakhon Pathom, Nonthaburi, and Pathum Thani. The second is a wider area comprising Samut Songkram, Ratchaburi, Kanchanaburi, Suphan-buri, Angthong, Ayuthaya, Saraburi, Nakhon Nayok, Chachoensao, and Chonburi. The third group includes the remaining 57 provinces plus the industrial estate at Laem Chabang on the eastern sea-board. The BOI offers an increasing range of industrial activities eligible for support between different zones, plus tax holidays for those in zone 3. Polluting industries are requested to go to industrial estates (e.g. Khongnirandsuk, 1992). Table 3 shows the distribution of BOI registered factories and industrial estates by region for 1989.

In January 1993, the BOI stated that it was attempting to produce regional industrial specialization in Thailand by deliberately directing specific industries to particular regions. Khon Kaen in the north east is aimed to specialize in aircraft manufacturing. Electronics are directed to the north of Thailand. Automobile construction is focused in Nakhon Ratchasima, Khon Kaen, and Saraburi provinces. Rubber companies are encouraged to locate in the south. Petrochemicals go to the eastern seaboard. Infrastructure projects are directed to the Bangkok metropolitan area.

Table 3:

BOI-registered factories and industrial estates, by region, 1989

(Factories: percent; industrial estates: number)

	Registered factories (% of total)	Industrial estates
Bangkok Metropolitan Region	51.91	12
Central Thailand	16.82	7
Northeastern Thailand	14.10	2
Northern Thailand	10.00	1
Southern Thailand	7.17	2

(Source: Phantumvanit and Panayotou, 1991:6, 36)

Policies to manage industrial pollution

Early legislation to control industrial pollution included the 1962 Factory Act, and 1972 National Environmental Quality Act, which helped create the Office of the National Environment Board (ONEB). The 1913 Navigation in Thai Waters Act also laid stipulations about the protection of land near waterways. Industrial pollution is defined in this chapter as waste and work practices damaging to life. It does not include sound pollution.

Section 19 of the IPA of 1977 concerned environmental protection. It stated that the BOI should incorporate "appropriate measures for the prevention and control of harmful effects to the quality of the environment in the interest of the common good of the general living of the public and for the perpetuation of mankind and nature." The BOI may also include provisions for the "prevention and control of damaging elements to the quality of the environment" (IPA, 1977; in EBG, 1993b:171).

BOI regulations in 1981 stated that certain investment projects needed a mandatory environmental impact assessment (EIA). These included hotels or resorts of over 80 rooms near rivers, coastlines, or national parks; mining; industrial estates; petrochemical industries producing more than 100 tons per day; oil refining and natural gas separation; chloralkaline industries; iron industries producing more than 100 tons per day or a kiln of more than 5 tons capacity; non-ferrous metal smelting producing more than 50 tons per day; pulp and paper manufacturing more than 50 tons per day; and cement industries (in EBG, 1993b:174). This list avoided pesticides.

In 1991, the BOI declared that measures taken by industry to control pollution or save energy would be eligible for tax deduction or exemption (BOI announcement 46/1991). It also stated that all investment projects with capital over 500 million Baht should investigate the likely environmental impact, and inform the BOI of the value of investment in anti-pollution machinery (BOI announcement 50/1991).

In 1992, the BOI defined projects eligible for its support as those that are "important, and beneficial to the country's economic and social development, and to national security." They are also required to be "economically and technologically appropriate, and have adequate preventative measures against damage to the environment." In April 1992, the BOI stated that it gave priority to projects which preserve, protect, restore or rehabilitate the environment, or conserve energy (BOI announcement 1/1992).

1992 also saw a more wide-ranging attention to environmental protection from the whole Thai government. The National Economic and Social Development Plan (the so-called 7th Five Year Plan) under prime minister Anand Panyarachun identified environment and quality of life as one of its three national priorities. The plan allocated US$17.2 million to the National Institute for Occupational and Environmental Medicine (NIOEM) to establish a staff of 200 and a national network to investigate and treat new cases of industrial poisoning (Forsyth, 1994). A series of new laws in 1992 also addressed the growing problem of industrial pollution: the Enhancement and Conservation of National Environmental Quality Act (the so-called 'Environment Act'); the Factories Act; and the Energy Conservation Promotion Act (Handley, 1992; Jolly, 1992).

Under the Environment Act, the old Office of the National Environment Board (ONEB) was absorbed into the Ministry of Technology, Science and Environment (MOSTE), which previously included the word 'energy' instead of 'environment'. MOSTE has three environmenta-related departments: the Pollution Control Department (PCD), a planning office (the Office of Environmental Policy and Planning – OEPP), and an information office (the Department of Environmental Quality Promotion – DEQP). The 1992 act also provided for the Prime Minister to chair a National Environmental Committee, composed of cabinet officials, representatives of business and non-governmental organizations (NGOs) with a mandate to ensure that environmental considerations are considered in government policy. Two new funds for environmental projects and energy conservation schemes were also set up to assist industry. The government could also establish 'pollution control zones,' and fine polluters or even close their factories.

Under the Factories Act, the procedure for factory inspection was made less cumbersome, making it easier for investors to open factories. The act referred to the Department of Industrial Works (DIW), which operates under the Ministry of Industry, and so a different sector of the government from MOSTE. Before the 1992 update to the act, the DIW had to give two license to a factory before it could start production or gain BOI incentives. After the act, the BOI promotional certificate could be given to a plant after just one inspection. Alternatively, the BOI could give a licenses to proceed to a factory which would then contact the DIW for extra inspection (EBG, 1993b:176). Also, in 1994, the Harbor Department, under the Ministry of Communications, brought actions against approximately 40 illegal wastewater discharging activities along the Chao Phraya river under the Navigation in Thai Water Act (Limvorapitak, 1994).

The Thailand National Report to the United Nations Conference on Environment and Development (UNCED) in 1992 (Thai Government, 1992) detailed Thailand's commitment to the manage-ment of hazardous waste through the 1992 legislation (cf Philippa England's chapter 4 in this book). The BOI also claimed to speed up efforts to attract anti-pollution industries to Thailand (*Bangkok Post*, 13 Dec. 1993).

INDUSTRIAL POLLUTION: OBSERVED TRENDS

The nature of Foreign Direct Investment

Foreign Direct Investment (FDI) in Thailand has risen substantially since 1970, but most markedly since 1987. Between 1975 and 1977, FDI inflow was 1,841 million Baht, between 1980 and 1982 4,874.3 million Baht, and between 1987 and 1989 27,343.8 million Baht. The share of FDI in gross domestic investment rose from 2.2% in 1980 to 7.6% in 1989 (Pupphauesa, 1993, in EBG, 1993b:189; Brummitt and Flatters, 1992; Akrasanee and Dapice, 1991).

1987 appears to be a watershed year for FDI in Thailand. An aggressive approach to investment by the Thai government (including, for example, 1987 as 'Visit Thailand Year') combined with the appreciation of the Yen currency and increasing labor costs in Hong Kong, Taiwan and Korea to make Thailand a comparatively attractive place for investment. Between 1987 and September 1991, 66% of joint ventures and 78% of foreign subsidiaries investing in Thailand came from Japan, Taiwan, Korea and Hong Kong (Brimble and Sibunruang, 1992:56, in EBG, 1993b:190).

Two main trends have become apparent since 1987. Firstly, the level of foreign involvement in promoted projects increased from less than 50% before 1987 to more than 80% by 1991. 21% of these were from subsidiaries of foreign parent companies, and 58% joint ventures with Thai companies. The second trend is that there has been a major increase in investment leading to exports from Thailand. The number of BOI-approved projects with at least 80% of annual sales exported rose from 437 in 1987 to 3,165 in 1991. Export-oriented industrialization is now replacing the earlier stated aim of import substitution (EBG, 1993b:191). Between 1985 and 1992, the quantity of merchandise exports from Thailand rose 450%, more than any other Asian country during that period. The second highest rise in exports, of 310%, came from Hong Kong (EIU, 1993:52).

The environmental impact of foreign investment

FDI into Thailand has increasingly been from industries that are associated with hazardous waste. Table 2 shows that the chemical, electrical appliance, and metallic and non-metallic manufacturing industries have grown in size since 1970. These industries are increasingly associated with foreign companies and with the manufacture of exports from Thailand. Figure 4 indicates the extent of foreign involvement in selected hazardous waste-intensive industries for the early year of 1986.

At its end-of-year conference in 1990, the Thai environmental think-tank Thailand Development Research Institute (TDRI) stated that BOI-promoted industries had encouraged the proportion of hazardous waste-generating industries to rise from 25% in 1987 to 55% in 1989. The manufacturing sector accounted for 90% of hazardous waste generated in Thailand, of which two thirds comes from the basic metals industry, and the remaining third from fabricated products, transport equipment, electrical machinery, chemical products, textiles, and printing and publishing. Most biodegradable wastes come from sugar factories (29%), pulp and paper plants (20%), and rubber processing (18%) (Phantumvanit and Panayotou, 1991:10; ESCAP/UNTC 1990: 321).

Table 4:

Indicators of significance of foreign affiliates in some hazardous waste-intensive segments of the Thai economy, 1986

(Percent of foreign affiliates in total)

	Assets	Sales	Exports
Chemicals	61.8	72.0	11.0
Metals	64.8	60.8	1.0
Non-metallic minerals	41.4	26.2	14.3
Electrical equipment	86.9	89.4	10.8
Mechanical equipment	85.4	80.3	0.4

(Source: EBG- World Investment Directory 1992, vol.1, in EBG, 1993b:198)

There is also a shift occurring from traditional pollutants such as wastewater to more complex pollutants such as heavy metals, toxic air, and water pollutants. Waste water impacts on the environment by increasing bio-chemical oxygen demand (BOD) and therefore reducing dissolved oxygen in water bodies below ambient levels. The Chao Phraya and Tachin rivers are at risk of becoming anaerobic in certain sections for parts of the year (Phantumvanit and Panayotou, 1991:11), which reduces plant and animal life.

Hazardous waste is defined as heavy metals, solvents, oils, and acids and alkalines which are non biodegradable. These are toxic to most forms of life, and they can remain in situ without breaking down for many years. There are various estimates of the quantity of hazardous waste in Thailand. TDRI (1991) estimated a total of 2 million tons throughout Thailand in 1990, increasing to 6 million tons in 2001. CIDA estimated 150,000 tons in Greater Bangkok in 1983, rising to 300,000 tons in 2000 (estimates in EBG, 1993a:15). The problem of industrial pollution may impact on the general and visual environment, and on the working and health environment of factory employees and local inhabitants (Woolman, 1992; OECCJ and TDRI, 1993). Table 5 shows one prediction for the regional distribution of hazardous waste.

Table 5:
Projected quantity of hazardous waste by region 1986-2001
(Thousand metric tons, Percentage of total)

	1986	%	1991	%	1996	%	2001	%
Bangkok	817.1	71	1413.7	71	2447.9	71	4236.3	71
Central	184.0	16	322.3	16	563.5	16	982.1	16
North	75.1	7	132.5	7	230.6	7	400.7	7
N.east	14.5	1	24.6	1	41.8	1	71.6	1
South	58.1	5	100.9	5	175.0	5	303.1	5
Total	1148.8	100	1994.0	100	3458.8	100	5995.8	100

(Source: Engineering Science Inc., 1989, in Phantumvanit and Panayotou, 1991:12)

The central province of Samut Prakan has been used as a case study of industrial pollution in Thailand (e.g. Limvorapitak, 1994a; EBG, 1993b:178-9). This province is just south of Bangkok beside the Chao Phraya estuary and on the approach to the eastern seaboard. It is the site of many factories and the Bangpoo industrial estate. In 1987, the Asian Development Bank (ADB) surveyed 1,400 factories in Samut Prakan and estimated taht these created 25,000 tons of hazardous waste per year. The top five hazardous waste-creating industries were fabricated metal products, electrical machinery, industrial chemicals, transport equipment, and textiles. The three main forms of waste were heavy metals, acid waste and oil. According to the governor of Samut Prakan, there are 4,000 factories in the province of which 2,000 cause annoyance to people living nearby and over 30 should be closed immediately because of pollution (EBG, 1993b:178). In September 1993, the Thai Council of Economic Ministers decided to relocate more than 300 industrial plants causing pollution in Bangkok and Samut Prakan to industrial estates within five years (*Bangkok Post*, 23 Sep. 1993).

New BOI-approved projects include at least one 100% foreign-owned factory producing only exports, and manufacturing glue, a well-known source of solvent poisoning (EBG, 1993b:179). In 1991, there was a major industrial dispute at the computer disk-drive assembly plant of Seagate Technology Inc., in Samut Prakan, partly because of workers' fears that deaths at the plant might have been caused by lead or solvent poisoning. Seagate Technology, from the USA, claims to be Thailand's largest employer and manufactures approximately 40% of its disk drives in Thailand. At another site in Pathum Thani, north of Bangkok, local authorities investigated a Union Carbide factory for suspected air pollution coming from solvents (*Bangkok Post* 24 May 1994).

The effectiveness of government control

In 1992, the Pollution Control Department temporarily closed a sugar cane processing plant and a pulp and paper plant in Khon Kaen province after they dumped inadequately treated wastewater into rivers (*Far Eastern Economic Review*, May 1992). Also in 1992, the tourist resorts of Phuket and Pattaya were declared pollution control zones, shortly followed by the province of Samut Prakan. So far these are the only factories to be closed because of the 1992 Environment Act, and the only districts to be declared pollution control zones. In February 1994, the PCD declared that Thailand would not accept toxic waste exported from other countries.

Government control on industrial pollution in Thailand is severely hampered by control of pollution being outside the agency which attracts investment. The BOI has no track record or personnel committed to enforcing section 19 of the IPA of 1977, but instead it relies on the judgment of other government agencies to be sufficient. The DIW and the PCD are considered to be line agencies for implementing industrial environmental regulations (EBG, 1993b: 176). EIAs are not available for inspection by the public. The BOI has rejected few, if any, projects on environmental grounds. It has been reported that in February 1993 senior BOI officials conducted a meeting to discuss if the environmental conditions should be dropped from BOI requirements because they may deter investors from proceeding with applications (EBG, 1993a:23). In a survey of transnational corporations in Thailand, of which only 33 respond-ed, only about 40% of respondents prepared EIAs for internal use. 20% said they did so only when required by authorities (ESCAP/UNTC, 1988).

Moreover, there is also confusion concerning which ministry or department has jurisdiction in each case. The DIW is in charge of factory inspection, yet the PCD can do this too, under the auspices of a different ministry. Currently, the Department of Public Works is responsible for implementing central waste treatment plants in cities where these are being built. However, at the end of 1994, the responsibility for these passed to the PCD. The Ministry of Industry stated in early 1994 that it intends to privatize the construction of hazardous waste treatment systems. Under the 7th Five-Year Plan, five hazardous waste treatment plans were proposed for the provinces of Ratchaburi, Rayong, Kanchanaburi, Surat Thani, and Chonburi. However, these have been postponed pending a decision concerning privatization, under which many more plants would be attempted.

NIOEM, government and citizen participation

On one occasion at least, it seems that confusion about which government agency was responsible for environmental monitoring was a result of deliberate government policy to aid investors rather than investigate potential environmental impacts of their investment. During the industrial dispute at the Seagate Technology disk-drive factory in Samut Prakan in 1991, the National Institute for Occupational and Environmental Medicine (NIOEM), under the Ministry of Public Health, investigated possible causes of deaths at the factory. It produced a report suggesting that Seagate may be responsible for chronic (long-term) lead poisoning. Although it is unlikely that workers would die from chronic (as opposed to acute, short-term) lead poisoning, the report indicated that industrial poisoning could be the causes of the deaths.

News of this report fuelled the industrial dispute, which the BOI feared would make Thailand less attractive to investors (e.g. *Bangkok Post*, 10 Sep. 1991). After weeks more of well-publicized demonstrations at the factory and outside parliament house, the NIOEM was removed from the investigation, and an alternative agency was brought in to investigate. This agency, the National Institute for the Improvement of Working Conditions and Environment (NIWCE), under the Ministry of Industry, employs industrial hygienists rather than physicians, and tested working conditions rather than the health of workers. Predictably, NIWCE reached different conclusions to NIOEM, and the Seagate factory was vindicated. Officials at NIOEM and workers at the factory claimed, however, that the factory had ordered workers most exposed to lead fumes and solvents to work in different sections of the factory to minimize the traceable effects of lead poisoning.

The event raised important questions of environmental policy and political will. The director of the NIOEM claimed that NIOEM was overpassed because of the direct intervention of the head of the BOI (Forsyth, 1994). The BOI denies this. However, since this incident in 1991, the NIOEM has yet to receive any of the funding or staff allocated to it during the 7th Five-Year Plan. The Ministry of Public Health claims that other sections of the Ministry have taken on the duties of NIOEM. But the director of NIOEM claims that there is still no agency available to investigate and treat new forms of poisoning resulting from Thailand's industrialization.

Such a gap became apparent when a similar case of alleged poisoning occurred in one of Thailand's new industrial estates two years after the Seagate incident. During 1993 and 1994, at least ten workers in the Northern Region Industrial Estate at Lamphun died from suspected lead or solvent poisoning. Virtually all worked in Japanese electronics factories, and some worked extra long hours to earn bonuses. Although the symptoms matched death from industrial poisoning, the Industrial Estate Authority of Thailand (IEAT) and the local Lamphun health authority blamed most of the deaths on AIDS, and opposed any investigation into poisoning of workers in the estate (Forsyth, 1994).

The Lamphun industrial estate is the most rural industrial estate in Thailand, and most of its workers are experiencing factory work for the first time. They therefore may not appreciate fully the potential hazards of working with modern manufacturing processes. One local activist noted that factory officials had sold a used chemical storage drum to a nearby hill-tribe village to store water. However, at the time of the deaths, there was no specialist equipment for testing or treating poisoning in northern Thailand. Revelations of poor waste management at the estate forced the PCD to announce plans for a general inspection of all industrial estates in Thailand (*Bangkok Post*, 12 April, 1994). Three inquiries into the deaths were inconclusive, but they did not rule out the possibility of poisoning. Industrialists at the estate still deny that poisoning occurred.

The Lamphun case provided more evidence for the emerging role of civil society in the resolution of environmental policy. Press reports of the Seagate and Lamphun deaths fueled public concern about the hazards of industrialization. Newspapers provided platforms for eminent academics or industrial specialists to speak out against government policy or to call for inquiries. In the case of Lamphun, such public outcry allowed the inclusion of the director of NIOEM in one of the official inquiries into the problem. Citizens also demonstrated outside the governor's office in Lamphun to draw attention to allegedly polluted water coming from the estate (e.g. Yangderm, 1994). Local people also invited journalists to a site near the estate where toxic waste had been dumped without adequate treatment, resulting in widespread media coverage and a resulting inquiry from the PCD.

In Lamphun, citizens have formed the NGO, "Lamphun Action Group" as a platform for discussion with government bodies. The power of the group is increased by having members, often natives of Lamphun, placed within other organizations, such as Bangkok's prominent universities who themselves may have closer links with media or international contacts.

Such independent action by non-governmental bodies also arose after the chemical fire in Klong Toey in southern Bangkok destroyed 600 shanty houses and left some 1,000 people with breathing difficulties in 1991 (Grassroots Development Institute, 1991). The NGO, "Grassroots Development Institute", began campaigning for better protection against chemical poisoning. Further action came when it was discovered that waste from this fire had been dumped in concrete containers on land owned by the army in Kanchanaburi province. In 1993, local people reported the containers were leaking and possibly contaminating a river. Press reports led to a national outcry, and also to a claim by some hospital officials, in March 1994, that current laws aiming to restrict industrial poisoning were inadequate (*Bangkok Post*, 17 March 1994). In April 1994, academics and professionals formed the "Toxic Chemical Watch Network" to spread information and to campaign for the proper treatment of hazardous waste.

Other NGOs include the Environmental Law and Development Center at Chulalongkorn University, which was established in 1993 to research and campaign for better environmental pro-tection. Rising public concern about water shortages throughout Thailand are increasing demands that water be unpolluted (e.g. Changsorn, 1993). The Thailand Environment Institute (TEI), a break-off from TDRI, is researching the practicalities of the 'polluter-pays-principle' (Phantumvanit and Olsen, 1994; Limvorapitak, 1994a,b). In all cases, the press has formed an important player in the debate concerning environmental pollution by revealing new causes for concern, and by calling on the government for action.

CONCLUSIONS

Since the establishment of the BOI in 1973, Thailand has become a major industrial power in South East Asia. Originally, industrialization was aimed to provide joint ventures with Thai companies and to manufacture goods normally imported into Thailand. Since the late 1980s this has changed to favour totally foreign-owned companies who manufacture exports from Thailand. Whilst these undoubtedly bring tax revenue and employment to Thailand, such industries are also increasingly those associated with hazardous waste or other forms of industrial pollution. Despite the review of environmental legislation in 1992, evidence suggests that Thailand still does not have the political infrastructure to control industrial pollution.

One major problem preventing the control of industrial pollution is the apparent difference in power between the government agency that promotes investment (BOI) and the agencies designated to enforce environmental standards (under MOSTE). The BOI does little to abide by the environmental section of the Industrial Promotion Act of 1977. The creation of the Pollution Control Department (PCD) in 1992 was an important step towards controlling pollution. However, its power has generally not been seen, and instead it seems that the BOI has greater political power within the Thai government at times when an important foreign investor is suspected of pollution. There is also confusion and an apparent lack of commitment within other government departments to delineate areas of responsibility for the control of hazardous waste and practices, or to adhere to the original details of the 7th Five Year Plan.

Another problem is a lack of awareness of hazardous waste and work practices among Thailand's previously agricultural workforce (e.g. Mekvichai, 1993; Parnwell, 1994). This is especially evident in the Northern Region Industrial Estate in Lamphun, where workers have not been aware of the health hazards posed by new industries from intensive work practices, especially using solvents. Thorough safety depends on adequate training of inexperienced staff. However, BOI plans to diversify high-technology industries to the rural areas of Thailand suggests that the government expects this new awareness of practices to take place rapidly. The government has tended to blame farmers' ignorance of hazards, and hence the farmers themselves, rather than take full responsibility for hazard awareness.

Representation of public concern about industrial pollution is still poorly developed. Trades unions are largely powerless in Thailand, and the reality is that large, foreign investors are more likely to adhere to safety legislation than smaller domestic producers (e.g. Forsyth, 1994). New NGOs are developing amongst the more educated classes, but their impact is still unclear. Perhaps change will come most rapidly only after emergencies illustrate the underlying problems, such as the Klong Toey chemical fire in 1991, or the Kader toy factory fire in 1993 (Clifford and Handley, 1993). Some forms of industrial poisoning such as by solvents, however, are difficult to detect, especially if occurring in rural locations where medical facilities are not extensive; local cultural preference to cremate bodies quickly after death exacerbates this by allowing insufficient time for autopsies. Moreover, the impact of industrial poisoning has to be considered against the current, more serious, impact of AIDS.

Recent policy changes show some positive thinking about managing industrial pollution. For example, the principle behind industrial estates is to concentrate pollution in one location where it can be controlled. Also, the 1994 suggestion to privatize the provision of hazardous waste treatment centres suggest attempts by part of the government to speed up the process by removing it from slow moving government bureaucracy. The actual success of such policies will be shown by how effectively the waste treatment centres can be implemented, or the pollution within estates controlled. Such measures can only benefit the long-term economic aims of the BOI by creating a controlled investment climate, and a motivated and settled workforce.

REFERENCES

Akrasanee, Narongchai, Dapice, David and Flatters, Frank, 1991, *Thailand's export-led growth: Retrospect and prospects*, TDRI (Thailand Development Research Institute) Policy Study No. 3, TDRI, Bangkok.

Bangkok Post, 10 Sep. 1991, "Trade unions may act against US firm"

23 Sep. 1993, "Thailand: 300 dirty factories to be relocated"

13 Dec. 1993, "Thailand: BOI to promote anti-pollution industries"

17 March 1994, "Health officials attack old toxic chemical laws"

14 April, 1994, "Team to be set up for factory inspection"

Board of Investment, Thai government (Various years), *Thailand investment: a directory of companies promoted by the Board of Investment*, BOI, Bangkok.

Brummitt, William E. and Flatters, Frank, 1993, *Exports, industrial change and Thailand's rapid growth*, TDRI (Thailand Development Research Institute) 1992 year-end conference: Thailand's economic structure – towards balanced development?, Background report, TDRI, Bangkok.

Changsorn, Pichaya, 1993, Factories warned on pollution of water sources, *The Nation*, 2 December 1993, p B2.

Clifford, Mark, and Handley, Paul, 1993, Burning questions: Thai factory give investors pause for thought *Far Eastern Economic Review*, 27 May 1993, pp 69-70.

EBG (Environmental Business Group Co. Ltd.), 1993a, *Study: Industrial pollution control in Thailand*, submitted to United Nations Industrial Development Organization, Vienna, by Paul Clements-Hunt and Peter Brimble, EBG April 1993, Bangkok.

EBG (Environmental Business Group Co. Ltd.), 1993b, *Project report: Environmental issues and sustainable development in Thailand: The role of the Board of Investment*, prepared for the Office of the Board of Investment and the ASEAN Promotion Center on Trade, Investment and Tourism, by Paul Clements-Hunt and Sonia Berry, EBG May 1993, Bangkok.

Economist Intelligence Unit, 1993, *Asia's investment flows*, EIU Report Q157, January 1993, EIU, London.

ESCAP / UNTC, 1988, *TNCs and environmental management in selected Asian and Pacific developing countries*, ESCAP/UNTC Publication series B, No. 13, Bangkok.

Far Eastern Economic Review, 1992, "Thailand shuts down pulp plant for polluting", 14 May 1992, p 20.

Forsyth, Tim, 1994, "Shut up or shut down: How a Thai medical agency was closed after it questioned worker safety at a factory owned by Thailand's largest employer", *Asia, Inc.* (Hong Kong-based monthly business magazine) April 1994, pp 30-37.

Grassroots Development Institute, 1991, *Information and documents: Chemical Explosion Klong Toey, Bangkok, March 2, 1991*, Grassroots Development Institute, Klong Toey, Bangkok.

Handley, Paul, 1992, New rules but old attitudes (Thailand: environment), *Far Eastern Economic Review* 29 October 1992, p 40.

Jolly, David, 1992, Cleaning up their act (Thailand: trade and investment), *Far Eastern Economic Review*, 20 August 1992, p 46.

Khongnirandsuk, Supranee, 1992, Sweeping the board: The BOI's new secretary general vows to do no less than bring perestroika to the country's bewildering bureaucracy, *Manager* (Bangkok-based monthly business magazine), No. 40, April 1992, pp 20-27.

Koomsup, Praipol (ed.), 1993, *Economic development and the environment in ASEAN countries: Proc. of the sixteenth conference of the Federation of ASEAN Economic Association*, The Economic Society of Thailand, Bangkok.

Limvorapitak, Qwanrudee, 1994a, "Application of polluter-pays-principle for industrial wastewater management in Samut Prakan province", *TEI Quarterly Environment Journal* 2:1 53-65, Thailand Environment Institute, Bangkok.

Limvorapitak, Qwanrudee, 1994b, *Draft report: Policy to promote business and environment in Thailand, No.1, Application of polluter-pays-principle for environmental quality management at the national level*, Thailand Environment Institute, Bangkok.

Mekvichai, Banasopit, 1993, "Is there hope for 'Green Urbanization' in Thailand?," pp 195-220 in Koomsup, Praipol (ed.), 1993, *Economic development and the environment in ASEAN countries: Proc. of the sixteenth conference of the Federation of ASEAN Economic Association*, The Economic Society of Thailand, Bangkok.

OOECCJ (Overseas Environmental Cooperation Center, Japan), and TDRI (Thailand Development Research Institute Foundation), 1993, *Strategy to promote eco-business in Thailand*, OOECCJ, Tokyo; TDRI, Bangkok.

Parnwell, Michael J.G., 1994, "Rural industrialization and sustainable development in Thailand", *TEI Quarterly Environment Journal* 2:1, pp 24-39, Thailand Environment Institute, Bangkok.

Phantumvanit, Dhira and Olsen, Erik, 1994, "The relationship between business and environment", *TEI Quarterly Environment Journal* 2:1 5-11, Thailand Environment Institute, Bangkok.

Phantumvanit, Dhira and Panayotou, Theodore, 1991, *Industrialization and environmental quality: Paying the price*, The TDRI (Thailand Development Research Institute) year-end conference: Industrializing Thailand and its impact on the environment, Synthesis paper No. 3, TDRI, Bangkok.

Thai Government, 1992, *Thailand national report to the United Nations Conference on Environment and Development (UNCED)*, June 1992, Various government agencies, Bangkok.

Woolman, Bruce, 1992, The wasteland: Some experts characterize hazardous waste as the most pressing problem facing the region, bar none, *Manager* (Bangkok-based monthly business magazine), No. 47, November 1992, pp 44-49.

Yangderm, Kheun, 1994, Grain to greed: Lanna is dying, *The Nation*, 18 Feb. 1994, pp C7-8.

THE POLITICS OF ENVIRONMENT IN NORTHERN THAILAND: ETHNICITY AND HIGHLAND DEVELOPMENT PROGRAMS

Anan Ganjanapan

INTRODUCTION

After 30 years of development efforts by Thai government as well as international agencies in the northern Thai hills, with an emphasis on eradicating opium production, the Thai government has recently launched its so called conservation policies for the highlands. This is clearly seen in such policies as ending logging concessions, expanding reforestation areas as well as increasing the areas of National Parks. It also involves relocating highland villagers out of those National Parks. These policies have raised many issues in the politics of environment and ethnicity, in part because of the contradictory nature of their implementation.

While denying poor uplanders access to utilise forest land for their subsistence farming, the Thai government encourages business interests to exploit the same resource. With heavy competition for utilisation of forest by both the poor and developers, forest encroachment and illegal logging are common, resulting in commercial interests enjoying benefits at the expense of the poor. On a political dimension, the developers have legal support (through the 1992 Forest Farm Act) to exploit forest in the name of industrial development, while the hill poor are, ironically, left without any legal means to safeguard their rights to conserve forest.

As a result of these political and economic contradictions, there is great inequality in the distribution of forest resources. Local ethnic groups endowed with customary rights to control and manage community forests are facing continuous pressure for exploitation from villagers both in their own communities and outside. The real threat, however, is from the government, which wants to use forest areas for various types of infrastructure construction such as roads and dams.

In addition to problems of inequity and conflict in sharing of forest resources, the development direction fostered by the government has increased the deterioration of natural forest. Without any legal means to protect their rights to forest and land tenure security because of conflicts between local customs and national laws, hill villagers tend to favor extensification over intensification of land use. Moreover, with intensified land markets for speculation, there is a strong pressure on villagers to sell their land to speculators and keep on clearing more forest land.

This is also a failure in the government's forest management policies that focus only on individual property rights while ignoring communal property. Furthermore, these policies are themselves contradictory, which can be seen in the land reform program and associated scandals and in the eviction of highland villagers from conservation forests. The two policies did not put a stop to the forest encroachment but, on the contrary, led to more destruction of forest and the violation of villagers' use rights.

Such contradictions have heightened conflicts between all the actors in hill areas, especially between different ethnic groups and government agencies as well as capital owners and between highlanders and lowlanders. During 1994-1995 several upland ethnic groups formed a loose network and organised mass demonstrations in Chiang Mai involving thousands of people who are affected by government conservation policies. This paper will attempt to examine critically contradictions and conflicts resulting from highland development programs, in the context of both the politics of environment and the politics of ethnicity.

AGRO-ECOLOGY AND ETHNICITY IN NORTHERN THAILAND

The region of Northern Thailand can be classified into three agro-ecological zones, namely the lowland, highland and intermediate zone. The lowlands are mainly the home of wet-rice growing Thai villages. The highlands, on the other hand, are the home of several ethnic minorities, including the Hmong, Mien, Lahu, Lisu and Akha who have been migrating into Thailand for a century. Most of these people traditionally practise swidden agriculture with rice, corn and opium as their main crops (Grandstaff 1976; Uraiwan et al 1988)

The intermediate zone is an upland area dominated mainly by the Karen and, to a lesser extent, the Lua. The Karen migrated into Thailand from Burma more than three hundred years ago, while the Lua are the indigenous people of this region. Both the Lua and the Karen have long been practising a combination of irrigated wet-rice farming and swidden agriculture. As a result, they are well known as conservationists because of their ability in the control and management of the watershed areas of their irrigation systems (Sutee 1993).

In 1995, the total population of all ethnic minorities on both highland and upland areas was estimated at 745,910 (Hilltribe Welfare Division 1995). Of this total, the Karen accounted for almost one half (cf. Kunstadter 1986: 17). In the past, these ethnic minorities were not considered Thai citizens and this was later changed by the Nationality Act of 1965. Despite an official announcement in 1970 that registration of all hill tribespeople as full citizens was a high priority, at present, only 61.2 percent are said to have Thai citizenship (Kammerer 1987 and Kampe 1992).

Without Thai citizenship, these hill people are unscrupulously treated by government officials. More than 70 percent have no access to formal Thai education and only about 60 percent can speak Thai. Even though most hill dwellers are actively engaged in agriculture, only about 35 percent own their own land. Instead, they are considered to be squatters on state property, whether National Reserve Forest or various forms of Conservation Forest (Sophon 1978). As a result, more and more hill people are forced into wage labour employment and join the ranks of upland poor, some of them in a form of rootlessness (Cooper 1984 and National Statistical Office 1989 cited in Kampe 1992: 159).

During the past 30 years, however, the highlanders have been consistently blamed for destruction of the forest, the growing of illegal opium and as a threat to national security (McKinnon 1987). To eliminate those problems, highland development programs were initiated by the Thai government, foreign agencies and recently by non-governmental organisations (NGOs). At the peak period of development during the 1980s, there was a total of 168 agencies from 31 government departments and 49 international donors and NGOs (Kampe 1992).

The first two types of agencies have as their main objective substituting other cash crops for opium and forcing the highlanders to adopt permanent settlements. On the one hand, underlying those objectives, the highlanders have found themselves increasingly integrated into the national market economy. On the other hand, they are facing the uncertainty of forced resettlement by government agencies (McKinnon 1987 and Eudey 1989). In contrast, the NGOs are looking for alternative development strategies, focusing on self-reliance and sustainable agriculture with strong sense of conservation.

In the process of highland development, road construction is at the forefront of the development mechanism. This results in several contradictions, as more development agencies and roads into the highlands allow lowlanders to take control over highlanders' land and cause more destruction of the forest, especially as the area of cash-crop farming – notably of cabbages – increases dramatically (Anan 1987). Not only ecologically marginalised, the highlanders and those ethnic groups in the intermediate zone are pushed further and further into poverty. While highlanders are forced to look for work in the town, lowlanders are increasingly looking for upland areas to be developed as orchards and resort areas (Kunstadter and Kunstadter 1983).

Although the development efforts of the past three decades have achieved significant results in reducing opium production down from 150 to only 30 tons per year, they are faced with rapidly increasing problems of addiction among ethnic minorities in the hills. Together with alienation from land and forest resources and limited access to the cash economy, these hill villagers are forced more and more into prostitution. In 1990, newspapers reported that 158 of 220 tribal prostitutes tested were founded to be HIV positive

(*The Nation*, 21 September 1990 and *Bangkok Post*, 1 October 1990, cited in Kampe 1992).

COMPETITION FOR CONTROL OVER LAND AND FOREST IN THE NORTH

In the name of conservation, the Thai government has tried to claim more control over forest areas in the highlands by using various legal means to protect the forest cover, such as designating a certain forest area as a national park or wildlife sanctuary, and classifying highland regions as restricted watershed areas. Underlying these measures is the concept of state property rights with little or no regard at all of local custom, which values common property and usufruct rights. This form of territorialisation is, in fact, an inherent aspect of modern Thai state power (Vandergeest and Peluso 1995). The government uses these laws as a threat to resettle the ethnic groups living in the conservation areas by portraying them as "enemies of the forest" and considering them both as violators of state land and destroyers of the environment. Although several government agencies have set up many types of development programs for the ethnic minorities in the highlands, no agency recognises any kind of ethnic rights over land in the hill areas.

While the laws are very strictly applied to the ethnic groups in the highlands, the government allows lowlanders and capital owners to utilise upland areas almost freely for many purposes, in the name of national development and the institutionalisation of private property rights. This can be clearly seen in the forest land allocation programs which issue land use rights (STK) certificates to individual occupants of national forest reserve land in certain areas but do not stop them from selling their rights and clearing more forest land (Anan and Mingsan 1992).

During the Chuan government's period in office (1993-1995), a land reform program was even introduced to legitimise the private land use by lowlanders, regardless of the harm lowlanders do to the environment. However, it became one of the biggest national scandals and the subsequent Banharn government put the program on hold. Under the land reform law, a certificate of occupation is supposed to be given only to landless farmers who have settled on the forest land, but the Chuan government gave the certificates to all occupants of forest land regardless of their status, and some of them were quite wealthy. Instead of allocating forest land to the poor, the land reform program encourages more competition to encroach on the forest. This kind of problem can be avoided if the government has a serious interest in conservation by allocating forest land, not only to individuals but also to local communities. What the government did indicates very clearly that it only favours private property rights and economic efficiency at the expense of equitable and sustainable use of the forest.

It is ironic to see the government allocating forest land to the better off while taking cultivable land away from the poor by relocating highland villagers out of the National Parks. This type of policy is carried out very arbitrarily because, in some other highland villages, the government even supports their development programs. It seems that the eviction policy not only violates villagers' use rights but goes also against the whole concept of equitable and sustainable development. Settlers in the conservation forest should be encouraged and recruited to participate more in the forest management if their indigenous systems can be proved sustainable. But the government tends to play more with the politics of conservation than to take seriously the dynamic nature of indigenous systems in forest management (Anan and Mingsan 1992)

No matter how active they are in the protection of their watershed areas, the ethnic minorities on the hills have never been treated the same as lowlanders. This is partly due to the lack of Thai citizenship by some of the hill dwellers. But the double standard in application of the law by the government, sometimes by the same agencies, leads to confrontations between the ethnic minorities and the state agencies. The practice suggests that ethnicity, in fact, may be utilised as a cover for the lack of real interest in conservation on the government's part.

However, the politics of conservation are not simply a confrontation between ethnic minorities and the state agencies, because they also involves intra-bureaucratic politics, as seen in a case of inter-agency rivalry between the Department of Forestry and the Ministry of Interior. The Department of Forestry tries to control more forest in order to give it better access to higher budgets and larger manpower. The Ministry of Interior would like, on the other hand, to have more control over the people regardless of where they live, as a way of extending its authority. While the Ministry of Interior encourages development programs in the highlands, the Department of Forestry in most cases does not, except in special pilot projects with an emphasis on forest management and development. Thus, while the Ministry of Interior looks mainly at controlling an area, the Department of Forestry will only look at trees. Both agencies pay little attention to the people who have been living in the highlands for generations (Anan and Mingsan 1992).

In this way, it becomes clear that the government has no proper conservation policy or even social development policy but has only an interest in legal ownership of forest and control of forest areas. Because real forest conservation is more than a mere legal protection and involves complex watershed management with full participation of all those involved, especially the forest settlers, it has to be more a social policy than a legal policy. So far only one government-sponsored development program subscribes to this social policy, that is the Sam Mun Highland Development Project in Chiang Mai. This is a pilot project in community forestry under the supervision of the Royal Forestry Department in support of local initiatives. With an emphasis on the participatory management of watershed areas, the project has encouraged hill villagers to participate in both development and agro-forestry programs as well as the management of their own watershed areas (Uraiwan et. al. 1988). This program is something of an exception and is only selectively applied to very limited cases.

The government's gain in control over the forest and highland areas, especially those within the conservation zones, namely the national parks, wildlife santuaries, and the watershed areas, does not guarantee the success of conservation policy. What is considered a government gain is a loss to the ethnic minorities. With less control over their common resources, the highlanders are even more marginalised. This situation allows powerful outsiders to fill the gap left by the highlanders. More lowlanders, particularly traders and capital owners, have managed to take over the control of forest land. The competition for control over forest land is most intense in the intermediate zone because its traditional occupants are mainly subsistence producers who have little experience in the market. Most of them are very poor and thus susceptible to the uncertainty of markets (Anan 1987).

Many minorities from these intermediate areas have become rootless, roaming the hills looking for employment. In contrast, the ethnic groups who are traditional opium growers do have some experience in the market and are able to adapt better to the commercialisation of the highlands. In fact, many of them even benefit from the development and can afford to move into the intermediate zone, under the government pressure not to grow opium in the highlands, at the expense of the Karen. Thus in the battle for control over forest land, the traditional conservationists have lost control of their land to the government, the land developers and other ethnic groups. The government has gained more legal control over the highlands but found more destruction of the forest.

It may appear that the Thai government has a socially based conservation policy when the RFD is seen as drafting a community forest law. But the fact of the matter is that there is at present practically no legal recognition of communal property. Most forest land is considered state property, but in practice it is more or less open-access. Under this situation, the strength of local organisations in protecting their community forest has increasingly been undermined by problems which are fundamentally embedded in the political and economic contradictions of the development process. The continuous emphasis on industrial development has, on the one hand, left rural producers deeper in poverty with strong pressure to exploit more of their forest resource, and on the other hand, encouraged business interests to exploit the same resources, which were once considered to be in the sphere of the poor (Anan and Mingsan 1992).

Although the politics of conservation played by the government have produced mostly negative impacts on the forest, the increasing pressure to evict settlers in conservation forests, together with the villagers' need for land tenure security because of their production for the market, has forced many hill communities to opt for conserving their forest as a strategy to bargain with the government in exchange for security of their settlement in the state forest areas. These communities, particularly highland ethnic groups, do not only reinforce their conservation of community forest but also increase their conservation practices in agriculture. The continued existence of this kind of indigenous system of forest management, however, requires appropriate government policies and legislation such as community forest law (Suthawan 1993).

Villagers do not always recognise the legitimacy of state claims over forest land. Villagers may justify their rights on customary and local practices, but they also have some ground in modern Thai laws. A serious study of Thai legislation, such as the Civil and Commercial Code that is still in use, also finds the existence of community rights and use rights in those laws which most Thai governments simply choose to ignore (Saneh and Yos eds 1993: 114-117).

Faced with increasing destruction of their environment, some ethnic minorities have turned to a campaign to save their livelihood. This can be clearly seen in the case of the Karen at Wat Chan area of Mae Cham district in Chiang Mai. The local residents, who are mainly Karen, have long managed to conserve a wide area of pine forest covering their watershed areas. In the early 1980s the Forestry Industry Organisation, a state-lumber agency, got Cabinet approval for logging of those pine trees as well as building of a saw mill in the area, all in the name of development. The Karen communities in the area, once they learned about the project, joined hands to oppose construction of the saw mill first by sending a petition to the deputy governor of Chiang Mai in 1989. The construction of the saw mill, however, continued. Not until 1993, when the villagers again sent a petition to the Prime Minister, was the saw mill's machinery withdrawn from the area and the construction temporarily abandoned (Prasan 1993). The Karen have a long history of opposing logging in their watershed areas (Anan and Mingsan 1992).

This kind of ethnic struggle cannot be simply regarded as a revival of a primordial idea but, on the contrary, confirms that, in an intensive competition for control over the forest, local communities do not always recognise the legitimacy of state claims. Increasingly faced with negative impacts of state-guided development, local communities have to rely more and more on the dynamic management and conservation of their natural resources and environment to maintain their livelihoods as well as to adapt to the outside market economy. Thus ethnic struggles shall be seen as local responses to the outside interventions with the ethnic idiom as a language of the discourse (cf. Moore 1994). For instance, during the long campaign to oppose the construction of the saw mill, in the case of the Karen at Wat Chan, the ethnic communities have employed ethnic symbols in various forms of ritual and have reinterpreted them to articulate their struggle (Prasan 1993).

CONSERVATION VERSUS COMMERCIALISATION OF THE HIGHLANDS

With an overriding aim to eradicate opium production in the highlands, most official development programs as well as foreign-aid development agencies, in their initial stage, paid less attention to conservation of the highlands than finding alternative cash crops to opium. The result is clearly seen in the increased commercialisation of the highlands. This is evident in several programs where the commercial interest has taken over the need for conservation (UNDCP 1994).

However, during the past decade, most development programs in the highlands have subscribed to conservation of the environment as their top priority. In practice, these development programs give only lip service to sustainable cropping patterns or agroforestry concepts as stated in their objectives, and they continue to rely mainly on the commercial production of cash crops, particularly coffee, fruit trees and temperate vegetables as a means to increase incomes for the ethnic minorities in the hills. This kind of development strategy is readily accepted by most traditional opium growers, who have long experience in the market system. Instead of sustainable land use, one finds the spread of commercial production of cash crops, especially cabbages, all over the hills. Moreover, such development programs encourage higher uses of chemical fertilisers and pesticides as well as water (Mingsan 1994).

The result is usually seen in some kind of ethnic conflict or lowland-highland conflicts, as in a well-known case of conflict between the Hmong of Ban Pa Kuai and lowland Thai farmers in Chomthong district of Chiang Mai. This Hmong village was studied by Cooper, an anthropologist, in the early 1970s and again by Renard, a historian, in 1987 (Cooper 1984 and Renard 1988). From those studies, the community was known to be recently settled with intensive opium production on very steep slopes. In 1984, with the introduction of a United Nations development project, Highland Agricultural Marketing and Production (HAMP), the Hmong villagers converted most of their old opium fields to cabbage and potato fields complete with a small reservoir feeding gravity-operated sprinkler systems. Stone contour fences were also constructed to check erosion. During 1985-1989, when Thai-Norwegian Church Aid Highland Development Project (with support of the United Nations Program for Drug Abuse Control, UNPDAC) took over development works from HAMP, the Hmong had extensively expanded their cultivation of cabbage (Renard 1988). As a result, they have to compete for forest land and resources as well as water with lowland villagers below their settlement.

Not only do people in the highlands and lowlands, who are mostly of different ethnic origins, have to compete for the use of water. The lowlanders are also quite outraged by the fact that their water sources have been contaminated. But the fact of the matter is not that simple, because in reality many lowland traders as well as farmers also have their vegetable plots on the hills. The lowland traders even subcontract the Hmong to farm for them. In this sense, the conflict should rather be seen in terms of competition for the use of water, which has become a major problem for most people in the North as they try to adapt to the increasing commercialisation of their region.

A classic case of the contradictory development process is found in Doi Luang National Park of Lampang province, where the Thai-Norwegian Church Aid Highland Development Project has quite successfully encouraged the Mien and Lisu, traditional opium growers, to turn to coffee production. This is seen as a first step towards establishing permanent settlement for the groups, who are highly mobile. This development strategy is also considered as a contribution towards a conservation objective. It took a period of more than a decade for the highlanders finally to stick to their permanent settlement because of the very high stake in their investment in coffee plantations, which have also turned land into a very valuable commodity. However, since 1990 the Mien have been faced with a threat from the National Park officials to be relocated outside the park area (Anan and Mingsan 1992).

While the Hmong at Ban Pa Kuai are still allowed to cultivate on the steep hills, the Mien villages of Mae San and Pa Daeng were finally relocated in 1994 to an upland area outside the Doi Luang National Park. The stated reason for the resettlement is conservation, but the real motive behind this move tends to be more commercial, that is tourist promotion as the park officials would like to save a waterfall's environment to attract more tourists. The Mien villagers had protested such a drastic action which put their livelihoods in jeopardy, because they found the land in the new settlement unsuitable for cultivation. Many of them had to turn to waged employment. After a long struggle the villagers have temporarily been allowed to harvest their coffee on their land in the national park.

It is also an irony in other cases, too, that implementation of the national forest protection policy has sometimes resulted in revoking from hill villagers their use rights of the land even though the villagers have participated actively in agricultural development working towards soil and forest conservation. In the Lahu village of Lo Pah Krai in Mae Ai district of Chiang Mai, for example, a sizable tract of land was simply taken away from villagers. The same land was granted as a concession to the state owned Forestry Industry Organisation, not for conservation purposes but for developing as a commercial *Eucalyptus* plantation (Kanok and Benjavan 1994: 91).

The above cases demonstrate quite clearly that the state agencies still subscribe to the idea that for forest conservation, people and forest cannot co-exist, especially those ethnic groups who are considered "enemies of the forest". But these agencies do not seem to mind the market as a mechanism for conservation management. In other words, while the presence of humans will do some harm to the conservation of forests, the commercialisation of the forest will not. Following this line of thinking, one can only conclude that the government has more trust in market-managed than people-managed conservation. In fact, most government officials do not think that people-managed conservation of forest is possible. The cases of large highland development projects, such as the Doi Tung project, will support this way of thinking since conservation and commercialisation of this hill area are fully integrated.

Here, one finds two lines of thinking about the conservation of the forest. Government officials think that either their agencies or the market can better conserve the forest and environment for the benefit of national development. The opposing line of thinking, subscribed to mainly by academicians and NGO workers, has more trust in the people's potential because the conservation of forest is not linked to commercial development but to rural development. These two views have fundamentally different concepts of property rights for the forest. The government only considers the forest as state property that the state alone can manage for the benefit of the whole nation. Scholars and NGO workers stand for the people's point of view in looking at the forest both as state property and as communal property, which is not recognised by the state. Thus the forest as communal property, or community forest, is an area where the relationship between environment and rural development should be re-evaluated. The government has, however, been very slow in promulgating such a law on community forests.

ENVIRONMENT AND COMMUNITY RIGHTS

Most highland development programs, whether they are under the sponsorship of the government or NGOs, are normally concerned mainly with technical aspects of environmental conservation such as looking for environmentally friendly and sustainable cropping patterns. But underlying the real politics of environment is the question of community rights, both property rights and human rights. Environmental conservation, particularly in the case of sustainable management of watershed forests of the northern Thai highlands, has rarely taken seriously the role of ethnic minority groups. This is because they are considered illegal migrants, even though most of them have been here for generations. Without the rights of citizenship, the hill people find no place in environmental conservation or rural development. Rather, they are relegated to labourers in commercial developments.

Under such conditions, scholars and some NGO workers propose to define rural development from the perspective of the rights of local communities. Here, rural development is seen as a way to strengthen the ability of local organisations to participate in the management of their environment. Because the hill environment, especially watershed forest, is not only state property but also communal property, the local communities should have customary rights to benefit from the resources that they help to protect. In this sense, rural development is an avenue where local communities can strengthen their rights in the management of their resources. However, the whole issue of rights on the part of ethnic minorities in the hills has always been caught up in the politics of environment, which are clearly manifested in controversies over swidden agriculture between the government on one hand and the local communities on the other, in their struggles over the control of forest resources.

Official lines of thinking are based mainly on a set of myths about villagers' land and forest management which government official themselves have created. The critical one is a myth of swidden agriculture as a main cause of destruction of watersheds. Many studies have long proved otherwise. The degradation of watersheds is not simply a physical problem of agriculture, or of construction of infrastructure such as dams and roads for that matter, but rather should be seen more as a social and political problem relating to the process of unequal development (Dove 1983; McKinnon 1989a). Shifting cultivation, as seen in many studies, is varied, complex and changing over time. In many cases, it has become a dynamic response to changing situations which local communities have employed as part of their coping strategies. In other cases, shifting cultivation is optional, as hill villagers have found several other agricultural alternatives as well as different ways of earning their income (Kanok and Benjawan 1994, and Kwanchewan 1996).

This kind of myth has kept government officials from understanding the rights of local people and the potentials of local knowledge in resource management and bio-diversity. By ignoring realities of local practices, the government has come up with uncompromising regulations in order to protect the watersheds. Villagers' tenurial rights on their swidden lands are often denied because they are considered not to be based on permanent agriculture. Moreover, officials often associate negative effects of shifting cultivation only with ethnic minorities on the hills but ignore the fact that both highlanders and lowlanders practise swidden agriculture. There are clear distinctions in shifting cultivation systems, with rotational shifting cultivation a more permanent and environmental friendly alternative (Kanok and Benjavan 1994, and McKinnon 1987 and 1989b).

The problem can also be seen in other controversies between government agencies and local villagers relating to the official classification of forest, which only allows community forestry in the so called economic forest and not in the conservation forest. Such classification of the forest will not only isolate an integrated biological system of an ecological region, like a watershed system, into artificial and unrelated units, but also ignores a holistic cultural system in the same region. In this sense, the official way of thinking does not match the fact that local knowledge is locality specific. To separate people from their locality will only weaken their knowledge in bio-diversity and their ability in forest management (Gurung 1994).

Underlying those official lines of reasoning are notions that only government agencies can be the legitimate guardian of the forest. But ethnic minorities, especially the Karen who are traditional conservationists, would also like to compete for the same role as the protector of the conservation forest to justify their rights of continued existence in the forest. At present, other highland ethnic groups, too, are trying to participate in the conservation of the watersheds as they are often threatened with relocation out of the conservation forests. Here, the role of environment seems crucial in lending legitimacy for both government agencies and ethnic communities in their struggles over the control of forests.

Since the 1980s, with growing global concern for the environment, government agencies have been stepping up their role in the politics of environment. The Royal Forestry Department (RFD) in particular has been busy with implementation of the national forest protection policy without much attention to social issues in terms of community rights and ethnicity. In 1986, in cooperation with the army, RFD began to put pressure on ethnic minorities in the hills by issuing eviction orders to the Hmong of Huai Yew Yee village in Huai Kha Khaeng Wildlife Santuary (Eudey 1989). The establishment of new national parks in some cases resulted in the relocation of hill villages. For example, the Hmong village of Khun Klang was relocated from Doi Inthanon National Park in 1989 (Chayan 1991). And most recently, this is evident in the case of the Mien villages of Mae San and Pa Daeng, which were evicted from Doi Luang National Park in 1994, as mentioned above.

In the name of environmental protection, government agencies have recently put more pressure on the hill population both through relocation from conservation forests and by revoking their use rights in the land. In response, the ethnic hill minorities have also demonstrated that they can play a role in the conservation of the forest, which can be seen in their active promotion of community forests and intensive efforts to experiment with sustainable agriculture.

However, much tension and scepticism still prevail on both sides, as seen in various incidents of confrontation while all actors tend to play with the politics of environment. In 1994, the ethnic minorities in the northern Thai highlands formed a loose network, and in 1995 they demonstrated their grievances in large numbers in the city of Chiang Mai. In addition to their rights in the participatory management of the forest in the form of community forests, the hill people also demanded their rights of existence in the forest where they have been for generations.

Thus, without simultaneous consideration of both the issues of environment and community rights, more conflict between the state and hill people will continue for the foreseeable future.

CONCLUSION

The conflicts in the northern Thai highlands are a clear case of the politics of environment in the sense that environment has played a role in lending legitimacy both to the government agencies and ethnic communities in their struggle for the control of forest resources. But an overall understanding, as well as appreciation of the social ramifications of the environment, have rarely been touched upon. The focus on particular technical issues has usually led to partitioning of all the related issues by taking each in isolation, without reference to others.

The conflict can be traced back to the official line of negative thinking about ethnic minorities in the hills by associating them with various vices, namely as enemies of the forest, opium producers and as a threat to national security. Thus government agencies always cite ethnicity against a role in conservation, which keeps them from appreciating ethnic-specific knowledge in the management of the forest. The emphasis is on development programs which produce even more devastating impacts on the environment because of their underlying commercial orientation. Shifting cultivation has always been distorted for having only a negative impact on the environment, disregarding the realities found in local practices which are varied, complex, adaptive and quite dynamic in many cases.

The ethnic minorities, on the other hand, keep raising the issues of community rights in relation to their role in the protection of the environment. Rarely are their voices recognised until serious conflict occurs, which can be seen particularly in cases of the eviction of minorities out of conservation forests.

Only recently have government agencies begun to show some positive concerns over the social issues of rights, as seen in the official pilot project on community forestry and the drafting of the

Community Forest Act. However, there is still no serious discussion of legal recognition of minorities' rights to live in the forest. Without full recognition of rights for the communities, there can be no guarantee that the real concern for and protection of the environment will be participatory in nature, which is so crucial to the idea of sustainable and equitable development.

REFERENCES

Anan Ganjanapan, 1987, "Conflicting Pattern" of Land Tenure Among Ethnic Groups in the Highlands of Northern Thailand: the Impacts of State and Market Intervention," *Proceedings of the 3rd International Conference on Thai Studies,* Australian National University, Canberra, Australia.

Anan Ganjanapan, 1992, "Community Forestry in Northern Thailand: Learning from Local Practices," in Henry Wood and Williem H.H. Mellink (eds.) *Sustainable and Effective Management System for Community Forestry,* Bangkok, FAO/RECOFTC.

Anan Ganjanapan and Mingsan Khaosa-ard, 1992, "A Study of Evolution of Land Clearing in the Forest Areas: Case Studies of the Upper North," in *Study of Conservation Forest Area, Demarcation, Protection, and Occupancy in Thailand, Volume 3:* Occupancy Study, Bangkok, Midas Agronomics Company, Ltd.

Chayan Vaddhanaphuti (ed.), 1991, *Nayobai Kan Chatkan Sapphayakon Bon Thi Sung Lae Thangluak Nai Kan Phatthana Chao Khao: Korani Khet Uttayan Haeng Chat Doi Inthanon (Policies on Highland Resource Management and Alternative Development for Highlanders: A Case of Inthanon National Park),* Chiang Mai, Social Research Institute, Chiang Mai university.

Chupinit Kesmanee, 1991, *Highlanders, Intervention and Adaptation: A Case Study of a Mong N'jua (Mong Ntsuab) Village of Patana,* Unpublished MA. Thesis, Victoria University of Wellington.

Cooper, Robert G., 1984, *Resource Scarcity and the Hmong Response: A Study of Settlement and Economy in Northern Thailand,* Singapore, Singapore University Press.

Dove, Michael, 1983, "Theories of Swidden Agriculture and the Political Economy of Ignorance," *Agroforestry Systems* 1, pp 85-99.

Eudey, Ardith A., 1989, "14 April 1986: Eviction Orders to the Hmong of Huai Yew Yee Village, Huai Kha Khaeng Wildlife Sanctuary, Thailand," in John McKinnon and Bernard Vienne, eds., *Hill Tribes Today: Problems in Change,* Bangkok, White Lotus.

Forsyth, Timothy, 1995, "The *Mu'ang* and the Mountain: Perception of Environmental Degradation in Upland Thailand," *South East Asia Research* 3: 2.

Grandstaff, Terry B., 1976, *Swidden Society in North Thailand*, Unpublished PhD. Dissertation, University of Hawaii.

Gurung, Jeanette D., ed., 1994, *Indigenous Knowledge Systems and Biodiversity Management*, Proceedings of a MacArthur Foundation/ICIMOD Seminar, Kathmandu, Nepal.

Hilltribe Welfare Division, Department of Public Welfare, 1995, *Tham Nieb Chum Chon Bon Pheun Thi Sung Nai Prathet Thai Pi 2538, (Directory of Highland Communities in Thailand in 1995)*, Bangkok, Ministry of Labour and Social Welfare, (in Thai)

Kammerer, Cornelia Ann, 1987, "Minority Identity in the Mountains of Northern Thailand: The Akha Case," in *Southeast Asian Tribal Groups and Ethnic Minorities, Cultural Survival Report 22*, Cambridge, MA, Cultural Survival, Inc.

Kampe, Ken, 1992, "Northern Highlands Development, Bureaucracy and Life on the Margins," *Pacific Viewpoint* 33:2 (Special Issue : Marginalisation in Thailand: Disparities, Democracy and Development Intervention)

Kanok Rerkasem and Benjawan Rerkasem, 1994, *Shifting Cultivation in Thailand: Its Current Situation and Dynamics in the Context of Highland Development*, IIED Forestry and Land Use Series No. 4, London, International Institute for Environment and Development.

Kunstadter, Peter, 1980, "Implications of Socio-economic, Demographic and Cultural Changes for Regional Development in Northern Thailand," in J.D. Ives (et. al.) *Conservation and Development in Northern Thailand*, Tokyo, The United Nations University.

Kunstadter, Peter, 1986, "Highland Populations in Northern Thailand," in John McKinnon and Wanat Bhruksasri, eds, *Highlanders of Thailand*, Singapore, Oxford University Press.

Kunstadter, Peter and Sally L. Kunstadter, 1983, "Hmong (Meo) Highlander Merchants in Lowland Thai Markets: Spontaneous Development of Highland-Lowland Interactions," *Mountain Research and Development* 3: 4.

Kwanchewan Buadaeng, 1996, "Changes in Shifting Cultivation and Coping Strategies," A paper presented at the second meeting of the sub-regional workshop on the cultural dimension of development in Asia and the cultural context of natural resource management, Social Research Institute, Chiang Mai University, Thailand.

McKinnon, John, 1987, "Resettlement and the Three Ugly Step-Sisters Security, Opium and Land Degradation: A Question of Survival for the Highlanders of Thailand," A paper presented to the International Conference on Thai Studies, Australian National University, Canberra, Australia.

McKinnon, John, 1989a, "Structural Assimilation and the Consensus: Clearing Grounds on Which to Rearrange Our Thoughts," in John McKinnon and Bernard Vienne, eds, *Hill Tribes Today: Problems in Development*, Bangkok, White Lotus.

McKinnon, John, 1989b, "Agriculture Development and The Impact on Land Use: Progress Report on Doi Chang," Chiang Mai, Tribal Research Instutite and Orstom Project.

Mingsan Khaosa-ard, 1994, 'Kan Suksa Khwam Yangyeun Khong Rabop Kaset Thisung,' (A Study of Sustainability of Highland Agricultural Systems). Bangkok, The Thailand Development Research Institute (TDRI).

Moore, Donald S., 1993, "Contesting Terrain in Zimbabwe's Eastern Highlands: Political Ecology, Ethnography, and Peasant Resource Struggles," Economic Geography 70, pp 380-401.

Prasan Tangsikbut, 1993, "Kan Chatkan Sapayakon Thammachat lae Singwaetlom Pak Nua," (The Management of Natural Resource and Environment in The North) in Singwaetlom'36, Proceedings of a seminar on the conservation of natural resources and environment in Thailand.

Renard, Ronald D., 1988, Changes in the Northern Thai Hills: An Examination of the Impact of Hill Tribe Development Work, 1957-1987, Chiang Mai, Research Report No 42, Research and Development Center, Payap University.

Saneh Chamarik and Yos Santasombat, eds., 1993, Pa Chumchon Nai Prathet Thai: Naothang Kan Phatana, Vol 1. (Community Forestry in Thailand: Directions for Development), Bangkok, Local Development Institute.

Sophon Ratanakhon, 1978, "Legal Aspects of Land Occupation and development," in Peter Kunstadter et. al., Farmers in the Forest: Economic Development and Marginal Agriculture in Northern Thailand, Honolulu, University Press of Hawaii.

Sutee Boonto, 1993, "Karen's Indigeneous Knowledge Forest Management System and Sustainable Development in Upper Northern Thailand," in International Symposium on Indigenous Knowledge and Sustainable Development, Cavite, Philippine, International Institute of Rural Reconstruction,

Suthawan Sathirathai, 1993, "The Adoption of Conservation Practices by Hill Farmers, with Particular Reference to Property Rights," Unpublished Ph,D, Thesis, Cambridge University,

Tapp, Nicholas, 1989, Soveriegnty and Rebellion: The White Hmong of Northern Thailand, Singapore, Oxford University Press.

Tapp, Nicholas, 1990, "Squatters or Refugees: Development and the Hmong," in Cohan Wijeyewardene, ed, Ethnic Groups Across National Boundaries in Mainland Southeast Asia, Singapore, Institute of Southeast asian Studies.

Thawit Jatuworapruek, 1995, Ritual of Reproductive Ethnicity Among the Poor Highlanders: A Study of Cultural Adaptation of the Lisu in Chiang Mai, Unpublished MA Thesis, Chiang Mai University (in Thai).

United Nations International Drug Control Programme (UNDCP), 1994, Two Decades of Thai-UN Cooperation in Highland Development and Drug Control: Lessons Learned, Outstanding Issues, Future Directions, A Seminar Organised by UNDCP.

Uraiwan Tan Kim Yong, Anan Ganjanapan, Shalardchai Ramitanondh and Sanae Yanasarn, 1988, *Natural Resource Utilisation and Management in Mae Khan Basin: Intermediate Zone Crisis*, Chiang Mai, Resource Management and Development Center, Faculty of Social Sciences, Chiang Mai University.

Vandergeest, Peter and Nancy Lee Peluso, 1995, "Territorialisation and State Power in Thailand," *Theory and Society* 24, pp 385-426.

WATERSHED MANAGEMENT IN PHETCHABUN, THAILAND: LOCAL STAKEHOLDERS AND THE INSTITUTIONAL ENVIRONMENT

Roger Attwater

INTRODUCTION

In Thailand, as in other countries with substantial rural populations, the processes of rural development are a major issue. The issue of rural development concerns the resource base, roles of local communities, and the broader institutional environment. One integrated approach to rural development that accommodates all these is a focus on watershed, or catchment, units. Watersheds are nested, open and complex systems, reflecting functional relationships between resources through landscape process, with patterns of settlement, property regimes and land use overlaying the landscape patterns. A watershed unit can be considered as a microcosm of broader institutional and socio-political arrangements, while contextually specific to local livelihoods. Within this microcosm, a range of social actors, or stakeholders, will hold different views of management opportunities, including those relating to local livelihood, responsibilities of government agencies, commercial interests, and broader ideological bases.

Watershed units have the characteristics of common pool resources, as described by Blomquist and Ostrom (1985) and Ostrom (1992), with a jointly consumed core resource, the watershed properties, and a flow of individually consumed resource units, the water resources. A focus on the flow of water resources commonly entails questions of appropriation and allocation between water use demands. The question of stakeholders' perceptions of management opportunities in upland watersheds, however, focuses on the maintenance of watershed properties through integrated activities that support local sustainable livelihoods.

The first section of this paper outlines the historical context of watershed management for rural development in Thailand, describing perspectives on current water resource development in terms of centralised strategies which reflect urban and industrial stakeholders downstream, and community-based perspectives supported by non-government organisations. This is followed by a brief description of a case study of a small rural watershed in Phetchabun Province, identifying community, agency and commercial stakeholders' perceptions of opportunities for collective and collaborative action. Discussion focuses on the value of catchment and stakeholder perspectives as a pragmatic means of determining legitimate and feasible collaborative action between differing stakeholders, within given institutional and socio-political arrangements.

WATERSHED MANAGEMENT IN THAILAND

Thailand has a long history of cooperative water resource management for rural development, and traditional forms of irrigation management can be considered as indigenous technical knowledge (Chantana 1988). Studies of the management of traditional irrigation systems in the north have included those by Abha (1983) and Vanpen (1986). One form of irrigation system, *muang fai rat*, was in existence in the northern Lanna period, over 1,400 years ago. Irrigation laws were established by King Mangrai in 1296 AD, the year Chiangmai was established as capital, and rules and penalties were documented in the *Mangraisart*. Other systems were established around 100 years ago, incorporating aspects of the irrigation law of the *Mangraisart* into weir agreements, *sanya muang fai*, between water users and the irrigation leader. Some of these weir agreements included specific issues such as conservation of forest in watershed areas *(paa ton nam)* (Vanpen 1986; Anan 1992).

At the turn of the century, irrigation development in the central region was encouraged by King Rama V, responding to foreign demand for rice. After the second world war the World Bank and the

IMF assisted with the country's development, leading to the first National Economic and Social Development Plan in 1961. From 1952 onwards, a number of dam developments were financed by the World Bank, including the Chaophraya Dam at Chainat and associated irrigation works in the Central Plains. Thailand has now developed at least 872 large and medium scale projects for irrigating more than 3 million hectares of farmland, and 39 large-scale hydro electric dams (Porntip *et al.* 1991).

Current water resource development

Current water resource development in Thailand reflects a tension between ideologies of centralised, growth-oriented development strategies, and community-based approaches supported by non-government organisations. The notion of water as primarily a resource for national economic growth tends to reflect the perspectives of urban and industrial stakeholders. The community-based ideology tends to focus on rural stakeholders upstream.

A focus on downstream industrial and urban stakeholders is a reflection of national strategies aimed at the continuing transformation of the Thai economy from an agrarian to an industrial and service-based economy (TDRI 1994). Urban and industrial users, both through direct consumption and indirect use through electricity generation, are a major political and economic force. Industry demand is expected to increase at about 10% per year, and as irrigated agriculture uses 30 times more water than industry to generate a unit of GDP (ESCAP 1991), the latter has been considered a more favourable end user. The demand for electricity generation is also expected to rise dramatically (Table 1). This has potentially major consequences for the development of new storages, and the timing of release from these storages.

The community-based perspective on recent water resource development has been that large-scale developments benefiting economically powerful industry, agro-industry, or urban groups, have failed to solve the problems of the majority of people and contributed to Thailand's ecological problems. The national irrigation and rural piped water projects have been perceived to

Table 1
Forecast water use demand by sector, 1990-2000 (ESCAP 1991)

Sector	Forecast water use needs (million m³ / yr)		
	1990	1995	2000
irrigation	30,000	34,000	38,000
rural domestic	62	383	938
urban domestic	1,468	2,180	2,967
industry	1,547	1,869	2,339
electricity	37,847	61,332	83,580

suffer problems of maintenance, wastage, inefficient collection of water charges, and other social problems within user groups (Vanpen 1986; Porntip et al. 1991; ESCAP 1991). *Muang fai* systems in the North, the volunteer irrigation systems in the Northeast, and water management on individual farms, have been alternatives that incorporate local decision-making, regulation, and utilisation according to needs. Local water users' groups are considered to be a 'foundation for community self-reliance', with these groups in the best position to take active lead roles in managing watershed forests, and regulating local use (Porntip et al, 1991; Chatchawan and Lohmann 1991).

Sustainable water resource management requires the integration of institutional arrangements for the identification and transfer of water rights, decentralised management systems, watershed management planning at a local level, and water resource information systems (Prakob 1994). Recently, two potential forms of water legislation have been proposed, one by the National Research Council (NRC), and one by the Law Faculty of Thammasat University. Both consider aspects of property rights, potential authorities, and policy instruments. The NRC proposal is based on common property (*sombat phaendin*), with civil law providing the basis for rights of utilisation, where every citizen has a right to use as long as negative effects are not imposed. The Thammasat version vests ownership in the State (*khong rat*) with the State granting use rights (Anon. 1994).

Both these legislative proposals include Basin and Sub-Basin Committees to oversee water allocation, operating under a central National Water Resource Committee. The Basin Committees would act to coordinate government agencies, and draw input from user groups for management and allocation of water resources. The major policy instruments proposed are transferable water permits, possibly based on local water authority rates. The Thammasat draft also included transferable permits for wastewater discharge. Potential problems of implementation include the cultural precedent of virtually free water, high administrative and political costs of the introduction of a comprehensive system of permits and charges, and the limited authority and incentive of Basin Committees, given that they may not be entitled to collect permit charges directly (Anon. 1994).

Agricultural expansion and forest management

The current status of watershed management in Thailand also needs to be considered in terms of the evolution of agricultural expansion and forest management systems. The history of settlement and agricultural expansion into the uplands is a result of changing social and economic relationships of the Thai economy, with resultant pricing policies, marketing structures and resource exploitation (Hirsch 1990a). This has been parallelled by an evolving system of forest management, which has been described in detail by Kamon and Thomas (1990). After the completion of logging concessions, which provided access roads, responsibility of these lands remains with the Royal Forestry Department as degraded forests (*paa seum soom*), as does a larger grouping of forest types, reserves, and steep land. Given the accessibility of land and favourable markets, many farmers migrated to these areas, often later abandoning sites to perennial grasses and bamboo (Hirsch 1990b).

The traditional view reflected by foreign development agencies is that deforestation and threats to watershed properties are due mainly to population growth and swidden agriculture. While such a rationale is maintained for foreign funded development projects, for example the inter-agency programme discussed by Viroj and Sitthichai (no date), Thai NGOs consider the resource crisis to be a function of conflicting policies geared to industrial expansion and aggressive economic development (Yos et al, 1991; PER 1991).

By the late 1980s, the contradictions and conflicts surrounding reserved forest were immense. Vast areas of reserve forest and logging concessions occurred in areas designated as protected areas, and large numbers of registered villagers, supported by government programmes, occupied areas of reserved forest and logging concessions (Kamon and Thomas 1990).

Agency responsibility and integrated projects

Currently, approximately a dozen government agencies have responsibilities that include watershed management to some degree. The major responsibility is vested in the Royal Forestry Department (RFD), with delineation of zones and watershed classification by topography (Kasem 1986). The Watershed Management Division of RFD tends to focus on watershed rehabilitation through plantation establishment (Van Ginneken and Uthai 1991). Soil and water conservation are the responsibility of the Department of Land Development.

In reviewing institutional and socioeconomic research on watershed management in Thailand, Nipon (1988) discussed the paucity of research dealing with attitudes towards watershed management and conservation, socioeconomic impacts, and institutional problems. Early programs in degraded forest areas included the forest village programme, initially established by the Forest Industry Organisation, and the Royal Forestry Department's *SorTorKor* [usufruct certificate] programme. Integrated projects in the North have included the Mae Cham Watershed Development Project and the Sam Mun Highland Development Project. There has also been an integrated watershed management project in Phu Wiang, northeast Thailand.

The goals of both the *SorTorKor* and forest village programmes included limiting land degradation, restricting illegal encroachment, consolidation of residents into permanent settlements to facilitate the provision of government services, and supporting national internal security policy. In studying these programmes within the Dong Mun Forest of Northeast Thailand, Hafner and Yaowaluk (1990) have discussed how the project goals seldom reflected the interests and needs of local people, and underinvested in the capacity of the local community to develop solutions to local problems.

The Mae Cham watershed project was supported by USAID and the Thai Department of Technical and Economic Cooperation (DTEC) from 1980 until 1989 (MCWDP 1989). The major soil and water conservation activities undertaken within this project were bench terracing and intercropping legumes. A study of attitudes of farmers within the Mae Cham project found that while the introduced activities were considered more effective than traditional methods, the local Karen were happy to provide labour, but local Thai farmers preferred to have the 'government do it all' (Sinth 1985).

Another ongoing project in the north is the Sam Mun Highland Development Project. This project was initially supported by the United Nations Drug Control Programme from 1987 until 1994, and is still supported by the Watershed Management Division of the RFD. The project has utilised village and watershed network committees, and community organisers, to try to promote involvement in planning and developing awareness of linkages upstream and downstream. Samer (1995) has described the need to spend time in developing lines of communication and trust, awareness among villagers, and understanding among officials and policy makers.

An integrated watershed management project in Phu Wiang, in the Northeast, was developed with the FAO to establish plantations and diversify local sources of income through sound utilisation of local resources. The villagers were lowland Thai, living in established villages outside the forest area, accessing forest areas by roads established by previous logging concessions. The establishment of plantations of eucalypts was planned to allow villagers to continue to interplant cassava until shaded out. The villagers, however, did not like the plantations, and perceived that they were being denied access to resources and were losing a source of income. Villagers preferred fruit trees, or local hardwoods, and while some aspects of conservation farming, crop diversification and agroforestry were developed, the major interest seemed to be due to the provision of free inputs. Activities which were well supported by villagers included the development of local sericulture resources, fruit orchards and fish ponds (Van Ginneken and Uthai 1991).

These examples reflect the general recognition of the need to incorporate participatory methodologies which can identify local sources of income, and means to promote communication and access between villagers, officials, and established agency services. While earlier technocratic approaches did not lead to sustained activity, the incorporation of participatory approaches can potentially lead to a mix of actions which support the goals of officials, villagers and project staff.

A RURAL CASE STUDY: KHLONG NAM THIN, PHETCHABUN

The focus of this study is two villages located in the upper watershed area abutting the Phetchabun Ranges, Ban Khao Kart and Ban Huai Khrai. These two villages are within Tambon Tabo, Amphoe Muang, Changwat Phetchabun. The stream in the case study catchment, Khlong Nam Thin, flows into the Pa Sak River just south of the Phetchabun township. This area has had no bilateral project activities, NGOs, or research activities, though contains aspects which reflect the range of rural and environmental issues, and institutional arrangements, common to Thailand.

Conceptual and methodological approach

The conceptual approach used builds upon contemporary approaches to participatory rural development and watershed management. A focus on 'sustainable livelihoods' has been part of a broad reconceptualisation of rural development through approaches such as 'farmer-first' (Chambers 1983) and people-centred development (Korten and Klauss 1984). These approaches support a conception of economic and social development as processes of change driven by actors' adaptive problem solving and social learning (Dunn 1984; Jamieson 1985; Chambers 1994; Scoones and Thompson 1994).

A recent workshop brought together experiences of participatory watershed management from a number of countries. Participatory watershed management was described as an approach which involved communities in the analysis of their own soil and water problems, supported by facilitating and catalytic external support. The emphasis is on the sustainability and equity of improvements, rather than on short-term benefits. Benefits which can occur without the help of payment or subsidies are aimed at as they are most likely to be sustained (Hinchcliffe et al. 1995).

In the context of rural development, Bromley and Cernea (1989) concluded that building rural managerial capacity needs to be an explicit objective of rural development projects, through emphasising both institutional arrangements and grass-roots organisations. The importance of building upon established, local institutions has been recognised for small-farm agriculture (Tendler 1993), and forest and fuelwood resources (Morse et al. 1987). Similarly, Amyot (1987) suggests that it is more appropriate to think in terms of the reorientation or reinterpretation of existing organisations, because they are part of rural village culture and consequently more in conformity with the social understandings and expectations of villagers.

This conception of development driven by actors' adaptive problem solving is also a key feature of institutional economics, which builds upon John Dewey's philosophy of pragmatism. An institution can be characterised by having a number of people doing something, rules providing some form of stable order, and ideologies or worldviews which justify the activities and rules (Neale 1987). Institutions thus include all forms of customs and traditions, rules of exchange, and legal frameworks. Rather than focusing on the question of economic efficiency, institutional economists recognise that efficiency is determined by the context of the institutional structures that define the distributional *status quo*. More important questions are: who controls the management rules (institutions) which determine the rates of use of natural resources, who receives the benefits, and who is exposed to the costs? (Bromley 1982).

The methodologies supported by institutional economics are quite different to those of neoclassical economics. Rather than deductive modelling of economic behaviour, institutional economics

Figure 1. <u>Khlong Nam Thin watershed, Phetchabun.</u>

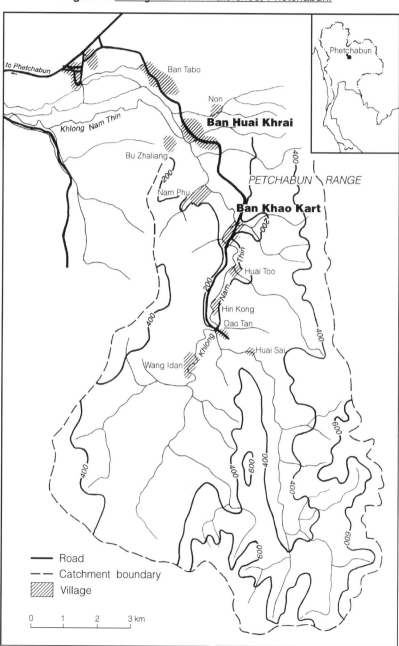

supports the use of inductive, pattern modelling methodologies (Wilber and Harrison 1978; Diesing 1991). Institutional economics also takes subjectivity and differences in ideology seriously, and therefore supports decision-making approaches which allow for the explicit identification of different stakeholders' perceptions (Soderbaum 1992).

An action research approach was used for this study, based upon documenting and discussing perceptions of resource and land use systems within a small rural watershed. Participatory action research has developed from a recognition of the inadequacy of classical research for development action, attempts to involve grass-roots groups in decision-making, and application of systems thinking to organisational behaviour (FAO 1978, Whyte 1991). 'Participatory' research can be considered the intent to involve target groups to integrate local knowledge in the research process. This alone, though, is considered meaningless to the target group if this exercise does not incorporate some form of participatory planning, followed by development action, which produces benefits for the local farmers (Verhagen 1984). An ethic for action-based rural research has been succinctly described by the late J. C. Mathur in his Small-Farmers Development Manual (FAO 1978), that the work should be of immediate benefit to small-farmers, and there should be gains from the process of the research as well as the outcome.

In introducing myself locally, I described my interest in terms of watershed health. This allowed a connection between healthy environment and water, subsequent healthy agricultural systems and healthy family livelihoods. Information collected documented local village organisation and livelihood strategies, perceived problems and opportunities of villagers and village leaders, and responsibilities, problems and opportunities perceived by a range of agency and commercial stakeholders. Opportunities were sought for meetings and discussions between agency staff and villagers, to facilitate the identification of mutually accept-able collaborative action.

Figure 2. Potential land reform zone and conservation zone

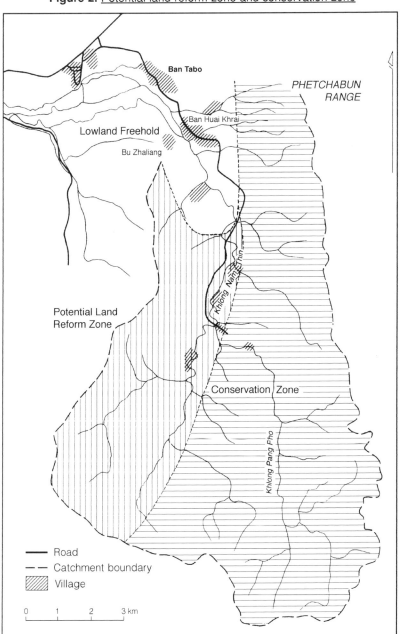

Khlong Nam Thin Watershed

The watershed site (Figure 1) is located at the base of the Phetchabun Ranges, rising from floodplain low terraces, up into high terraces of old alluvium, transitional colluvial deposits, and finally the Phetchabun Range. The Range runs south from the Luang Phetchabun Ranges in Laos, and separates the Central region of Thailand and the Chaophraya basin from the Northeast region (Donner 1978).

While the lowland village, Ban Tabo, has been established for over 300 years, Ban Huai Khrai was established 100 years ago, and Ban Khao Kart was only isolated households in the forest until a forest concession established a road in the mid-1960s. Many people migrated from the Northeast to plant maize around this time, though most upland areas have been abandoned since, with bamboo and perennial grass succession. Mungbeans were introduced in the early 1970s, tamarind gardens in the late 1970s, and soybeans about 1990. The logging concession only finished with the nationwide logging ban in 1989, having totally removed commercial timber from the watershed area. Only degraded remnants and regrowth are now found within the watershed.

Ban Khao Kart and Ban Huai Khrai are village administrative units, each having about five housing groups (*klum ban*), with upstream housing groups more widely distributed. These two villages are combined with another six as Tambon Tabo, with the commune leader (*Kamnan*) living in Ban Tabo. The main point of contact between government-recognised local officers and representatives of the bureaucracy is at the Tambon meeting hall. The chain of command is strongly hierarchical, with meetings designated by district level officers, and the *Kamnan* then calling upon village leaders.

While lowland freehold is established around the downstream Ban Tabo, Ban Khao Kart lies entirely within a forest conservation zone. Ban Huai Khrai, while mostly outside the conservation zone, does not have established freehold. Currently rezoning is expected to occur to transfer most of the area immediately surrounding Ban Khao Kart into a land reform zone, with authority transferred from the Royal Forestry Department to the Agricultural Land Reform Office (Figure 2). This rezoning of peripheral areas of the Phetchabun Ranges is also part of a broader strategy to establish a reserve in the Phetchabun Ranges, between Phetchabun and Chaiyaphum. From June 1993 onwards, a concerted effort by the Provincial Government, Royal Forestry Department officers and police systematically evicted all households and settlements in the highlands to the east of the Khlong Nam Thin watershed.

Local household livelihood strategies are a complex mix of cropping and agricultural activities, heavily supplemented with casual labour in Bangkok. Some older men also worked for Thai logging companies in Cambodia. Local land use is based upon a complex mix of formally and informally recognised rights to parcels of land with use rights or land tax certificates, within the degraded conservation zone. Though some individuals seasonally migrate between the villages and Bangkok, many households have at least one young individual who remains working in Bangkok most of the year, only returning home for major festivals such as the new year.

STAKEHOLDERS' PERCEPTIONS OF OPPORTUNITIES

The information strategy used was based upon iterative and open-ended interviews, documentation, and retranslation into Thai for rechecking. The information presented below focuses on perceptions of opportunities, which build upon stakeholders' perceptions of responsibilities and problems.

Village stakeholders

Perceptions of village stakeholders was undertaken through iterative interviews. These included discussions with village leaders either alone or together with their deputies, and a leader of the local women's group. Perceptions gathered were further developed through meetings with village councils and/or public meetings, supported by household interviews. Village leaders were questioned as to their perceptions of problems and opportunities as they related to local economic conditions and livelihood, water resources, agricultural systems and the local environment. The following are summary development aims drawn from interviews with village leaders which were later used with council and public meetings to discuss the information, technical, financial and organisational needs to achieve these broad objectives.

- *Livelihood.* Local developments planned and undertaken by local people to manage water, local funds, agricultural produce and skills to generate economic activities and income for local households.

- *Water resources.* Development of small-scale dams and weirs to store rainy season flows for use during the dry season, while assisting the quality of the water through reducing the use of chemicals.

- *Agriculture.* Development of diversified and integrated small scale agricultural enterprises which include more animal enterprises, vegetables, and fruit trees which have resilient and productive lives longer than current cropping activities, with experienced people to help develop appropriate new enterprises.

- *Local environment.* Conservation of remaining natural areas, while replanting degraded forest to help the environment, and generate economic activities.

The wife of Khao Kart's village leader, nominally the leader of the village women's group, discussed how opportunities for skills development and activities by village women were crucial. She expressed interests in raising small livestock for school children's lunches, funds for medicines, and traditional technologies such as weaving.

Household surveys were also undertaken for a small number of households in each housing group. Opportunities identified by villagers tended to focus more on agricultural or economic activities that households could undertake. Opportunities included secure land tenure, cattle and cattle groups/banks, fruit orchards, integrated agricultural systems with a range of small animal enterprises, vegetables, and local water resources. More public needs were also mentioned, including bridges to cross streams, a clinic, and activities in which old people could participate.

Agency and commercial stakeholders

Agency representatives were interviewed to ask them of their responsibilities, and how they perceived opportunities for watershed management within the Khlong Nam Thin watershed with which they could assist. Agency stakeholders' perceptions tend to reflect the institutional environment within which villagers' livelihood strategies are developed. The grouping of agency stakeholders in the following section reflects the institutions of public administration (District Government), education (local school teachers), land use zoning (Royal Forestry Department and Agricultural Land Reform Office), soil and water conservation and agricultural development (Department of Land Development, Royal Irrigation Department, Department of Agricultural Extension), State-led community development (Department of Community Development), and State-initiated commercial resource exploitation (Thai Plywood Company).

- *District Government.* The District Deputy discussed how key opportunities were land reform to improve land tenure, and local water resource development. Water was perceived to be the key to developing agricultural activities, providing income for basic needs and children's education, in turn providing opportunities for the household in the future.

- *Khao Kart School.* The local school teacher perceived the roles of local information and organisation as crucial for developing local livelihood. The school plays a central role in the provision of information to both children and local villagers, as well as planning and information support for local organisation. A focus of the school's attention is the development of a local piped water supply, together with the establishment of a water users group.

- *Royal Forestry Department.* The district forestry officer discussed how the strengthening and policing of conservation reserves was necessary for upland conservation.

- *Agricultural Land Reform Office.* The provincial ALRO officer discussed how the major opportunity was the rezoning of previous conservation zones to allow the establishment of a land reform zone. This could provide both improved land tenure and the development of road and water resource infrastructure which was not possible within conservation zones. The provincial officer expressed an interest to visit the villages and explain the land reform process.

- *Department of Land Development.* Officers discussed how DLD could provide support for a range of soil and water conservation programs in which villagers could participate. On the basis of plans submitted through the Tambon Council, DLD could provide technical support for contour planting of vetiver grass, perennial legumes, and support the development of small scale water sources.

- *Department of Agricultural Extension.* The local agricultural extension officer mentioned the key need for water resource development and the provision of low interest loans to farmers without land tenure as collateral. The officer is involved with farmers' groups, but very few villagers in Ban Khao Kart or Ban Huai Khrai were involved as yet.

- *Royal Irrigation Department.* The officer expressed an interest in meeting the local villagers to discuss local needs and the submission of plans through the Tambon Council. One major obstacle which needed to be overcome was the need for Forestry Department permission for any water resource development in areas under their control.

- *Department of Community Development.* The representative of the DCD explained the current activities of the Department, focusing on women's group activities, savings groups, and a new project to be established which would focus on the uppermost village Ban Khao Kart, with a fund for agricultural loans. Irrigation and bores for drinking water were also mentioned.

• *Thai Plywood Company:* the local manager of the Thai Plywood Company described how his company could support village tree planting through the provision of seedlings, technical support, and an assured market, based on five year rotations of coppice regrowth. This could be undertaken on any land with slope less than 35 degrees. Steep lands were the responsibility of the Royal Forestry Department. Local organisation was also considered a key opportunity, with village, government and company representatives supporting tree planting, animal management or other local activity-based groups.

Identifying feasible options

Based upon the perceptions of these agency and commercial stakeholders, opportunities were sought for village visits so that agency stakeholders, village leaders and the school teachers could discuss feasible options for collaborative activity. Visits by Irrigation and Land Development officers who were interested to meet local village leaders were organised, and interview information collected was collated and distributed to all interviewees. This was followed by a catchment forum, held at the house of the village leader, Ban Khao Kart, and chaired by the District Deputy, where the Provincial Officer of ALRO, and officers from the Departments of Land Development, Irrigation, Agriculture and Community Development spoke to villagers and answered questions posed by village leaders and teachers.

A number of technical and organisational options emerged from this dialogue, including: land reform; local management of revolving funds; water supply and management through user groups; contour planting and demonstration; and enterprise groups such as cattle banks. At the time of the forum, a Thai worker also began to work to maintain communication and planning support between village leaders and agency staff. Plans for irrigation and soil conservation demonstrations have been formalised, and funding for a local water supply has been received.

The local water supply scheme, being implemented in the school housing group, is a good example of the development of a local plan which integrates both resource and organisational aspects. Technical and planning support were provided by the Irrigation Department and school teachers, as well as visits by members of the village council to other villages in the district which had developed a low cost local water supply. Funds from the Australian Embassy's Small Activities Scheme are being used to establish a weir, major supply line and water filter, as well as a supporting revolving fund to use these water resources to raise chickens for school lunches. A water users group is being established, with villagers who connect to the water supply paying for the lateral pipes and a meter. This payment will be made to the water users group.

CONCLUDING REMARKS

At the scale of aggregate water resource development, the divergence of ideologies makes the consideration and accommodation of different stakeholders' perceptions difficult. At the scale of the small rural watershed, however, a stakeholder approach can be a useful way to identify the needs of local villagers, and the opportunities for legitimate and feasible action with agency stakeholders. The value of a stakeholder approach to rural watersheds is the attempt to consider the differing agencies' activities, local villagers' livelihood systems, and the way that these interact within a particular local context.

In Thailand, the major influence on the way that any dialogue can occur is constrained by pervasive, hierarchical patron-client relations. Rigg (1991) has discussed the problems of applying populist conceptions of empowerment or participation at the grass roots level. It is critical to work with established protocols if the aim is some form of continuing support for development activities. In research which follows a stakeholder approach, however, opportunities can present themselves to initiate collaborative action. This can occur through facilitating occasions for meetings and dialogue in peripheral upland villages which traditional public administration protocols may rarely, if ever, provide. This can promote local awareness of potential management options, supported by the possibility for legitimate plans through traditional channels, funding to initiate small locally identified projects, and future interaction with agency staff.

Three examples from this study reflect different forms of dialogue in relation to different institutional arrangements. The most top-down of relationships is that of rezoning to a land reform zone. This rezoning will be communicated formally from the Royal Forestry Department to the Agricultural Land Reform Office (ALRO), from whom information will flow through standard public administration channels. In this case, interviews with the ALRO Provincial Officer identified an opportunity for him to talk to the villagers, providing some personal contact, and the possibility of his patronage. A second example is that of collaborative activity between villagers and agencies which is reliant upon an exchange of information between the two. Plans for irrigation and soil conservation demonstrations were of this form. While the initial meeting was facilitated through this research process, formal local requests needed to support village visits by agency officers. Through this meeting village leaders were able to learn of how they could submit proposals, a process of which they had no previous experience. The third example is more similar to projects undertaken by non-government organisations. A local need for dry-season water supply to a housing group together with temple and school led to funding support for a local water supply scheme. Local school teachers worked with village council members to visit other villages and government offices in the region which had local or technical experience, and to develop plans for both technical aspects and local organisational management.

The case of Khlong Nam Thin shows that watersheds are a useful planning unit for attempting to coordinate agency activities and to integrate local decision-making to promote locally appropriate technology (Prakob 1994). Throughout Thailand, with the establishment of Basin Committees there will be the potential to integrate concerns for the appropriation and allocation of water resources with the enhancement of degraded watershed properties through local watershed management. The dynamic interplay of the exploitation of forest resources and agricultural expansion has led to a large number of households living in degraded upland 'forest reserves'. The future management and protection of core watershed resources lies in the ability of agency representatives and these upland communities to develop collaborative solutions. Solutions based on integrated, locally appropriate activities which promote sustainable livelihoods are perhaps the key to sustainable watershed management.

Acknowledgements

I would like to acknowledge the support of my research patrons who made it possible for me to undertake this study: Khun Wanarat Thothong, Department of Land Development; Ajarn Saneh Chamarik, Local Development Institute; and Ajarn Anuchat Pongsomlee, Mahidol University. I would also like to thank Ajarn Suwattana Thadiniti, Chulalongkorn University Social Research Institute.

REFERENCES

Abha Sirivongs Na Ayudhaya (1983) *A comparative study of traditional irrigation systems in two communities of northern Thailand*, Chulalongkorn University Social Research Institute, Bangkok.

Anan Ganjanapan (1992) "Community forestry in northern Thailand: learning from local practices", in: Wood, H., Mellink, W.H.H. (eds.) *Sustainable and effective management systems for community forestry*, pp 83-88, RECOFTC Report No. 9, Regional Community Forestry Training Centre, Kasetsart University, Bangkok.

Anon. (1994) "Water crisis: blame it on poor water management", Thai Development Newsletter 25, pp 14-19.

Amyot, J. (1987) "Issues of rural development", *Journal of Social Research* 10 (1-2): pp 28-40, Chulalongkorn University Social Research Institute, Bangkok.

Blomquist, W. and Ostrom, E. (1985) "Institutional capacity and the resolution of a commons dilemma", *Policy Studies Review* 5(2): pp 383-393.

Bromley, D.W. (1982) "Land and water problems: an institutional perspective", *American Journal of Agricultural Economics* 64 (December), pp 834-44.

Bromley, D.W. and Cernea, M.M. (1989) *The management of common property natural resources: some conceptual and operational fallacies*, World Bank Discussion Paper no. 57, The World Bank, Washington, D.C.

Chambers, R. (1983) *Rural development: putting the last first*, Longman Scientific and Technical, Harlow U.K.

Chambers, R. (1994) "Participatory rural appraisal (PRA): challenges, potentials and paradigm", *World Development* 22 (10): 1437-1454.

Chantana Banpasirichote (1988) "The situation of indigenous knowledge in Thailand" in *Indigenous knowledge and learning*, Chulalongkorn University Social Research Institute, Bangkok, and Centre for the Study of Education in Developing Countries, The Hague.

Chatchawan Tongdeelert and Lohmann, L. (1991) "The muang faai irrigation system of Northern Thailand", *The Ecologist* 21 (2): pp 101-106.

Diesing, P. (1991) *How does social science work? Reflections on practice*, University of Pittsburgh Press, Pittsburgh.

Donner, W. (1978) *The five faces of Thailand: an economic geography*, University of Queensland Press, St. Lucia, Queensland.

Dunn, E.S. (1984) "The nature of social learning", in Korten, D.C., Klauss, R. (eds.) *People-centred development: contributions toward theory and planning frameworks*, Kumarian Press: West Hartford Connecticut.

ESCAP (Economic and Social Commission for Asia and the Pacific) (1991) Assessment of water resources and demand by user sectors in Thailand, Report ST/ESCAP/1068, Economic and Social Commission for Asia and the Pacific, Bangkok.

FAO (Food and Agriculture Organisation) (1978) *Small farmers development manual*, Vol. 1. field action for small farmers, small fishermen, and peasants, RAFE No. 36, FAO, Bangkok.

Hafner, J.A., and Yaowalak Apichatvullop (1990) "Migrant farmers and the shrinking forests of Northeast Thailand", in Poffenberger, M. (ed.) *Keepers of the forest: land management alternatives in Southeast Asia*, pp 187-219, Kumarian Press, Connecticut U.S.A.

Hirsch, P. (1990a) *Development dilemmas in rural Thailand*, Oxford University Press, Singapore.

Hirsch, P. (1990b) "Forests, forest reserve and forest land in Thailand", *The Geographical Journal* 156 (2), pp 166-174.

Hinchcliffe, F., Guijt, I., Pretty, J.N., and Shah, P. (1995) *New horizons: the economic, social and environmental impacts of participatory watershed development*, Gatekeeper series no. 50, International Institute for Environment and Development, London.

Jamieson, N. (1985) "The paradigmatic significance of rapid rural appraisal", in Proceedings of the 1985 International Conference on Rapid Rural Appraisal, Khon Kaen University, Thailand.

Kamon Pragtong and Thomas, D.E. (1990) "Evolving management systems in Thailand", in: Poffenberger, M. (ed.) *Keepers of the forest: land management alternatives in Southeast Asia*, pp 167-186, Kumarian Press, Connecticut U.S.A.

Kasem Chunkao (1985) "Watershed management in Thailand: principles and problems", in Thawatchai Santisuk, Tem Samitinan, and Brockelman, W.Y. (eds.) *Nature conservation in Thailand in relation to social and economic development*, The Siam Society, Bangkok.

Korten, D.C. and Klauss, R. (1984) *People-centred development: contributions toward theory and planning frameworks*, Kumarian Press, West Hartford Connecticut.

MCWDP (Mae Cham Watershed Development Project) (1989) Proceedings for the summarisation of the Mae Cham watershed development project model and establishment of directions for continuing development of the Mae Cham Watershed, Payap University Research and Development Centre, Chiang Mai.

Morse, R., Charit Tingsabadh, Vergaro, N. and Varun Vidyarthi, et. al. (1987) *Peoples' institutions for forest and fuelwood development: a report on participatory fuelwood evaluations in India and Thailand*, East-West Center, Hawaii, and Appropriate Technology Development Association and Chulalongkorn University Social Research Institute, Bangkok.

Neale, W.C. (1987) "Institutions", *Journal of Economic* Issues 21 (3) : 1177-1206

Nipon Tangtam, N. (1986) "Status of socio-economic-institutional research and identification of needed researches for watershed management in Thailand", *Kasetsart Journal* (Social Sciences) 7: pp 217-226, Kasetsart University, Bangkok.

Ostrom, E. (1992) "The rudiments of a theory of the origins, survival, and performance of common-property institutions", in Bromley, D.W. (ed.) *Making the commons work: theory, practice and policy*, pp 293-318, Institute for Contemporary Studies Press, San Francisco.

PER (Project for Ecological Recovery) (1991) *People and the future of Thailand's forests: an evaluation of the state of Thailand's forests two years after the logging ban*, Project for Ecological Recovery, Thailand.

Porntip Boonkrob, Chatchawan Thongdeelert, Pratuang Narintrangkul Na Ayuthdhaya and Orawan Sripim (1991) "Local water resource management, Thailand", in International Forum Case Studies: Water, People's Forum, Oct 8-17, 1991, Bangkok.

Prakoh Wirojanagud, P. (1994) "Four major tools for sustainable water resource management", Thai Development Newsletter, 25, pp 36-38.

Rigg, J. (1991) "Grass-roots development in rural Thailand: a lost cause ?" *World Development* 19(2/3), pp 199-211.

Samer Limchoowong (1995) *Watershed management by local communities*, paper presented at the UNESCO UNITWIN International Workshop on Water Quality and Catchment Management, 2-5 May 1995, Hat Yai, Thailand.

Scoones, I. and Thompson, J. (1994) "Knowledge, power and agriculture – towards a theoretical understanding", in Scoones, I., Thompson, J.(eds.) *Beyond farmers first: rural people's knowledge, agricultural research and extension practice*, pp 16-32, Intermediate Technology Publications, London.

Sinth Sarobol (1985) The attitudes of farmers towards highland soil and water conservation in the Mae Cham Watershed Development Project, research report supported by the Ministry of University Affairs.

Soderbaum, P. (1992) "Neoclassical and institutional approaches to development and the environment", *Ecological Economics* 5, pp 127-144.

TDRI (Thailand Development Research Institute) (1994) "The TDRI 1993 year-end conference 'Who gets what and how?: challenges for the future", *TDRI Quarterly Review* 9 (1), pp 3-7.

Tendler, J. (1993) "Tales of dissemination in small-farm agriculture: lessons for institution builders", World Development 21(10):1567-1582.

Van Ginneken, P., and Uthai Thongmee (1991) "Attempting integrated watershed development in Phu Wiang, Thailand", *Unasylva* 164, Vol. 42, pp 8-15.

Vanpen Surarerks, (1986) *Historical development and management of irrigation system in northern Thailand*, Ford Foundation, Bangkok.

Viroj Pimmanrojnagool and Sittichai Ungphakorn (no date), "Uplifting Thailand's disadvantaged villagers: an inter-agency highland development programme", in Rao, Y.S., Hoskins, M.W., Vergara, N.T., Castro, C.P. (eds.) *Community forestry: lessons from case studies in Asia and the Pacific region*, pp 221-234, RAPA, FAO, Bangkok and East-West Centre, Hawaii.

Verhagen, K. (1984) *Co-operation for survival: an analysis of an experiment in participatory research and planning with small farmers in Sri Lanka and Thailand*, Royal Tropical Institute, Amsterdam.

Wilber, C.K., Harrison, R.S. (1978) "The methodological basis of institutional economics: pattern model, storytelling, and holism", *Journal of Economic Issues* 12 (1), pp 61-89.

Whyte, W.F. (1991) *Participatory action research*, Sage Publications, Newbury Park California.

Yos Santasombat, Wichean Saengchot and Therapon Sawanruengrang (1991) "Community forestry: a dimension of alternative development" (abstract), in Vitoon Panyakul (ed.) (1991) *Development as if people mattered*, pp 22-24, abstract conference papers, The People's Forum, Oct. 8-17 1991, Thai NGO-CORD and Chulalongkorn University, Bangkok.

A COMPARATIVE STUDY OF INDIGENOUS AND SCIENTIFIC CONCEPTS IN LAND AND FOREST CLASSIFICATION IN NORTHERN THAILAND

Santita Ganjanapan

INTRODUCTION

For decades, growth-oriented development models and centralised control of natural resources have been criticised for undermining the livelihood security of peripheral people and for causing pervasive environmental degradation (Anan 1995; Preecha 1994). In the past few years, academics, NGOs and grassroot organisations have called for a shift in development paradigms toward decentralisation, people-centred development and legal recognition of community rights over local resources (Wiwat 1993).

One of the latest and more promising strategies for sustainable community-based resource management is applying indigenous knowledge (Seri 1993). The concept is based on the premise that local people are able to manage their resources. Thai bureaucrats, however, are still sceptical about local people being stewards of nature as well as about the value of indigenous knowledge itself. The knowledge is often regarded as inefficient, inferior to scientific knowledge and an obstacle to development.

This article examines and compares both knowledge systems, based on case studies in the upper northern region of Thailand, in order to inrestigate whether indigenous knowledge offers some potential for local resource management, and how local people utilise both knowledge systems to negotiate for the interests of their community. The case studies come from a survey of four villages in the foothills of the mountainous upper northern region of Thailand, and represent different ethnic groups. The first two cases involve groups of Karen people in Mae Sariang village in Mae Hongson province, and Mae Ai village in Chiang Mai province. The third case is a combination of Thai Leu and Lao people in Thawangpha village in Nan province. The last case is Mae Chan village which belongs to northeastern people who migrated to Chiang Rai. Except for the Mae Chan village which is twenty years old, the other villages are old settlements dating back about eighty to over two hundred years.

HISTORY OF KNOWLEDGE SYSTEMS

Diverse ethnic groups in the mountainous upper northern region of Thailand practice various resource management systems within different ecological zones. The lowland northern Thai have practiced *muangfai* irrigated farming systems supplemented by upland short cultivation-short fallow swidden and permanent tree crop gardens (*miang* tea gardens) on hillslopes at middle elevations. In the upper terraces and foothills of the middle elevations, Karen and Lua people subsist on irrigated farming systems and short cultivation-long fallow swidden. Other ethnic groups who migrated much later into Thailand, such as Hmong, Mien, Akha, Lahu and Lisu, occupy upper elevations and practice long cultivation-long fallow swidden system (Kunstadter and Chapman 1978). The management of land and water and the protection of forest is inherent in the culture of these ethnic groups.The law of King Mangrai, dating back almost 700 years, forbids lowland northern Thai from violating '*Pa Sua Ban*', or forests dedicated to guardian spirits of each community (Shalardchai et al 1993). In other ethnic cultures, there are reports of varying degrees of forest protection by Karen (Prasert 1991; Shalardchai et al 1993), Lua (Somkuan 1991), Akha (Aju 1991), Mien (Thawil 1991), Lahu (Charoen 1991), Lisu (Sakda 1991) and Hmong (Prasit 1991). Even newcomers like the northeasterners who migrate and settle down in the upper north have their way of protecting forest (Shalardchai et al 1993).

The practices of indigenous resource management systems gradually declined in many parts of Thailand, except in peripheral areas, when Thailand began seriously to adopt western, scientific knowledge systems during the reigns of King Mongkut and King

Chulalongkorn in the last third of the nineteenth century. In response to pressures and challenges of a modern, expanding, imperialist Europe, Siam endeavored to strengthen its nation by modernisation through educational, administrative and other kinds of reforms. At the time of boundary negotiations between the British and French, King Mongkut began to appoint European teams to survey and map frontiers and other parts of Siam. Urban and transportation growth also required increasing use of mapping technology (Thongchai 1994). In the need to centralise political power of the nation, the government took gradual control of nationwide natural resources, thus establishing new property regimes. The establishment of the Royal Forestry Department in 1896, headed by Mr. H. Slade, marked the beginning of a state property regime as all forests belonged to the nation (Bawornsak 1993). A private property regime was officially confirmed with the establishment of Department of Lands in 1901 and the initiation of cadastral survey, land registration and titling (Tongroj 1990). Extensive resource inventory and planning using modern technology began with the First National Economic and Social Development Plan (1961-1966). The Department of Land Development (DLD), established in 1963, is responsible for soil surveying, mapping soils, land use and land capability. The classification techniques are based on the U.S. soil taxonomy system, FAO's land evaluation techniques, remote sensing and geographic information systems. Forest lands are continually inventoried by the Royal Forestry Department (RFD) while cultivated areas are surveyed by the Office of Agricultural Economics. With the need to cope with soil erosion and water depletion, the Office of the National Environmental Board (ONEB) has been a facilitating agency in classifying and managing watershed areas in the whole country since 1982 (ONEB 1990). Other agencies are responsible for particular aspects of land, water and forest. One study reports that there are as many as 19 government agencies involved in land management (TDRI 1988).

The use of western, scientific technology equips the bureaucracy with enormous power to manage resources. As the state hegemony extends increasingly into villages, scientific knowledge is encouraged to take supremacy over indigenous knowledge. When policies fail, the bureaucracy often claim that local people do not possess knowledge and thus are backward. In this way, indigenous knowledge of the poor and the marginalised is not recognised by the state.

During the 1980s, there was a revival of interest in indigenous knowledge because centralised, technocratically oriented solutions failed to improve the prospects of many rural people. Some academics, NGOs and local people believe that local wisdom may indicate local peoples's potential to cope with or resist external forces or changes (Seri 1993; Chayan 1993). Even some sectors in the bureaucracy have become interested in aspects of indigenous knowledge, such as the Office of the National Culture Commission (ONCC), and the Ministry of Public Health (Suwit and Komatr 1987; Office of the National Culture Commission 1991).

COMPARISON OF LAND CLASSIFICATION SYSTEMS

It is not easy to compare the two knowledge systems because they are based on different concepts of land and soils. A local knowledge system employs the concept of land and soils as habitat for crops because the livelihood of local people depends upon agriculture in any particular micro-environment. On the other hand, scientific classification is based on the concept of soils as natural bodies (Brady 1974). The latter concept aims for appropriate, efficient and sustained use of land according to soil properties from local to regional scales. In other words, it aims for universal applicability rather than agriculture *per se*. The best use of land from an indigenous perspective may not correlate with the best use of land from a scientific perspective, as the former is influenced by dynamic land use interests of communities. For example, short cultivation-long fallow type of upland cultivation which is appropriate from the Lua and Karen perspectives may be susceptible to erosion from a pedological perspective. This is because the cultivation is on slopes exceeding 35 percent where in principle rangeland, agroforestry or forest protection should be practiced instead.

Each system employs a different set of evaluative criteria. The scientific system depends upon field collection of concrete, quantifiable data on physical and chemical properties of land and soils. The analysis is based on the total soil profile from surface layers down to parent materials. Special attention is given to a broad range of physical factors such as terrain types, soil texture, structure, particle and bulk densities, porosity, consistency, colour, moisture and profile arrangement. Chemical properties include organic matter content, mineral content, reaction, salinity and other properties. The indigenous systems tend to analyse only discernible characteristics of surface soils since local people are concerned mainly with agriculture. Some physical factors may be similar to the scientific system, but analysis is much simpler, using human senses. Such factors are terrain, slope, aspect, soil texture, soil taste, color, temperature and vegetation cover. What makes them differ from the scientific system is the observation of signs, for example from animals and human dreams. To some ethnic groups, these observations may indicate possible misfortune related to use of a certain piece of land for agriculture.

The communication of scientific analysis of land is normally based on maps and reports with standardised soil nomenclature derived from pedogenetic criteria. For example, Ustic Dystropepts, or Phayao series, suggests clayey-skeletal, mixed soils originating from acidic bedrocks under tropical climate (Erb 1990). Added to this are soil series, associations and capability and suitability classes. These semantic classes are meant for universal applicability. The communication of indigenous analysis is normally a simple description of land and soils (Tables 1-3), and on the level of mental mapping. Description and analysis of land and soil qualities is tied to exact place names. For instance, Karen farmers in Mae Sariang village define *din dam* as a good paddy soil found in lowland areas such as along a stream called *Jimaejokro* (Shalardchai et al 1993). This taxonomy reflects dynamic land use considerations of the communities. In addition, certain place names may conjure up the association of soils, terrains, land uses and other natural resources in the mental mapping of farmers. To Thawangpa villagers, *Na bon* is a specific lowland area in the village where soils are good for growing rice, chili, onion, garlic. Fish, crabs and frogs are also available in that place. Mental mapping of a local resource inventory can be precise. One villager in this village can tell from afar, at the sound of a falling tree in a certain direction, what species and where that tree is.

Table 1
Indigenous Land Classification of Thawangpha Village

Terrains	Soil Textures and Colors	Land Uses
teud (lowland)	*din dam, din dak, din hae din khi pong, din ruan, din pon hin*	paddy
term or *merng* (gentle slopes)	*din daeng* *din sai* and *din pon hin*	paddy and upland crops upland crops
jing (steep slopes)	no available data	forest
tad (cliff)	no available data	forest
san (mountain tops or ridges)	no available data	upland crops, forest

Table 2
Scientific Land Classification of Thawangpha Village

Terrains	Soil Series	Nomenclature	Paddy Suitability*	Land capability for upland crops*
floodplains	alluvial soils	not available	P I, P IIIs	U IVd
semi-recent terraces	Hang Dong	Typic Tropaqualfs	PI	UIIId
old terraces	Mae Rim	Oxic Paleustults; loamy-skeletal, mixed	P Vt	U VIs
mountains	slope complex	not available	PVt	UVIIe

* Codes used are as follows:
1. Soil Suitability Grouping for Paddy Rice (P)
   PI = soils very well suited for paddy land, having no significant limitations for rice production. There is sufficient water available from rainfall and/or irrigation for at least one high-yielding crop of rice in most years.

Table 3

Indigenous Evaluation of Suitable and Unsuitable Characteristics of Land for Agriculture

Features	Suitable Characteristics	Unsuitable Characteristics
terrain	floodplain, river terrace, mountain top	steep slopes
aspect	east	west
soil color	black, reddish	gray, orange, yellowish
soil taste	bitter	acidic, saline
soil texture	clayey loam	sandy, gravelly
vegetation	Dipterocarpus alatus Roxb. Dipterocarpus turbinatus Polyalthia virides Craib bamboos bananas	Pentacme suavis Dipterocarpus obtusifolius Schoutenia hypoleuca Pierre Shorea obtusa Wall.

PIIIs = soils moderately suited for paddy land, having moderate limitations that restrict their use for rice production and/or require special management In this case, s = soil limitations in the root zone, such as shallowness, unfavourable texture, stoniness or low fertility that is difficult to correct.

PVt = soils generally not suited for paddy land, having very severe limitations that preclude their use for rice production with ordinary methods. In this case, t = unfavourable topography. They are soils of which relative position or relief (macro or micro) limits use for crops and paddy in particular.

2. Land Capability Classification for Upland Crops (U)

UIVd = soils poorly suited for upland crops, having severe limitations that restrict the choice of crops and/or require very careful management. In this case, d = impeded drainage. These are soils of which use for upland crops is limited by excess water due to high water table, slow permeability or slow surface drainage or a combination of all three limitations.

UIIId = soils moderately suited for upland crops, having moderate limitations that reduce the choice of crops and/or require special management. 'd' has the same meaning as in UIVd

UVIs = soils having severe limitations that make them generally unsuited for cultivation and limit their use to pasture, woodland, wildlife food and cover and water supply. 's' = soil limitations in the root zone. Similar to PIIIs.

UVIIe = soils and land types having limitations that preclude their use for commercial plant production and restrict their use to recreation, wildlife food and cover and water supply. 'e' = erosion. These are soils with an erosion hazard or past erosion damage.

COMPARISON OF FOREST CLASSIFICATION SYSTEMS

The interpretation and meaning of forest between indigenous and scientific systems differ significantly. Forest functions as an integral part of peasant subsistence farming systems in the mountainous regions interspersed with narrow valleys (Anan 1992). Rice production in the valleys, under the condition of limited land and uncontrollable water supply, is made possible by the *muangfai* irrigation system. However, rice production from irrigated land in small river valleys may not suffice, and supplementation with upland rice and crops is vital. Forest is thus indispensable to both irrigated lowland paddy fields and upland swidden plots. While watershed forests yield water to irrigated farmland, soil fertility under fallow swidden plots recover through forest succession. By contrast, technocrats in the bureaucracy have regarded forests as an important source of state revenues since 1896. Forest land is a potential supply of capital resources for economic development such as supply of land for land allocation schemes, hydropower, irrigation, and commercial tree plantations since 1954 (Komon and Thomas 1990). Thus, scientific classification of forest serves the role of maintaining forests as state property, for production, protection and allocation purposes on a much broader scale than indigenous classification.

The indigenous classification of land and forest resources is done in terms of ecology, land use and land tenure. The ecological classification of forest corresponds with classification for utilitarian purposes. In terms of land use, there are three broad categories of forests : watershed forests, sacred forests and village woodlots. Watershed forest (*pa khun nam, pa ton nam,* or *pa sap nam*) is usually forest at the headwaters from which villagers draw domestic or irrigated water supply. Identification of such forest includes its headwater location as well as denser forest structure. Thawangpha villagers identify it as dense headwater forest with large trees, the half-circumferences of which measure more than 10 *kams* (a *kam* is a hand length of approximately four to five inches. This type of forest usually covers a large area of evergreen or mixed deciduous forests. A survey of 153 community forests found that the sizes of watershed forests range from 40 to 40,000 *rai* (6.25 *rai* = 1 ha) depending upon whether such watershed forests are managed separately by a single village, or the management of a piece of contiguous forests is shared by several villages or several tambons (Shalardchai et al 1993). In addition to headwater forests, forests in the vicinity of springs (*nam sap* or *nam jam*) as well as forest along stream banks may be included. Watershed forest is strictly protected by communities, and minimal uses are allowed only in some cases. For example, a group of users can harvest *luk tao* (seeds of *Arenga Pinnata* sugar palm) in a watershed forest of Thawangpha district in Nan province (Shalardchai et al 1993).

The second type of forest is sacred forest whose size is generally much smaller than watershed forest, ranging from 15 to 200 *rai*. However, it may form a part of watershed forest or woodlot forest, or it may stay in the vicinity of the village compound. This forest may correspond with either evergreen forest patches or patches of mixed or dry deciduous forest. It is preserved mainly for such religious or ceremonial purposes as *pa pra that* (site of a pagoda containing the Buddha relics), *pa aphaiyathan* (Buddhist temple ground forest where all lifeforms are forgiven and protected), *pa sua ban* (forest of village guardian spirits), forest around cremation grounds, and forest for keeping the belongings of the dead (the last is related to Karen culture). Also included in this category are individual trees that are significant to the life of an individual person. For example, Karen people keep the umbilical cord of a new born baby on a large tree with the belief that it contains *kwan*, or life essence, of that person. The wellbeing of the tree means the wellbeing of that person (see Pratuang in this volume). Other studies mention different types of sacred forests. Hmong people preserve *Ntoo Seeb* tree near the village (Prasit 1991). Akha people stictly protect forests near such sacred objects as a sacred well and a village gate (Aju 1991). The category also includes haunted forests that are not for ceremonial purposes. Disturbance is forbidden for fear of misfortune. For example, Lahu people dare not disturb forests around banyan trees and places where unnatural death occurs (Charoen 1991).

The third type of forest is *pa chai soi*, or village woodlot, where grazing, timber cutting, gathering of food, medicinal plants, firewood and other forest products are allowed to a certain extent and to specific groups of users. The vernacular name of this forest may vary. For Mae Sariang villagers, the name is *pa kep tong* because they gather leaves of *Dipterocarpus tuberculatus* to wrap around food or to thatch roofs. For some villagers who raise cattle in the forest, the forest may be called *pa liang sat*. The size of this type of forest may range from 100 *rai* to 5,000 *rai*. It is normally a dry dipterocarp forest covering lateritic soils that is unsuitable for cultivation. Also included in this category is *pa hua rai plai na*, or groups of trees at the edge of paddy and upland crop fields. Many communities protect this forest, thus allowing forest to regenerate.

The boundaries among these types of indigenous forest are not mutually exclusive. There are cases where they physically overlap. For example, patches of sacred forest may occupy a place within a village woodlot. In terms of ownership, *pa hua rai plai na* is private property, the exclusivity of which depends on local rules. All the other types of forests are common property resources whose boundaries are agreed upon by members of communities. The boundary lines may not be physically discernible, but they have been recognised by nearby communities since former times. The boundaries are agreed upon based on such natural features as mountain divides and stream channels.

Scientific classification of state forest consists of a classification system in terms of ecology and management. Ecological classification encompasses lower montane, coniferous, dry evergreen, moist mixed deciduous, dry mixed deciduous and dry deciduous dipterocarp forests (Tem et al 1978). There are several classification systems in terms of management. In 1964, forty percent of land area in Thailand was allocated for conservation and economic forests. The National Forest Policy of 1985 specifies that conservation forest should occupy fifteen percent of total forest land, whereas economic forest should cover the remaining 25 percent (Komon and Thomas 1990). The percentage was reversed between these two categories in 1989, and in 1991, the percentage of gazetted conservation forests was futher increased to 27.5 percent (Apichai

1995). Demarcation by remote sensing techniques did not exclude settlements in the forest. This leads to conflicts between RFD and forest occupants. In an effort to solve land rights problems, the Ministry of Agriculture and Cooperatives reclassified forest areas into three broad types, based on agricultural suitability of land and degree of forest encroachment: economic zone, land reform zone and preservation zone (MIDAS Agronomics Company 1991). Land in the economic zone is still covered with forest, and it will remain a forest reserve. The land reform zone consists of land that is encroached and is suitable for agriculture. It must be placed under the RFD land usufruct certificates program (STK), or under the land reform program of the Agricultural Land Reform Office (ALRO). The preservation zone includes national parks, wildlife sanctuaries and watershed areas. In response to soil and water problems in watershed areas, the government issued cabinet resolutions between 1985 and 1991 to classify watershed areas in the north, northeast, south and central regions respectively (Midas Agronomics Company 1991). The watershed classification is quantitatively calculated, based on six physical criteria including slope, elevation, landforms, soils, geology and existence of forest cover. It classifies land into five watershed classes (Office of the National Environment Board 1990). Only the area designated as class I is protected forest. It is under forest cover and is usually at high elevation with steep slopes. The class is subdivided into class 1A and class 1B. The former is a forest with no significant occupation or agricultural activities. The latter covers forest area with significant agricultural clearings or other disturbances that require special soil conservation protection measures. Management of the remaining watershed classes differs in degrees of activities on them. In addition, demarcation of scientifically classified forest relies not only upon natural landmarks but also on signs on trees, and stakes buried at intervals in the ground (MIDAS Agronomics Company 1991).

Although protection of watershed forest in scientific and indigenous systems is strict, the bureaucracy allows some land use exceptions. For example, mining, roads or uses by some state agencies in class I watershed forest may be permitted by the cabinet. The indigenous system cannot afford such flexibility in the watershed forest because survival of communities depends upon the health of the microecosystem. For example, two factions in the Thawangpha village have different opinions on the use of dead and windblown trees in the watershed forest. One faction wants to use the trees to avoid cutting timber in the village woodlot. Another faction prefers to use a restricted quantity of woodlot timber instead of using dead and fallen trees in the watershed forest. They argue that in order to move the trees from the watershed forest, some living trees must be cut to provide some support for sawing, thus the watershed trees will be destroyed. The factions cannot agree, so the watershed forest is left undisturbed.

Other than to watershed forest, the scientific classification system offers no protection of forest corridors along stream channels. By contrast, in many indigenous systems, the protection of a forest corridor helps conserve water collection zones in the drainage basin. Moreover, the protection of forest around springs helps keep moisture and prevents their sedimentation.

Classification is meant for management purposes. Rules and guidelines for indigenous resource management are far from scientific methods of management. In the scientific system, technocrats have played important roles for decades in classifying and planning at the national, regional or provincial levels without public participation. As the state declares forest land to be state property, centralised management is necessary. A number of implementing agencies are responsible for narrowly defined aspects of forest land. For example, the RFD is responsible for existing forest land. ALRO deals with degraded forest land that is degazetted for land allocation purposes. The Forest Industry Organisation is responsible for commercial wood production. The Interior Ministry extends its administration into forest settlements providing infrastructure, administration and services. In addition, there are other agencies using forest land for particular purposes such as road construction, dams and reservoirs, electricity transmission, communication, schools and others. The management of forest land, therefore, is not coordinated or integrated among government agencies. Adding to the problem are insufficient funds and personnel. This results in inefficiency and ineffectiveness in forest management.

Indigenous systems, on the other hand, deals with the local level which is more manageable. Management decisions are traditionally carried out by institutions within the village such as irrigation groups, groups of elders and temple groups. Members of communities participate in establishing customary rules to conserve and utilise communal forest, allowing their members exclusive rights and duties to forest resources. Thus, only those who help protect the forest have a right to benefit from it. The rules are based on sustainable use for communal benefits and not for individual benefits. To illustrate, trees in *pa chai soi* may be cut for such communal uses as repairing temples and weirs. Individual use of timber is restricted in amount and is reserved for the poor and for new couples only. Villagers are allowed to collect forest products for domestic uses. For example, a fair amount of bamboo shoots can be collected for consumption, but they cannot be sold because this will exceed the carrying capacity of the forest. As villagers often go into the forest for forest products, they can keep an eye on intruders or violators. In places where conflicts arise, patrolling groups may watch at regular, though secret, intervals. Leniency is used with violators. They may be warned, fined or sanctioned depending on repetition of violation. Villagers seldom report to the police about violation. This is partly because at the present time they have no legal rights to protect forest. Moreover, legal measures are only used as the last resort since villagers value good social relations in the area.

COSMOLOGY OF FOREST MANAGEMENT

When compared with the scientific system, indigenous systems are more holistic in that they encompass physical, human and supernatural spheres. The scientific system tends to emphasise physical more than human considerations. The supernatural sphere is absent as it is considered not scientific. The bureaucracy pays attention to the application of technology in solving resource problems based on the concept that humans dominate nature. In contrast, indigenous people perceive their environment as a part of a complex system where people cannot be separated from nature. Another important element in the system is that nature is owned, guarded and regulated by supernatural power. This power comprises not only good spirits of watersheds, paddy land, weirs, and trees, but also evil spirits haunting streams, springs and salt licks ready to punish intruders. In order to use resources, humans must ask permission and blessings from good spirits. At the same time, they must also try to avoid disturbing bad spirits. Violation of rules over resources leads to punishment from spirits such as drought and famine. In this way, the disturbance of any of the three components will have impacts on one another. Scientific systems are not as integrated as indigenous systems. Even ecology, which is an integrative science, regards the interrelationship of people and nature only from a material perspective.

Nevertheless, the cultural and moral values of indigenous resources has weakened in recent years with the increasing incorporation of villages into the national polity and economy. As rural labour migrates toward cities, and competition and conflicts over local resources intensify, traditional beliefs in supernatural power have gradually eroded, especially among the younger generation. However, many local people still remain committed to community forest protection. This indicates the potential of villagers to translate their sense of belonging to their community into action. There are many cases in northern Thailand where villagers try to cope with outsiders who want to exploit their land and forest resources. Many of the disputes stem directly from the use of classification systems.

CONFLICTS ARISING FROM CLASSIFICATION SYSTEMS

Soil and land classification schema of the two knowledge systems do not come into conflict, because the 1983 Land Development Act provides land use guidelines without giving power to enforce it. However, forest land classification does create conflict. Conflicts between indigenous and scientific forest classification systems dates back to the 1960s and competing land ownership claims between communities and the central government. With the passages of the 1960 Wildlife Preservation Act, the 1961 National Park Act and the 1964 Reserved Forest Act, the government has continually enclosed more forest areas to conserve natural forest and solve deforestation problems. These laws facilitate rapid mapping and gazetting by reducing land claim verification requirements (Komon and Thomas 1990). Many older settlements already existed in the gazetted forest areas (Midas Agronomics Company 1991).

In terms of property regimes, many community forests, particularly indigenous watershed forest, overlap with state conservation forest. Consequently, confrontation between local communities, the RFD, and other parties such as forest concessionaires about rights over resources is inevitable. The disputes intensified during the 1980s when RFD realised the scale of forest depletion and shifted emphasis to conservation policies following the implementation of the 1985 National Forest Policy, and the 1985 declaration of an official Watershed Classification System. Eviction from conservation forests and reforestation with fast-growing species in the economic forest have become widespread as the state tries to establish hegemony over forest resources.

At the root of the conflicts lie the debates on definitions of forest, property regimes, and the question of whether people can or cannot live in the forest. Legal definition of forest is land which is not owned by anyone under the 1941 Forestry Act, regardless of presence or absence of vegetation cover. Therefore, completely deforested land continues to have the status of forest. For some officials, forest is a collection of trees growing together which may not be a plant community and may include both natural forest and tree plantations. For indigenous people, forest means a plant and wildlife community, found on an extensive open space, which provides food, medicine, forest products, and water. Therefore, the cultivated cropland of a forest settlement, which is not a forest from an indigenous perspective, may end up being within the boundaries of state forest land from a legal perspective. Strong protests can also take place with development projects in reserved forest, such as forestry concessions, if they overlap with communal watershed forest or other types of communal forests. The 1993 survey found that protection of 64 out of 153 community forests in northern Thailand (42 percent) was initiated by protests against logging companies in the watershed areas (Shalardchai et al 1993).

One example from this research is the overlapping boundaries between a reserved forest and the upland cultivated plots in Thawangpha village. About 100 *rai* of the land was left under fallow, and secondary forest started to regenerate. RFD hired labour from other villages to cut small trees, and planted with commercial species such as teak (*Tectona grandis*), *mai sor* (*Gmelina arborea*), *takian* (Hopea adorata Roxb.) and *pradu* (*Pterocarpus macrocarpus*). Villagers are forbidden to continue cultivating the land, even though they still pay land utilisation tax on that land. Without sufficient care for the planted species from the RFD side and negligence from the people's side, the seedlings soon died and the whole plot reverted to secondary forest. During early 1990s, a national park was to be formally established in the area. This would overlap with a large expanse of community forests and cultivated plots of many communities at the edge of forest in several districts along the north-south boundaries of the proposed national park. Local people have been negotiating with RFD to excise villages, cultivated land and communal forest from the national park area. However, RFD tends to excise only villages and paddy fields, whereas upland cultivated areas and community forests will become national park. Villagers harbour bitter feelings towards the future enclosure of these two types of land. They mention that the transformation of communal forest and private cropland into state land will create an open-access regime where anyone can exploit the forest that they have protected for a long time. As the cultivation of upland crops is discouraged, villagers have to migrate to find jobs outside villages, weakening the forest surveillance activities.

The use of two knowledge systems as instruments of competing, unequal social groups has culminated in the debate on the Community Forestry Bill. The Bill is expected to provide a common ground between the state and villagers by granting some degree of local rights over management of natural resources. The RFD, academics, NGOs and local people have been discussing the Bill for several years around several issues. The presence of the RFD's and the people's versions of the Bill indicates that the RFD still wants to cling to its power over forests. After prolonged debates and negotiations, involved parties agreed to draft a new version of the Community Forestry Bill together in April 1996.

CULTURAL REPRODUCTION AND ADAPTATION OF INDIGENOUS KNOWLEDGE

In an effort to defend their customary rights to control and protect forest resources for members of their own community and to assert the point to the bureaucracy that people and forest can coexist, villagers use two strategies: application of their traditional values to more formal practices, and adoption of scientific method. The formalisation of traditional values and practices can be seen in various forms. First of all, many communities start to translate their customary regulations of forest resource management into written form. Informal groups are transformed into more formal organisations such as village councils and, in some cases, tambon councils (see Apichai in this volume). Special organisations are set up for conservation purposes. Analysis of these formal organisations in research sites found that members of irrigation groups and temple groups overlap with those of village councils. Moreover, religious rituals are applied to conservation such as *buad ton mai* (tree ordainment) and *seub chata maenam* (river life blessings) (see Taylor in this volume). Despite the gradual erosion of beliefs in guardian spirits, villagers are still able to retain the sense of communality by asserting the rights of human guardians of resources. Only those who protect and look after resources have rights to benefit from them. Therefore, outsiders who do not take care of resources have no rights to use and must be excluded. This concept is crystallised into slogans. An example of a Karen slogan is "We drink from streams, we must protect streams. We eat from the forest, we must protect the forest".

Apart from application of traditional values and practices, confrontation with outsiders prompts villagers to adopt some scientific techniques to improve their strategies in defending their customary rights. One example is the resource mapping of their own community and the construction of cardboard or wooden models of their communities. Shown on the maps and models are land use types including different community forests. These techniques have spread to many communities in the North. They are imitations of maps and models seen in some RFD projects such as the Sam Mun Highland Development Project in Chiang Mai and Mae Hong Son. The preparation of most models is assisted by government officials and facilitated by NGOs and academics. Some communities, such as Mae Chan village, have made maps and carried out ground demarcation of *pa aphaiyathan* forest with the cooperation of RFD personnel. As for the demarcation, a growing number of villages add new types of demarcation. For example, they adopt roads, signs on trees, tree lines, and stakes. Mae Chan village has used a combination of land tax collection zones and a stream channel to demarcate boundaries between neighboring villages and forest.

Another technique that villagers try to adopt is reforestation, but their interpretation is not similar to that of RFD. In addition to allowing natural forest recovery, villagers learn to keep nurseries and plant tree seedlings. Reforestation strategies differ among villages. Mae Chan villagers planted commercial trees propagated by monks in the temple nursery. Mae Ai villagers used fast-growing species that the RFD gave to them. Thawangpha villagers used fruit trees, such as mango and tamarind, obtained from the local agricultural extension service to delineate boundaries between the national park and their community forest and private cropland. Mae Sariang villagers neither keep nurseries nor obtain seedlings from state agencies. They transplanted native plants that are believed to retain soil moisture from spring areas to watershed forest during the rainy season. They were successful as all the native trees survive.

CONCLUSION

Scientific knowledge has served as an important instrument of the state in managing natural resources. Technocrats have played important roles in centralised decision-making with minimal public participation. Indigenous knowledge has been a well-integrated instrument of local people that has proven effective in the past.

Competition for local resources in modern Thailand affects the lives of rural people. Their coping strategies involve the reproduction and adaptation of their cultural and moral values in the new context. Even though some communities succeed and some fail, this cultural reproduction indicates their potential as resource managers. Such potential should be enhanced as the state cannot work successfully by itself. The state should provide an opportunity for local people's participation by granting them rights to manage their own resources with some technical assistance from the bureaucracy. Collaborative management will strengthen people's organisations, which is essential to the solution of local environmental problems.

REFERENCES

Aju Jupo, 1991, Akha Livelihood and Mountain Forests, *Life on the Mountain* 6, pp 20-21, (in Thai).

Anan Ganjanapan, 1992, Community Forestry Management in Northern Thailand, In Amara Pongsapich, Michael C. Howard, and Jacques Amyot (eds), *Regional Development and Change in Southeast Asia in the 1990s*, pp 75-84, Social Research Institute, Chulalongkorn University, Bangkok.

Anan Ganjanapan, 1995, Social Change and Potential of the Thai Community Potential, In Chalong Suntharawanit (ed.), *Critiques of Thai Society*, pp. 151-191, The Social Science Association of Thailand, Bangkok , Amarin Printing and Publishing, (in Thai).

Apichai Puntasen, 1995, Forest Crisis and Future Solutions, In Samai Apapirom and Yaowanan Chetharat (eds.), *State of the Thai Environment 1995*, pp. 112-125, The Green World Foundation, Bangkok , Amarin Printing and Publishing, (in Thai).

Bawornsak Uwanno, 1993, Notes on Legal and Policy Issues on Natural Resources, In Wiwat Khatithammanit, ed, *Community Rights: Decentralisation of Power to Manage Resources*, pp 491-502, Bangkok, Local Development Institute, (in Thai).

Brady, Neil C. 1974, *The Nature and Properties of Soils*, 8th ed, New York, Macmillan Publishing.

Charoen Dhammabandit, 1991, Lahu, *Life on the Mountain* 6, pp 16-19, (in Thai).

Chayan Vaddhanaphuti, 1993, Traditions of Village Study in Thailand, In Philip Hirsch (ed.), *The Village in Perspective , Community and Locality in Rural Thailand*, pp 9-38, Social Research Institute, Chiang Mai University, Chiang Mai.

Erb Khiew-reunrom, 1990, *Soils of Thailand: Characteristics, Distribution and Uses*, Department of Soil Science, Kasetsart University, Bangkok, (in Thai).

Komol Pragtong and David E. Thomas, 1990, Evolving Management Systems in Thailand, In Mark Poffenberger (ed), *Keepers of the Forest , Land Management Alternatives in Southeast Asia*, pp. 167-186, Connecticut , Kumarian Press.

Kunstadter, Peter and E.C. Chapman, 1978, Problems of Shifting Cultivation and Economic Development in Thailand, In Peter Kunstadter, E.C. Chapman, and Sanga Sabhasri, *Farmers in the Forest: Economic Development and Marginal Agriculture in Northern Thailand*, pp 3-23, East-West Center, Honolulu , University of Hawaii Press.

MIDAS Agronomics Company, 1991, *Study of Conservation Forest Area Demarcation, Protection and Occupancy in Thailand, Volume I, Main Report*, Prepared for the World Bank, Bangkok, Thailand.

Office of the National Culture Commission, 1991, *Indigenous Knowledge, Cultural Work and Rural Development*, Bangkok, Amarin Printing Group, (in Thai).

Office of the National Environment Board, 1990, *Cabinet Resolutions Concerning Watershed Classification*, (in Thai).

Prasert Trakarnsupakorn and Pala Arunworarak, 1991, Conservation Wisdom of Karen Communities, *Life on the Mountain* 6 , 4-9, (in Thai).

Prasit Leepreecha, 1991, Hmong under Changes, *Life on the Mountain* 6, pp 25-27, (in Thai).

Preecha Piampongsarn, 1994, Poverty, Environment and Development, In Jaturong Boonyaratanasoonthorn (ed.), *Methodology in Thai Studies , New Directions in Development* (2nd ed.), pp 81-195, Bangkok, Edison Press Product.

Sakda Saenmee, 1991, Forest Conservation According to the Beliefs and Rituals of Lisu People, *Life on the Mountain* 6, pp 22-24, (in Thai).

Seri Pongpit (ed.), 1993, *Indigenous Knowledge and Rural Development*, Phumpanya Foundation and Village Foundation, Bangkok, Amarin Printing Group, (in Thai).

Shalardchai Ramitanond, Anan Ganjanapan and Santita Ganjanapan, 1993, *Community Forestry in Thailand , Directions of Development, Volume 2, Community Forestry in the North*, Bangkok, Local Development Institute, (in Thai).

Somkuan Charoentempiam, 1991, Soil Conservation of Lua People, *Life on the Mountain* 6, pp 10-11, (in Thai).

Suwit Wiboolpholprasert and Komatr Jeungsathiansap (eds), 1987, *Traditional Thai Medicine , Wisdom of Self-Reliance*, Bangkok , Morchaoban Press, (in Thai).

Thawil Chotichaiwibul, 1991, Customs and Forest Conservation, *Life on the Mountain* 6, pp 12-15, (in Thai).

Tem Smitinand, Sanga Sabhasri, and Peter Kunstadter, 1978, The Environment of Northern Thailand, In Peter Kunstadter, E.C. Chapman, and Sanga Sabhasri (eds.), *Farmers in the Forest: Economic Development and Marginal Agriculture in Northern Thailand*, pp 24-40, East-West Center, Honolulu, University of Hawaii Press.

Thailand Development Research Institute, 1988, *Thailand Natural Resource Profile,* Bangkok.

Thongchai Winichakul, 1994, *Siam Mapped, A History of the Geo-Body of a Nation*, Chiang Mai, Silkworm Books.

Tongroj Onchan (e.d), 1990, *A Land Policy Study*, The Thailand Development Research Institute Foundation Research Monograph No. 3, Bangkok, The Thailand Development Research Institute Foundation.

Wiwat Khatithammanit, ed, 1993, *Community Rights: Decentralisation of Power to Manage Resources*, Bangkok, Local Development Institute, (in Thai).

SUSTAINABLE AGRICULTURE IN THAILAND

Nitasmai Tantemsapya

INTRODUCTION

Agriculture was once the largest and most important sector of the Thai economy. Only a generation ago, three quarters of the country's working population were engaged in agricultural production and earning about one third of the national income, while agricultural exports were the major source of foreign exchange earnings.

Due to structural changes in the Thai economy which started in the 1960s, the industrial and service sectors began to supplement agriculture as significant income and employment generators. The government implemented systematic plans aimed to develop the physical infrastructure and move the country towards industrialisation, not realizing that in the long-term this development would partly injure the country's agricultural sector and the environment.

Thailand shifted its agricultural *modus operandi*, which formerly concentrated on food production for domestic consumption, to export-oriented agricultural systems in order to boost economic growth. Agricultural strategies which did not take into account the possible environmental impacts and effects of intensive production backfired: a country once endowed with plentiful natural resources and blessed with large expanses of fertile land and ideal growing conditions is currently facing a whole host of problems: natural resources over-exploitation, environmental degradation, deforestation, rural poverty, social imbalances, and many others.

Sustainable agriculture, a new approach for the development of agricultural practices, has been deemed to be the cure for these problems. In Thailand, such approaches have been carried out for several years, but only on a very small scale. Chemical farming culture persists. Sustainable agricultural practices are still not popular among the majority of farmers. Local NGOs have, to a certain extent, contributed to the development of the sustainable agriculture movement in the country. The government, on the other hand, continues to support conventional, high-input agriculture. Although there has been rising concern amongst consumers as to the dangers of chemical-grown produce, it will be a long time before pesticide-free vegetables and hygienic produce become a staple in Thai households.

AGRICULTURAL DEVELOPMENT IN THAILAND

Agricultural growth in Thailand since the 1960s

After the Second World War, many countries in the Third World became preoccupied with the problem of feeding a rapidly growing population. The solution was to increase per capita food production. The means was the green revolution. This focused mainly on the three interrelated actions of breeding programs for crops which produced high-yielding varieties, organization and distribution of packages of high pay-off inputs, such as fertilizers, pesticides and water regulation, and implementation of technical innovations (Conway and Barbier 1990: 19). The green revolution made exceptional impacts on the Third World. Overall per capita food production in developing countries has risen by 7 percent since the mid 1960s (Conway and Barbier 1990: 20), and by more than 27 percent in Asia.

Similarly to other developing countries, Thailand entered the green revolution determining to resolve the problem of feeding a rapidly growing population. From 1947 to 1961, the country's population increased from 17.4 million to 27 million. By 1989 that number had further risen to 55.2 million (Amphol 1993: 14). In response, there needed to be an expansion in per capita food production. The Thai government implemented a policy supporting farmers expeditiously to produce various kinds of crops beside rice At the same time, it supported forest clearance to make more land available for agricultural purposes.

Agricultural development thinking in Thailand during the 1960s focused mainly on increasing the production of upland crops and perennial crops. During the 1970s and the 1980s, western countries played a major role in organizing agricultural research networks throughout Asia and the Pacific under the supervision of the Consultative Group on International Agricultural Research (CGIAR). The group provided support in terms of consultation and financial assistance to Thai research institutes located in various parts of the country. Agricultural development and research directions during those times similarly put emphasis on increasing the production of upland crops and perennial crops, which included sorghum, groundnut, potato, sweet cassava and other root and tuber products. However, local research centres carried out numerous agricultural research projects which neither profited nor raised the level of the country's economy, but rather benefited industrialized countries and large multi-national companies (Policy Analysis and Recommendations for the Development of Alternative Agriculture 1992: 50). The Thai government supported a policy for large-scale agriculture and agro-industries for export. Contract farming was introduced as another farming system.

After the government implemented the First National Economic and Social Development Plan in 1961, Thailand shifted from a country with an agricultural system which mainly concentrated on food production for domestic consumption supported by rice exports, to a country which emphasized export-oriented agricultural development. Consequently, as agricultural production was geared towards cash-crop farming, the country became even more dependent on the use of external resources and technological inputs such as imported farm equipment and seeds. The use of chemical fertilizers and insecticides had increased drastically. Intensive application of technology, capital and chemical pesticides began to supersede the limits of the environment.

The consequences of unsustainable agricultural practices

Agricultural development and strategies which did not take into account the possible environmental impacts and displacement effects of increased production in the past two decades in Thailand contributed to a relative retardation of the country's agricultural sector. Until the 1970s, agriculture accounted for 40 - 50 percent of Thailand's GDP. Today, that number has decreased to less than 15 percent. In the next decade, it is expected to fall below 10 percent (Boonsawasdi et al., 1993: 40). A number of impacts are associated with past patterns of agricultural development.

Impact on land

The government policy of rapidly increasing agricultural production for export from the 1960s led to an enormous increase in agricultural land area. Expansion of cash cropping for export and the push for food production without proper management techniques or agricultural practices depleted the nutrient content of the most fertile land and caused soil erosion and exhaustion problems. Together with the import of chemical fertilizers and insecticides, coupled with the lack of effective regulation and mindful implementation of these compounds, this brought about a less than optimal allocation of land use and resulted in land damaged by salinity and soil degradation.

Impact on forest

The strategies to achieve rapid increases in export crop production also led to the problem of forest encroachment and deforestation. Forest areas were turned into agricultural land for growing rice, upland crops, perennial crops, palm and rubber. Between 1961 - 1989, national forests decreased from about 187.5 million *rai* to only 90 million *rai* (Amphol 1993: 18). From 1989 to 1991, they further decreased to approximately 85 million *rai* (Office of Agricultural Economics 1992: 226). In 1991, forest land constituted only 26.64 percent of the country's total land area, compared to farm land which made up 41.50 percent of the total land area (Office of

Agricultural Economics 1992: 215). The rest of the total land area (31.86 percent) was unclassified land, which is composed of swamp land, sanitary district area, municipal area, railroads, highways, real estate, public area, and others (Office of Agricultural Economics 1992: 214). Tables 1 and 2 show change in forest area and regional land classification. What had been left of forest land in the country could not restore the balance in the ecosystem. As a result, Thailand was left to face many natural disasters, namely drought, floods, loss

Table 1:

Forest Land Area in Thailand From 1982 - 1991

Unit: 1,000 *rai*

Year	Total Land	Forest Land	Percentage
1982	320,697	97,875	30.62
1983	320,697	96,597	30.31
1984	320,697	95,409	29.68
1985	320,697	94,291	29.37
1986	320,697	92,765	29.06
1987	320,697	91,295	28.43
1988	320,697	89,877	28.12
1989	320,697	89,636	27.81
1990	320,697	87,489	27.18
1991	320,697	85,436	26.56

Source: Royal Thai Survey Department & Royal Forestry Department: LANDSAT 3,4 in 1982, LANDSAT 4,5 in 1985, 1988 and LANDSAT-TM in 1989.

Table 2:

Land Utilisation in Thailand by Region, 1991

Unit: *rai*

Region	Total Land	Forest Land (%)	Farm Holding Land (%)	Un-classified Land (%)
North-East	105,533,963	14.38	60.91	36.08
North	106,027,680	51.12	31.17	30.13
Central Plain	64,938,253	9.86	18.60	13.71
South	44,196,992	3.72	7.66	8.16
Whole Kingdom	320,696,888	26.64	41.50	31.86

Source: Royal Thai Survey Department and Royal Forest Department: LANDSAT; 1988, 1989, and 1991.

of vegetation and biodiversity, and environmental pollution such as air and water contamination.

Impact on water resources

Inappropriate use of agricultural inputs produced negative impact on the country's water resources. Erosion associated with intensification of food crop production ultimately caused canals and rivers to silt up. Pesticide misuse and the use of agricultural chemicals polluted water supplies. Fertilizer run-off caused problems of groundwater contamination, eutrophication of surface water, damage to fisheries and biological diversity. Diversion of scarce water supplies to irrigation has led to competition with other uses, notably industrial and domestic consumption.

Impact on human health

The increased dependence on the use of agrochemicals to boost export-crop production not only undermined the natural agricultural resource-base and destroyed natural resources over a wide area. In many circumstances, their use also caused human illness and death.

From 1981 to 1990, the supply of formulated pesticide increased from 26,996 tons to 67,969 tons (Office of Agricultural Economics 1992: 118) (See Figure 1) Between 1982 and 1991, agricultural consumption of chemical fertilizers increased from 1,042,503 tons to 2,487,082 tons (Office of Agricultural Economics 1992: 116) (See Figure 2)

Pesticides have been shown to be associated with cancer, genetic mutation and birth defects (Department of Medical Services 1993: 104). Without proper handling and protection techniques, the application of pesticides can lead to acute toxicity among farmers. Studies carried out by the Agricultural Toxic Substance Division, Department of Agriculture, found a highly significant correlation between death rates among rural people and increasing pesticide use (Policy Analysis and Recommendations for the Development of Alternative Agriculture 1992: 113). Statistics obtained from the Epidemiology Division, The Ministry of Public Health, illustrated

Figure 1:
Supply Quantity of Formulated pesticide, 1981-1990

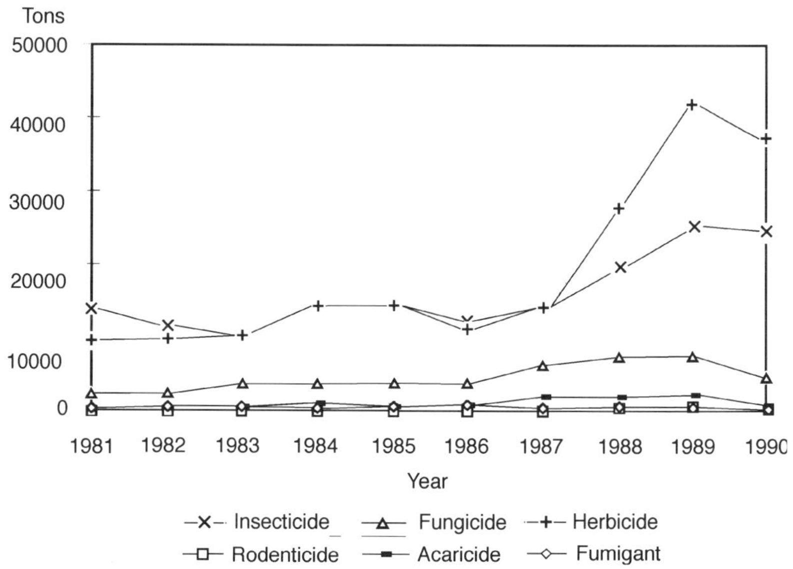

Source: Department of Agriculture, 1992

that in 1975, 518 people suffered from pesticide poisoning while 18 people died. Thirteen years later, in 1988, while the number of patients increased to 4,234, the number of deaths rose to 34 (Policy Analysis and Recommendations for the Development of Alternative Agriculture 1992: 113). Within 13 years, the number of people who suffered from pesticide poisoning grew 8 times while the number of deaths doubled (See Figure 3). Organochlorine and DDT were the two types of pesticides found to have most effect on human health.

Figure 2:
Agricultural Used of Chemical Fertiliser, 1982-1991

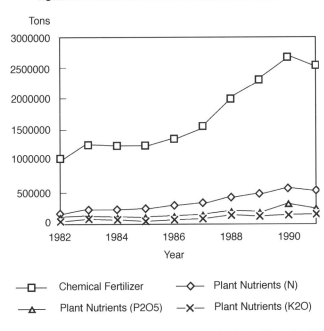

Source: Agricultural Economic Research Division, Office of Agricultural Economics, 1992

Impact on society

Unequal land distribution and the ineffective management of natural resources widened the income gap between rich and poor people and induced conflicts amongst various groups. Rural poverty resulting from falling agricultural income provoked farmers to migrate into Bangkok and other urban centres seeking labouring jobs. Life styles changed. The rural family structure transformed from what used to be extended family into nuclear family, and the divided family emerged with migration of young people into large urban places. Farmers had to increase their dependence on forest products from the dwindling unencroached forests and from off-

Figure 3:

Number of Deaths and Ill-patients Suffering from Pesticide Poisoning in
Thailand, 1975-1991

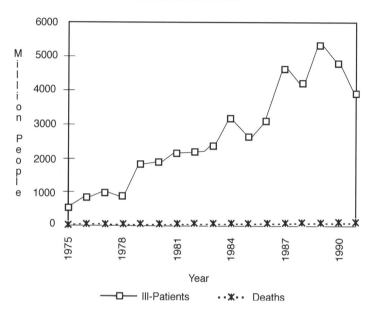

Source: Epidemiology Division, The Ministry of Public Health, 1993

farm employment (Dhira and Panayotou 1990: 27). Many faced
problems of reduction of income, the risk of losing land ownership
and debt overload. This was exacerbated by the "scissors effect" of
rising inputs and declining yields.

SUSTAINABLE AGRICULTURE APPROACHES IN THAILAND

Sustainable agriculture represents a new phase in development
thinking, contrary to that associated with the green revolution. It is
an approach that is equally revolutionary but very different in its
conceptual and operational basis. It places greater emphasis on

sustainability and equity. It is also an approach which takes both economic and social factors into consideration and, at the same time, protects and improves the environment through efficient capital stock management (Thanwa and Dejrat 1994: 19). Similar to indigenous farming systems that are diversified and efficient, sustainable agricultural development takes into account every interacting factor, internal or external to the agricultural system. It imitates the ecology of natural forest in terms of its biodiversity, depends on an optimum amount of external resources, encourages multicropping instead of monocropping, applies intercropping and multistory cropping systems and puts emphasis on integrated technologies with high potential sustainability (Phrateep 1993: 23).

The problems associated with conventional or modern agriculture in the early 1980s led to the re-emergence of sustainable agriculture in Thailand. Whether integrated farming, agroforestry or natural farming, all emerged out of a need to break out of the "vicious circle" of debt and health risks and vulnerability to external shocks and stresses. These approaches may be different in terms of practices, but they all share the same principles: reducing market dependency, strengthening self-reliance and rehabilitating the ecosystem by cutting down on chemical uses.

Integrated farming

Integrated farming generally involves the integration of multi-cropping and livestock production. The benefit of growing two or more crops on the same piece of land is based on the principle that the crops exploit different soil, water and light resources or mutually interact with one another. They also serve to control pests and weeds. Integration of crops and livestock production reduces the risk of production loss due to environmental fluctuations. Farm animals can be turned into a valuable source of food and income. While crop residues can be converted into marketable products and allow recycling of nutrients, animal wastes are made into invaluable fertilizer. The success of integrated farming depends on the physical, biological, economic, social and natural resource components of the system. If effectively managed, not only can integrated farming reduce the risk of production loss due to fluctuations associated with environmental cycles, but it can also increase the efficiency in resource management and decrease labor migration (Boonsawasdi et al. 1993: 48). Despite its benefit to sustainable agricultural production, however, integrated farming requires certain conditions: sufficient land, capital, labor and market availability. Also, farmers needed to be diligent and enduring.

A successful case of integrated farming in Thailand

In a study of sustainable agriculture in Thailand, Vichaen and Boriboon (1993: 306) found one of the more successful cases of integrated farming in Surin, a province located in the Northeast. A farmer by the name of Mahayou Suntornchai started to practice integrated farming many years ago on his 93 *rai* farm. He planted food crops such as chili, egg-plant, ginger, galanga, lemon grass and bergamot. He also raised farm animals such as pigs, chickens, ducks and fresh water fish. These crops and animals were used as sources of both food and income. They also provided an ecological symbiosis. Animal wastes were turned into natural fertilizer, while the animals themselves helped destroy plant pests. Mahayou planted a number of different garden crops around the fish ponds. These crops protected the soil from eroding, and at the same time they could be converted into natural fertilizer and provide shade for fish in the ponds.

Mahayou's marketing strategies were thought out in accordance with his production plans. For example, rice products would be stocked and sold at the end of the year because their value would be higher during that period; fish would be caught and sold after other farmers had sold theirs; to guarantee that prices would be stable, duck eggs would be primarily sold to bakery factories and local schools; and poultry products would mainly be sold during the Chinese New Year in order to fetch higher prices.

Integrated farming has proven to be successful for Mahayou. He was able to manage the use of resources properly, control his inputs and outputs, avoid the need to put out any mortgage, produce stable agricultural products with the system which has the least impact on the environment and generate sufficient income for his family and workers.

Agroforestry

Agroforestry is a practice of intercropping where annual herbaceous crops are grown interspersed with perennial trees or shrubs (Boonsawasdi et al., 1993: 54). This system includes trees as the main component in a multi-crop production process. The trees are needed to protect the soil from the impact of rain. Because certain tree species can fix atmospheric nitrogen and enrich the soil, while others prevent nutrient loss from the system and draw nutrients to the surface, the interaction between the trees and other components of the system leads to soil protection and water conservation. Agroforestry in Thailand sometimes incorporates perennial and agricultural crop production with livestock production.

A successful case of agroforestry in Thailand

Vichean and Boriboon (1993: 308) found that one of the most successful cases of agroforestry practices in Thailand belongs to a village headman by the name of Viboon Kheamchalearm. Viboon could be considered to be a pioneer of agroforestry. In the late 1960s, Viboon sold 200 *rai* of land in the province of Chachoengsao (located approximately 80 kilometers east of Bangkok) to pay off his debts, which had been incurred from the failure of conventional chemical-based agricultural practices. He was left with no assets and only a small piece of land (about 9 *rai*). In 1969, Viboon started to practice agroforestry by planting perennial crops combined with a wide range of fruit trees, particularly those that would attract birds. The intention was to use the birds as a form of biological pest control. In addition to growing fruits and vegetables, he also planted herb and other garden crops. Today, Viboon's land has become a real forest. He was able to achieve self-sufficiency. Everything that grows in his farm has a use – as food for himself, goods to sell and even medicine.

Natural farming

Natural farming is an approach to sustainable agriculture following the principle of integrated crop and livestock management in consonance with nature. Presently in Thailand, the natural farming approach is not as widely used as integrated farming or agroforestry. The practice of natural farming in Thailand mainly concentrates on the "Kyusei Natural Farming System", developed in Japan by Teiruo Hikna in 1989. The principle of this system gives "full play to the great powers inherent in the soil itself" (Kanayama 1993: 31). Natural farming makes use of effective micro-organisms in fertile soil to halt soil degradation while increasing soil nutrients. This is based on the principle that soil has various dynamic functions contributing to maintenance of the eco-system, such as the conservation of aquatic environments, the conservation of atmospheric circulation, preservation of nutrients and water and the habitat of micro-organisms (*ibid.*). Through proper implementation of this system, certain targets can be attained: the production of chemical-free agricultural products, establishment of a pollution-free environment and efficient management of resources.

A successful case of natural farming in Thailand

Vichean and Boriboon (1993: 309) describe how hopelessness and debt overload led Khamduang Phasi into reforming his past agricultural practices with natural farming. After having read a book written by Masanobu Fukuoka, and with inspiration from his sister who is a Buddhist nun, Khamduang tried out natural farming on his two pieces of land (18 *rai* and 12 *rai*) in Buriram province. He grew rice on his farm in combination with mung beans and soy beans. Three to four weeks before the grain could be harvested, Khamduang would sow black and red beans into the rice fields, and the legumes would serve as natural fertilizers. He refrained from soil tilling, avoided the use of chemical fertilizers and insecticides and left weeds to grow on the farm.

Three years after his experimentation with natural farming, Khamduang was able to pay back all his debts, had decreased his household expenditure and increased the micro-organism habitat of the soil. Not only did his production expand, he was physically and mentally healthier. Khamduang has set an example for other farmers in the village. He has shown that natural farming is an effective approach to overcome the dry conditions of northeastern Thailand.

DIVERSITY OF RESPONSES TOWARDS SUSTAINABLE AGRICULTURE IN THAILAND

NGOs' contribution to sustainable agriculture

The role of local NGOs in the promotion of sustainable agriculture in Thailand is important. Since the late 1980s, they have played a significant role in providing background analysis for decision making and in shaping the direction of sustainable agriculture. They helped farmer leaders such as Mahayou to develop their farming techniques and encouraged several others to adopt sustainable agriculture practices through the development and promotion of pilot farms applying sustainable agriculture techniques. NGOs launched campaigns for support from the general public and forged informal collaboration with universities and research institutions (Vitoon 1993: 3).

Among the pioneers who promoted sustainable agriculture in Thailand was the Alternative Agriculture Network (AAN) (Vitoon 1993: 9). Since its inception in 1984, AAN's main activities have been focusing on technical experience sharing among NGOs and farmers on policy advocacy through information dissemination, and organization of discussion groups with academics in public fora, such as the "Alternative Agriculture Forum" held in November 1992. Most advocacy campaigns in which AAN has been involved concern the government's agricultural development plans, particularly those relating to the dominance of agribusiness, such as the campaign opposing establishment of a National Agricultural Council (Vitoon 1993: 11).

Today, there are over 50 NGOs working on sustainable agriculture in Thailand, with most employing an extension strategy to promote sustainable agriculture through a farmer-to-farmer approach. However, this strategy has its limits. Many farmers are still reluctant to change their practices due to factors which inhibit adoption of a new approach, including economic barriers, technical uncertainties and market outlets. Sustainable agriculture is more complicated than intensive chemical-farming. Farmers are often too concerned with stability and productivity to adopt new innovations.

Hence, sustainable farming still accounts for a very small proportion (0.4 percent) of the national farming population when considered in terms of households (Vitoon 1993: 11). The numbers of farmers switching to sustainable agricultural practices are increasing, but the rate of change is still low.

The government's involvement

In principle, according to the Seventh National Economic and Social Development Plan (1992-1996), the government puts emphasis on recovering and improving Thailand's agricultural systems through the implementation of sustainable agricultural approaches. It stresses the importance of interdisciplinary research, the use of natural pest control methods and organic fertilizers, and environmental preservation.

In practice, although the Seventh National Economic and Social Development Plan (1992-1996) has included the term "integrated farming" in its agricultural development plan, this is something of a superficial target in that there are no concrete policies or measures to implement the plan. Substantively, this plan aims to foster the development of agribusiness and agro-industries through the intensive application of higher agricultural technology rather than to pursue any genuine sustainable agricultural programs (National Economic and Social Development Board 1992: 33). Not much progress has been made in terms of policy settings either. Only a few attempts have been made on the part of the government to promote sustainable farming. For example, in 1991, the Agriculture Department and the Agricultural Extension Department have launched promotional projects to produce hygienic vegetables. The aims were to reduce chemicals and promote consumption of safer produce domestically, while promoting exports of Thai fresh food to overseas markets where hygiene and chemical level standards are very strict.

In January 1992, the Ministry of Agriculture and Cooperatives established a "Committee on Sustainable Agriculture" to respond to the need to rectify the consequences of past agricultural development. Chaired by the Permanent Secretary of the Ministry of

Agriculture and Cooperatives and the Director-General of the Department of Agriculture, the Committee is responsible for sustainable agriculture policy and planning in terms of research and development and the promotion of cooperation with the private sector and international organizations such as the International Mokichi Okada Association, the Natural Farming International Research Foundation, and the MOA National Diet Members Federation for Protecting Food (Busaba 1993: 297).

Presently, the Ministry of Agriculture is considering a "Green and Clean Thai Agriculture" strategy to increase competitiveness of Thai farm products in international markets. This government-supported project will begin with fragrant rice and will be promoted among farmers who are members of cooperatives (Sukanya and Walailak 1995: 28).

In reality, agricultural development programs in Thailand implemented by the government continue to be biased against sustainable agriculture. The drive to maximize crop productivity by chemical applications remains the government's main agricultural development strategy. According to the Commerce Ministry, Thailand's 1994 imports of chemical fertilizers and pesticides totalled 18 billion baht, an increase of about 1.5 percent over 1993. For vegetables alone, the Agriculture Toxic Substances Division has identified up to 60 chemicals which included DDT, Aldrin, Captan-Folpet, Endrin, Heptachlor and Lindane (Sukanya and Walailak 1995: 28). Also, there is an increasing trend toward agribusiness involvement in the farm economy, where farming is being geared towards producing excessive flow of raw materials for manufacturing industries (Vitoon 1993: 31).

The role of consumers

Thai consumers have recently become more serious about selecting hygienic food, due largely to fear of cancer from consuming too many chemical substances. A survey carried out by the Agriculture Department recently showed that people with higher educational and income levels tend to be more health-conscious (Sukanya and Walailak 1995: 28). Because of limited supply, some organically grown vegetables and other foods are expensive and only those with higher income can afford to buy them. For example, a two-kilogram package of organic brown or fragrant rice costs 75 baht, compared with 65 - 75 baht for five kilograms of normal fragrant rice.

Presently, there exist alternative markets for hygienic produce in Thailand operated by both non-governmental organizations and business group such as the "Thammada" Shop in Chiang Mai, the "Payao Group" Shop in Payao and in Khon Kaen provinces, the "Phalan Boon" shop, and the "Green Garden Shop" and "Trinity Way Supermarket" located in Bangkok (Vitoon 1993: 37). However, these outlets are still inadequate and it is difficult for people to buy hygienic and organic produce on a daily basis.

Entrenched consumer habits and few sales outlets are one of the causes of slow growth in consumption of pesticide-free vegetables. Today, hygienic vegetables have captured only about one percent of the total market for vegetables sold in supermarkets (Sukanya and Walailak 1995: 28). In order to increase consumption of pesticide-free produce, people's preference for buying only attractive-looking vegetables would probably have to change.

CONCLUSION

Sustainable agriculture clearly represents a serious alternative to the environmentally destructive chemical-dependent monocultures that have dominated past agricultural practice in Thailand. Approaches such as integrated farming, agroforestry and natural farming present a challenge to dominant developmental influences in the rural sector, even though they remain outside the mainstream. Moreover, this challenge has been taken up in various ways by a diverse set of social actors, including farmers, non-governmental organisations, government agencies and urban consumers.

While diversity of interest strengthens sustainable agriculture as an environmental alternative, such diversity also presents a number of contradictions. The notion of what constitutes truly sustainable agriculture is itself fraught with ambiguity. The extent to which it could serve as an alternative on a wide scale has yet to be tested. Perhaps most fundamentally, because it goes so squarely against the mainstream of agricultural and wider economic development, labour-intensive and subsistence-oriented sustainable agriculture is likely to sit uneasily with the dominant trends of ever greater market orientation, diversion of labour from agricultural to industrial and service sector occupations, vertically integrated production through agribusiness and new developments such as those resulting from genetic engineering. As a movement, however, it remains a significant element of Thailand's new environmentalism.

REFERENCES

Amphol Seanarong, 1993, "The Impact of Past Agricultural Development." *Sustainable Agriculture: The Future of Thai Farmers.* Bangkok: The Department of Agriculture pp 14 - 19.

Amphol Seanarong, 1993, "Thailand's Agricultural Development." *Sustainable Agriculture: The Future of Thai Farmers.* Bangkok: The Department of Agriculture, pp 8 - 12.

Amphol Seanarong, "Towards Sustainable Agriculture." *Sustainable Agriculture: The Future of Thai Farmers.* Bangkok: The Department of Agriculture, 1993 pp 3-6.

Boonsawasdi Ajvalaka, et al., 1993, "Agricultural Systems for the Development of Sustainable Agriculture", in *Sustainable Agriculture: The Future of Thai Farmers.* Bangkok: The Department of Agriculture, pp 8 - 63.

Busaba Varakornvoravuthi, 1993, "Sustainable Agriculture: The Initiative of the Department of Agriculture." *Sustainable Agriculture: The Future of Thai Farmers.* Bangkok: The Department of Agriculture, pp 295 - 301.

Conway, Gordon, and Edward Barbier, 1990, *After the Green Revolution: Sustainable Agriculture for Development.* London: Earthscan Publications Ltd.

Department of Medical Services and the Occupational and Environmental Medicine Association of Thailand, 1993, "Toxic Substances Related Diseases and the Prevention." *Occupational and Environmental Medicine.* Bangkok: Health Education Division, pp 104 - 108.

Dhira Phantumvanit, and Theodore Panayotou, 1990, "Natural Resources for a Sustainable Future: Spreading the Benefits." A Synthesis Paper. Bangkok: TDRI.

Kanayama, Shigenobu, 1993, "Soil Building: Key Practice in Developing Sustainable Agriculture." *Sustainable Agriculture: A New Generation of Survival.* Bangkok: His Majesty's Royal Development Projects Board, pp 39 - 40.

National Economic and Social Development Board, 1992, *The Seventh National Economic and Social Development Plan (1992 - 1996)*. Bangkok: Office of the Prime Minister.

Office of Agricultural Economics, The Ministry of Agriculture and Cooperatives, 1992, *Agricultural Statistics of Thailand Crop Year 1991/92*. Bangkok: Chuanpim.

Policy Analysis and Recommendations for the Development of Alternative Agriculture, 1992, Bangkok: Alternative Agriculture Forum.

Phrateep Virapattananiran, 1993, "Sustainable Agriculture." *Sustainable Agriculture: The Future of Thai Farmers*. Bangkok: The Department of Agriculture, The Ministry of Agriculture and Cooperatives, pp 21 - 31.

Sukanya Jitpleecheep and Walailak Keeratipipatpong, 1995, "Healthy Harvest." *Bangkok Post* 16 January 1995, p 28.

Thanwa Jitasaknuan, 1992, "Policies for Sustainable Agriculture in Thailand: A Synthesis Paper". Bangkok: The Department of Agriculture.

Thanwa Jitasaknuan, and Dejrat Seukkamnerd, 1994, "Sustainable Agriculture and Thailand's Food Policy." *Kasetsart University Journal of Economics* 1, pp 19 - 36.

Tassanee Vejpongsa, 1995, "Freedom from the Shackles of Debt." *Bangkok Post* 10 January 1995, p 29.

Vichaen Sasiphrabha and Boriboon Somrit, 1993, "Cases of Farmers Who Engage in Different Approaches of Sustainable Agriculture". *Sustainable Agriculture: The Future of Thai Farmers*. Bangkok: The Department of Agriculture, pp 305 - 327.

Vitoon Panyakul, 1993, "Sustainable Agriculture in Thailand: Past and Present." A paper presented to the 1993 IFOAM Asian Continental Meeting, 19 - 22 August 1993.

INDEX